PENGUIN REFERENCE BOOKS
THE SLANG THESAURUS

Born in 1948 and educated at Oxford University, Jonathon Green has been working as a writer, journalist and broadcaster since 1969, and has contributed to a wide variety of magazines and newspapers ranging from the defunct 'underground press' to Fleet Street. He published his first book in 1976 and since then has specialized in dictionaries of quotations and compilations of professional jargon and contemporary slang.

The Slang Thesaurus

JONATHON GREEN

PENGUIN BOOKS

PENGUIN BOOKS

Published by the Penguin Group
Penguin Books Ltd, 27 Wrights Lane, London W8 5TZ, England
Penguin Books USA Inc., 375 Hudson Street, New York, New York 10014, USA
Penguin Books Australia Ltd, Ringwood, Victoria, Australia
Penguin Books Canada Ltd, 10 Alcorn Avenue, Toronto, Ontario, Canada M4V 3B2
Penguin Books (NZ) Ltd, 182–190 Wairau Road, Auckland 10, New Zealand

Penguin Books Ltd, Registered Offices: Harmondsworth, Middlesex, England

First published in Great Britain by Elm Tree Books/Hamish Hamilton 1986
Published in Penguin Books 1988
7 9 10 8 6

Printed in England by Clays Ltd, St Ives plc

For Lucien and Gabriel

Contents

Introduction

Dr Peter Mark Roget published his *Thesaurus of English Words and Phrases* in 1852 with the intention of classifying and organising the English Language. His topic encompassed the great spread of standard English, and for all that the Thesaurus has become a basic adjunct to anyone seeking a polished style, his initial aim was to reveal through the relationships of words a new and simpler means of communication for everyone.

Since then, the Thesaurus has gone through a number of revisions, the most recent being published in 1982. It remains a vital helper for every type of writer – both professional and general – who seeks the most apt, the most accurate, the most telling and the most elegant expression of their thoughts. In essence, a comprehensive wordlist, arranged as to topic – with all the words that deal with the same idea (and sometimes their opposites and correlatives alongside them) grouped together – the Thesaurus format remains massively popular.

The intention of *The Slang Thesaurus* is the adapting of the thesaurus technique to the slang vocabulary. Unlike a dictionary, which provides a meaning for a given word, the thesaurus provides a variety of words, all of which express a given meaning. As the editor/compiler of a number of dictionaries of alternative language, including *Newspeak: A Dictionary of Jargon* (1982) and *The Dictionary of Contemporary Slang* (1984), I have come to realise that there exists a definite, and often-voiced demand for a book that would provide just such a 'reverse dictionary'. This book attempts to meet that demand.

The range of slang that has been amassed in the *Thesaurus*, with the particular effect of grouping like with like, is intended to offer a variety of appeals to scholars and less professional logophiles, as well as all those many people who simply enjoy browsing through such collections of more or less arcane, exotic and even obscure words and phrases. As the tabulation of the contemporary slang lexicon gradually developed it became interesting to note the way in which certain areas of human life create seemingly disproportionate vocabularies. While all aspects of the language – taking in the prosaic as well as the more dramatic – have been duly included, specific categories do stand out.

'The chief stimuli of slang are sex, money and intoxicating liquor,' opined Dr J. Y. P. Greig in 1938. Bowing to current events one must add drugs to that list. Coupling such pleasures with a good ration of blasphemy, scatology and euphemism, one has a fair cross-section of slang origins. And, given those additions, Dr Greig's sources are still remarkably constant, as the word lists make clear. There remain only a few parts of the body, and a limited number of functions for their employment, but the language such parts and functions create is still evolving without restraint. Although my intention has been to restrict the *Thesaurus* to contemporary usage, many of the words originate in earlier periods. Slang, like more standard usage, develops over the years, responding in kind to the vagaries and developments of the society in which it is created and used. Listing it in this form only underlines such development.

The *Thesaurus* is divided into sections and groups of categories based roughly, although obviously not completely following, on those used for *Roget's Thesaurus*. These are arranged according to the principal or dominant idea that they convey. Within the sections of these categories are words and phrases that are definitely synonymous; they are entered in alphabetical order. In such cases that the words within a given section require a more specific definition other than that offered by the keyword, this will be given. All categories and sections and the vocabulary listed in them will be cross-referenced whenever necessary. As well as the usual abstract categories – 'Volition', 'Emotion' and the like, I have added listings of several specialist vocabularies – 'Crime', 'Prostitution', 'Commercial Sex', 'Drugs', 'Commerce' and 'Gambling'. All of these fall outside the purlieus of the traditional Thesaurus but are repositories of large amounts of popularly used slang and therefore demand inclusion.

A thesaurus, by definition, is a compilation of facts – in the form of listed, connected words – rather than of etymologies, discursive explanations of the development and origin of a word or of similar philological exposition. For such information one must look to the ordinary slang dictionaries. On the other hand, this comprehensive organisation into specific categories and sections of the enormous body of slang is designed to appeal not merely to wordsmiths but to have, like any of its peers, a practical function. The genesis of *The Slang Thesaurus* was in the requests of those who said to this compiler 'I enjoy the definitions in a slang dictionary, but what I really want is the reverse, something that gives me the slang for the normal word.' Such appeals have been many. It is the aim of *The Slang Thesaurus* to meet them.

The bulk of the material included in the *Thesaurus* has been derived from my own *Dictionary of Contemporary Slang*, much enhanced by subsequent delvings and accretions. To thank each individual for their contributions would be impossible, grateful though I certainly am, but I must thank David Robbins for opening up an area that had hitherto defeated me, notably the patois used by West Indians in England.

Finally I offer my profound thanks to John Nicolson, without whose invaluable efforts, clichéd acknowledgement though this may be, the compilation of the *Thesaurus* would truly never have been possible.

JONATHON GREEN
March 1986

Abbreviations

abbrev.	*abbreviation*
adj.	*adjective*
adv.	*adverb*
aka	*also known as*
Aus.	*Australian*
backsl.	*backslang*
betw.	*between*
Can.	*Canadian*
derog.	*derogatory*
eg	*example*
esp.	*especially*
euph.	*euphemism*
excl.	*exclamation*
facet.	*facetious*
fr.	*from*
milit.	*military*
mod.	*modern*
n.	*noun*
occ.	*occasionally*
phr.	*phrase*
poss.	*possible*
rhy.sl.	*rhyming slang*
S.Afr.	*South African*
Sp.	*Spanish*
spec.	*specifically*
UK	*United Kingdom*
US	*United States*
USMC	*United States Marine Corps*
v.	*verb*
vi	*verb intransitive*
vt	*verb transitive*
Yid.	*Yiddish*
WI	*West Indian*

Abstract Relations

TIME
1. Duration
n. 1. *period of time:* go, space, stretch, trick
2. *long time:* blue moon, born days (all one's), coon's age, month of Sundays
3. *short time:* brace of shakes, jiffy, less than no time, two shakes of a lamb's tail, in a tick, wake-up; spec: mo, sec; short (short service commission)
4. *work time:* hitch (milit.), forty-eight, (milit), gaol break (movies), graveyard shift, lobster shift, swing shift, R&R (milit.)
v. 5. *spend time:* spec. 29 and a wake-up (prison use: period betw. receiving notice of parole and release)
adj. 6. *new, novel:* brand spanking, bran-new, fresh as paint, hot, hot off the press, wen (backsl.)
7. *old:* dillo (backsl.) has-been, over the hill, past it
adv. 8. *during; while:* punch the clock
9. *for a long time:* for donkey's years, for yonks, since God knows when
10. *forever:* for keeps, till the cows come home, till hell freezes over
11. spec. short (near the end of prison term/milit. service)

2. Relative Time
n. 1. manana
2. *crucial time:* nick (of time)
v. 3. *to be late:* stand up
adv. 4. *formerly:* already; spec: space, while back

5. *long ago:* donkey's years, way back, year dot
6. *after:* later! when morning comes (US bl.)
7. *now:* on the dot, this is where we came in (the same time)
8. *soon:* in a brace of shakes
9. *any time:* any old
10. *immediately, shortly:* before you can say Jack Robinson, chop-chop, first crack out of the box, in a jiffy, a jiffy, in a brace of shakes, in less than no time, like a shot, like a shot out of hell, one-two-three, on the knocker, on the nail, PDQ (pretty damn quick), pronto, right off the bat, stat (medical)
11. *suddenly:* bam, bang, bang off, blam, caplunk, kerblam, kersmack, plop, plunk, pop, powee, slap, slap-bang, slap-dab, smack, smack-dab, smacko, socko, wham, whang, zap, zoom, zowie
12. *seldom, occasionally:* once in a blue moon, – a coon's age, a month of Sundays; since God knows when
13. *early:* bright and early; previous
14. *prompt, punctual:* in the nick of time, Johnny on the spot, on deck, on the dot, – nail, – nose, – the spot, pronto, right there
15. *late:* Harry Tate

3. Divisions of Time
n. 1. *day:* good day for it, – for the race; spec. roaster, scorcher, swelterer (a hot day); nice day for ducks (a wet day)
2. *days of the week:* when the crow shits (Aus. payday), Mother's Day (US black), poet's day (piss off early today), TGIF (Thank God It's

Friday); spec. sickie (Aus.: a day's sick-leave)

3. *festival days:* hols, Xmas; spec. buck's night (Aus.: stag night)

4. *week, month:* moon; spec. Hell Week (US college); leo-time (August); play-away (UK society use: weekend in country); beno (menstrual period, there 'be no' fun); wallflower week (menstrual period)

5. *seasons:* dog days, lamb time, silly season

6. *weekend:* dirty weekend

7. *morning:* ack emma, morning after the night before, rooster time, small hours, sparrow fart

8. *afternoon:* arvo (Aus.), pip emma

9. *night:* crash time, flop time, hay time; spec. dog-watch (media: post-midnight broadcasts)

10. *hour:* half (in telling time: half-five, -six, etc); spec. happy hour (cheap drinks period in a bar); mad minute (milit. use: free-fire test period for weapons)

11. *minute:* cock linnet (rhy.sl.)

ORDER
4. Arrangement; Order; State of Affairs

n. 1. *conditions:* how-do-you-do, kettle of fish, lay of the land, lie –, size of it, way the wind blows; spec. lineup, set-up

2. *orderliness, good condition:* apple-pie-order, apples (Aus.), apples and rice (Aus. rhy.sl. = nice), fine as wine (US black) hunky-dory, jake, nice going, squeaky-clean, ticketty-boo, top whack

3. *cleaning, neatening:* doing up, pearl diving (washing dishes in restaur.), policing (milit.), tarting up

v. 4. *to arrange, to clean:* do up, doll up, police up, pretty up, tart up

5. *be consistent:* hang in there, – together, – tight, – tough, hold water, get in line, put one's money where one's mouth is, stand up

adv. 6. hitting on all four (cylinders), up to scratch, – snuff; spec. runner (of a second-hand car)

7. *orderly:* in apple-pie order, kosher

8. *consistent:* according to Hoyle, boilerplate, by the book

5. Disorder

n. 1. Chinese fire drill, dog's dinner, grunge, Horlicks (UK upperclass use), pig's ear, pit, (right) two-and-eight (rhy.sl. = state), scrunge, schmutz, what the cat brought in

v. 2. *to get out of order, get into a mess:* make a dog's dinner (out of), screw up

3. *to disarrange:* arse (ass) up, ball up, foul up, fuck up

4. *to dirty, to soil:* crap on, – over

adv. 5. *messy, out of order:* all to cock, all over the place, – the shop, any how, arsy-versy, cockeyed, everywhichway, fouled up, fubar (fucked up beyond all recognition), gfu (general fuck-up), gmbu (grand military balls-up), gmfu (– fuck-up), grungy, out of whack, raspy (US black), ratty, samfu (self-adjusting military fuck-up), sapfu (surpassing all previous fuck-ups), screwed up, screwy, scruff, sky-west and crooked, sleazy, snafu (situation normal, all fucked up), susfu (situation unchanged, still fucked up), tarfu (things are really fucked up)

6. *infested:* crawling (with)

IMPROVEMENT
6. Improvement

v. 1. *to improve:* be on the mend, – on the up-and-up, get oneself into shape, – together, get one's act together, – arse (ass) in gear, – shit together

2. *recover:* perk up, pull oneself to pieces (facet.), pull oneself together, pull out of it, pull through, snap out of it

3. *repair, mend:* do up, rev, revamp

4. *strengthen:* beef up, jack up, jazz up

7. Impairment

n. 1. *defective object:* dead duck, fuck-up

2. *accident:* balls-up, cobblers, cock-up, howler, mons

3. *wreck, collision:* pile-up, smash-up

4. *ruin, destruction:* blooie, blow-out, blow up, blue ruin, brodie, bust, bust-up, conk-out, fold-up, knock-out, smash-up, washout

v. 5. *deteriorate:* conk (out), die on the vine, pull a fadeout, fade, go blah, peg out, peter –, spec. deteriorate rapidly: do a brodie, go down the chute, – the tubes, hit the skids, take a nose-dive

6. *get out of order, break:* blow (up), bust, conk (out), crack (up), crap out, fold up, get out of whack, go blah, – blooie, – on the blink, – haywire, poop out, screw up

7. *to degenerate, go to ruin:* (to be) all up, (be) washed up, conk out, fold up, go boom, – phfft, – phut, go to the devil, – to the dogs, – the deuce, – to hell, – to pieces, – to pot, – to smash, – to the pack (Aus.)

8. *to spoil, disorder:* balls up, blow, do up (brown), bugger up, foul up, fuck up, gum up (the works), louse up, put the kibosh on, – the skids under, queer up

9. *to hit:* bash, whack

10. *to ruin, destroy:* belt out, christen, clean out, crab, diddle, ding, dish, do, – a job on, – brown, – in, – over, – up (like a kipper),

gimp, knock off, murder, put the kibosh on, – the skids under, sew up, total, trash, wipe out

11. *have a crash:* have a bust-up, – crack-up, pile up, smash-up, total; spec. collide: collect (Aus.), run smack-dab into, tear into

12. *to spoil, upset:* crab, piss on one's parade

13. *broken, out of order:* arsed up, ballsed up, banjaxed, beat up, bollixed, bollocksed (up), buggered up, bust (up), clapped out, cockeyed, fouled up, fucked (up), gone blooie, – haywire, – to fuck, – (all) to shit, on the blink, – the fritz, out of whack, screwy, shot, upgefucked

14. *in poor condition:* all wet, beat up, cheesy, crappy, crummy, low rent, punk, trashy

15. *ruined:* all to hell, – to pieces, – to smash, bought and sold (and done for), done, – up, conked out, finito, fucked, gone phut, – to the devil, – to hell, – the dogs, – to pot, – to smash, (all) shot, washed up

phr. 16. that's torn it

SEQUENCE

8. Sequence; Succession

n. 1. *list:* sked(s), slate

2. *turn:* go, hand, stretch, whack; spec. buying drink: shout; Buggin's turn (next in line for a job)

v. 3. *to follow:* gumshoe, pussyfoot, string along, tag, tail

4. *continue:* go with the flow, hang in (there), keep the ball rolling, stay with it

adv. 5. *in succession:* on the trot

9. Beginning; Commencement

n. 1. first base, first crack (out of the box), git-go, (on the) ground floor, ground zero, jump, jump street, square one, starters

2. *preface:* openers; spec. opening

remarks: er, gosh, hell, I mean, look, you know

v. 3. *to begin:* cut loose, dig in, do it, fire away, get the lead out, – the show on the road, – one's arse in gear, – one's finger out, – on one's bike, go for it, hit it, kick off; spec. jump the gun (to begin prematurely)

4. *at the beginning:* early bird, from the word go, in front, off the top, right from the giddyap, when the balloon goes up

10. End; Termination

n. 1. blowoff, curtains, end of the line, in the death, – the stretch, kiss off, payoff, wrap

2. *stop, cessation:* bust-up, fold, knockoff, quits

3. *conclusive end:* all bets are off, capper, clincher, crunch, end-around, KO, living end

4. *suffixes used in slang words:* -aroo, -eroo, -erino, -ette, -fest, -iferous, -ino, -terino, -inski, -itis, -nik, -o, -ola, -ski

v. 5. *to end:* ace it up (Aus.), bust up, conk (out), fold (up), go over the top, – the limit, take the count

6. *to cease, stop:* call it a day, – quits, drop (it), get one's cards, hand in one's chips, hang it up, knock (it) off, pull the plug (on), put the brakes on, stow it, wind up

7. *to terminate:* break (it) up, call all bets off, clean up (on), floor, fold, knock (it) on the head, polish off, put (it) away, – on ice, – the brakes on, say goodbye (to), wash up, wind up; spec. kill (turn off lights, machinery, etc)

adv. 8. *ended:* all over bar the shouting, all bets are off, all torn up, all up (with), done (for), down the drain, – the pan, – the tubes, in the bag, kiboshed, pegged out, up the spout

excl. 9. can it!, cheese it!, come off it!, cut it out!, drop it!, forget it!, hold on!, hold up!, kill it!, knock it off!, – on the head!, ace it up! (Aus.), lay off!, leave it out!, – off!, – over!, less of it!, stow it!

phr. 10. curtains for you, that's your lot, the deal's off

CHANGE

11. Change

n. 1. *experience:* picnic, set-up; spec. dead man's shoes (US black: an unavoidable unpleasant experience); university of life (learning by experience)

v. 2. *to alter:* go through changes, snap out of (it); spec. go fish (gay use: to act as a woman)

3. *to happen, to turn out:* come down, go down, pan out; spec. peak (to reach the limit of an experience)

12. Substitution

n. 1. *substitute:* dupe, front, ringer, switcheroo

v. 2. *to replace:* ad lib, cover up, double (for), front for, pinch-hit, ring (in)

adj. 3. *fake:* bogue

13. Permanence

v. 1. hang in there, – tight, stay with (it)

RESEMBLANCE

14. Kind; Sort

n. 1. character, lot, number, piece; spec. situation: layout, outfit, scene, set-up

15. Similarity

n. 1. *likeness:* dupe, lookalike, (dead) ringer

2. *duplicate:* ditto, dupe; spec. knockoff (antiques/clothing trade)

3. *imitation:* copycat, takeoff; spec. shamateur (sporting use)

v. 4. *resemble:* not tell t'other from which, stack up (with)

5. *to copy:* make like, me-too
adj. 6. plastic, strictly from

QUANTITY: SIMPLE
16. Quantity; Number
n. 1. *collection:* ballpark figure, caboodle, grab-bag, whole kit and caboodle, whole bag of tricks, – ball of wax, – bang shoot, – boiling lot, – shebang, – shooting match
2. *zero, nought:* damn all, dick, diddley-squat, doodley-squat, jack shit, nisht (Yid.), not a sausage, squat, sweet FA, – Fanny Adams, zilch, zip, zot; spec. cricket: blob, duck, pair of spectacles (two scores of 0 in the same match)
3. *small denominations:* flach (backsl. = half), country cousin (rhy.sl. = 12), oat (backsl. = 2), roaf (backsl. = 4), net (backsl. = 10), ace, deuce, tray, finif, fiver, nickel (5 as number or quantity), neves (backsl. 7), half a dollar, – a bar, – a sheet, – a yard, – a cock (£5), half saw, sawbuck, quid, tenner, cock and hen (rhy.sl. = ten), cockle and hen, pony
4. *large denominations:* big bucks, telephone number(s), Nelson (111), big one, C, century, G, grand, K, ton, monkey, yard, mill; spec. gambling: nickel ($500), dime ($1000), big nickel ($5000), big dime ($10000)
5. *indefinite numbers:* points (percentages), tall (US black use: large numbers, often of cash), jillion, squillion, umpteen, zillion
v. 6. *count:* dope out, figure out, guesstimate, reckon, tote (up)
mod. 7. one (as in 'You won't get dime one out of me!')

17. Degree
n. 1. cut above, notch above
adv. 2. *to a degree:* that (when = extent: 'I was that pissed!'), the

devil, – deuce, – hell, – on earth (when preceded by 'what . . .')
3. *at the most:* tops

QUANTITY: GREATNESS
18. Greatness
n. 1. *something large:* blockbuster, boomer (Aus.), cheese, gorilla, humdinger, monster
2. *large amount, many:* all sorts, and then some, bags, barrels, heaps, loads, oodles, devil of a lot, heck –, hell –, hulluva, thumping, fat lot, gobs, lashings, more than you can shake a stick at, neat sum, tidy –, pile, pot (of), rafts, scads. tons, wads
3. *something/body important:* ace, biggie, big cheese, – deal, – enchilada, – league, – noise, – shot, – stuff, – time, – wheel, – wig, full two bob (Aus.), something to write home about, your (yer) actual; spec. important facts: brass tacks, nitty-gritty
4. *eminence in degree:* (preceded by 'as', 'like', etc) all creation, all getout, beans, billy-o, blazes, a house on fire, nobody's business, in spades
v. 5. *to be important:* beat all. – the band, cut a lot of ice
6. *to feature:* headline, put in lights, – on the map, hit the high spots
mod. 7. *large, huge:* bumper, ginormous, gross, humungous, dirty great, tearing, thumping (great). whopping, whacking
8. *great in degree:* almighty, bally, big-time, blankety, blazing, blessed, blinking, bloody, blooming, boiling, clinking, crying, father and mother of, flaming, heavy, hellacious, hell-fired, holy, motherfucking, mollyfogging, motherless, mother-raping, pepper-kissing, perishing, rip-snorting, ruddy (great), serious, some
9. *to a great extent:* and how, and

then some, damn tootin', darn (durn) tootin', as all getout, something awful, – fierce, – terrible, to beat all creation, the worst way, over the fence (Aus.), up the gazoo

10. *very, exceedingly:* all-fired, bang, beastly, blame, blankety, bleeding, blind, blinking, bloody, bust-out, darned, dashed, dead, double, dynamite, ever so, fonky, for sure, goddam, Harry ... -ers, hell-fired, helluva, pigging, powerful, right, screaming, slamming, spanking, socking, sodding, steaming (great), stiff, stinking, stone, TNT (US black = dynamite), thundering, veddy, way, well, whacking, whopping (great), wonelly

11. *excellent:* raspy

19. Smallness; Insignificance

n. 1. *something small:* (big) hunk of nothing, (long thin) streak of piss, no great shakes, nothing to shout about, – to write home about, not worth a plugged nickel, – a bumper (Aus.), – a hill of beans, small potatoes, small-time

2. *something worthless:* boloney, blah, bushwa, crap, garbage, trash

3. *small amount:* dribs and drabs, bits and bobs, smidgeonette; spec. cough and a spit (theatre: a small role)

v. 4. *not to matter:* cut no ice, (don't) hold no air, no great catch, – great shakes, not amount to a hill of beans, not worth a bumper, not worth a fart in a noisemaker, – in a thunderstorm, – a hill of beans, – a light, – a pisshole in the snow

5. *to lose importance:* to go down the chute, – the tubes, to hit the skids, poop out

adj. 6. *small, insignificant:* airy-fairy, chickenfeed, dinky, footling, half-cocked, – -pint, – -portion, one-horse, milk and water, penny-ante, piddling, pissy-ass, popcorn, sawn-off, teensie-weensie, thin on the ground; spec. -ette (suffix)

7. *cheap:* bargain basement, dime-a-dozen, dime-store, five-and-dime, nickel-and-dime, reach-me-down, two-bit, weak

---

QUANTITY: COMPARATIVE

20. Superiority

n. 1. *act of surpassing:* licking, fading, screwing, shafting, skinning, whitewashing

2. *the best:* A1, capper, cream, daddy, grade A, gravy, monte, payoff, pearler, topper, tops

v. 3. *to beat, surpass:* beat all to hell, – eight ways from Sunday, – out, give a black eye, get the jump on, hammer, have one cold, hype (US black), kick (one's) arse, knock for a loop, knock sideways, – the spots off, – the stuffing out of, lick, run rings round, put away, – one's nose out of joint, put it over (on), steal the show, sweep the board, take the shine off, whitewash

4. *to be best:* beat all, – all get out, cop the lot, take the cake

adv. 5. *superior to:* ahead of the game, a cut above, two jumps ahead

6. *best:* A1, ace, top of the tree, tiptop, up in the paints

phr. 7. *I've won:* read them and weep

21. Inferiority

n. 1. spec. sport: wooden spoon

v. 2. *to be surpassed:* licked, skinned, get on the short end, take a bath, – a back seat, – it on the chin, – one's lumps, – the fall, – the gas, – the knock, (to be) taken to the cleaners

adj. 3. *inferior:* bush, out of the money, – the picture, not in the game, – the picture, – the same league, pipped

QUANTITY: COMPLETENESS

22. Completeness; Sufficiency

n. 1. *sufficiency:* earful, enuff, full house, noseful, nuff

2. *superfluity:* bellyful, chokka, enough and then some, too much of a good thing, up to one's neck, skinful, snootful

3. *everything:* ballgame, business, everything but the kitchen sink, full monte, full two bob (Aus.), guntz (Yid.), hook, line and sinker, issue (Aus.), SRO (standing room only), whole bag of tricks, – ball of wax, – bang shoot, – boiling lot, – kit and caboodle, – shebang, – schmeer (Yid.), – shooting match, – works

adv. 4. *satiated:* lousy with, jam-packed, crawling with

5. *excessive:* gross, mondo, over the top, OTT, far out, too much, out of sight, outasite, mega-, too-too

6. *complete:* all-fired blinking, blooming, dead, plumb, regular, straight-out, straight-up

7. *completely:* abso-bloody-lutely, bang up, clean (to), clear to hell, flat, from arsehole to breakfast time, from soup to nuts, – the ground up, – the word go, slam,

23. Incompleteness; Insufficiency

n. 1. *share:* cut, divvy, piece (of the action), slice, split, whack

2. *quantity used in a given portion:* crack, edition, go, jag, shot, slug, sniff, throw, toot, toss, whack

3. *nothing:* bugger all, not a lick, – a smell, – sniff, sod all, sweet fuck all, sweet FA, zero, zilch, zip all

v. 4. *to lack:* be clean out of, fresh out of, shy of, light, to be hungry for, hung for

QUANTITY: VARIATION

24. Increase

v. 1. throw in

phr. 2. all that jazz

25. Decrease

n. 1. dent (in one's wallet), knockdown, knockoff, letup

2. *riddance:* brush-off, the big E, – dust, – elbow, – rubout, – runaround, – slip,

v. 3. *separate, divide:* cut up, cut up touches, divvy up, go halves, – fifty-fifty

4. *eliminate, discard:* axe, blow (out), boot (out), can, chuck, chunk (US black), clean house, count out, cut loose, deep six, ditch, dump, get shot of, give the air, – the bump, – the hook, – the brush-off, – the elbow, – the slip, – the (old) heave-ho, – the heave, – the knife, put the skids under, – rollers under, – the shears to, scarf (US campus), unload; spec. censorship, editing: blue-pencil; throw the baby out with the bathwater (to discard the useful along with the useless)

adv. 5. *used up:* all out (of), all shot, done for, fresh out (of), washed up

26. Equality

1. *inequality:* another story, a something else (again), a whole new ballgame, two other guys, a horse of a different colour

2. *on equal terms:* even-Steven, fifty-fifty, halvers, quits

QUALITY

27. Goodness

n. 1. *something excellent:* ace(s), beaut, bee's knees, bells (US black use), belter, the berries, big time, bobby dazzler, but good, cat's pyjamas, – whiskers, corker, cracker, daisy, dilly, duck soup, fave rave, the goods, gravy, humdinger, jim-dandy, kayo (KO), lily, lulu, McCoy, oldie but goodie, pea (Aus.), peach, pip, pippin, real McKay, real McCoy, rip-snorter, scorch (US black use), Shovel City (which one really 'digs'), some thing to shout about, – to write home about, topper, trimmer (Aus.),

v. 2. *to be excellent:* beat all, – the band, go over big, – like a million bucks, hit the spot, make it big, take the cake

adj. 3. *excellent first-rate:* A1, all fine and dandy, all wool and a yard wide, AOK, apples (Aus.), – and rice (Aus.), awesome, back of the net, bad, baddest, bagged, bang on, – up, bat, beaut, bitchen, bitchin, bitchin twitchin, blinding, bod, boffo, bonaroo, bonzer, boss, brahma, brill, bully, cas (casual), choice, classic, clearly, cold, completely, cool, copacetic, crackerjack, crazy, d, dandy, dead set (Aus.), def, death, deaf (US black), doog (backsl.) doog eno (backsl.), ducky, dynamite, electric, ex, fab, fantabulous, foxy, gaff, gear, godawful, good as all getout, great shakes, grouse (Aus.), groovy, handsome, hellacious, high-tone, hot-shit, hotsy-totsy, hunky-dory, irey (Jam.), jolly d., just like mother makes it, – the job, – the ticket, – what the doctor ordered, keen(-o), killer, king, knockout, live, mad (Aus.), magic, major, marvy, massive, mean, mega-, mind-blowing, mondo, nasty, neat, number one, numero uno, on the money, outasite, out of sight, – state, – the box (Aus.), – this world, peachy, peachy-keen, pimp, primo, rad (radical), rich, right up one's alley, righteous, ripper, scrummy, serious, sexy, shit-hot, smashing, socko, solid, spiffy, splendiferous, spot on, superfly, sweet, swell, TB (très brill), that's the ticket, to die, tons, top drawer, top hole, top notch, top shelf, total blowchoice, totally, tough, triff, trippy, tubular, unreal (Aus.), v., vg., vicious, Wee Georgie Wood

(rhy.sl. = good), wicked, wizard, yummy

excl. 4. encore!, far out!, fuckin(g) A!, perfecto!

5. *quite good:* better than a poke in the eye with a blunt stick, – a slap in the belly with a wet fish, close but no cigar, not so dusty

28. Badness

n. 1. *something bad:* asshole, baddie, baloney, bomb, bosh, bum, bushwa, chazerai (Yid. = rubbish), cheapie, cold, cold case, crap, crock (of shit), crumb, dead duck, double-whammy, doodley-shit, dreck, kaker (Yid.), no big deal, nowhere, pain (in the arse), – (in the neck), schlock, small beer, – change, – potatoes, snot, stinker(oo), tinhorn

adj. 2. *poor, mean, second-rate:* bad-ass, basic, bit previous, blamed, blankety, bodger (Aus.), bum, brummy (Aus.), bush league, chump-change, coffeeand, cold, cotton-picking, crappo, crappy, Crow McGee, cruddy, crumbum, crumby, crummy, dashed, dicky, dipshit, ditso, dodgy, dog-ass, g, godawful, gross, gnarly, half-baked, hard-boiled, hole-in-the-wall, iffy, jerkwater, low down, – rent, mean, Mickey Mouse, naff, NG (no good), NBG (no bloody good), no bon, no go, not much chop (Aus.), number ten, on the outer, pisspoor, poxy, punk, rank, ribby, rinky-dink, ropey, schlocky, shag, shitty, stinko, suck-ass, ticky-tacky, tinhorn, two-bit, two-bob (Aus.), unreal, upta (Aus. = up to shit), yucky, zero minus

3. *mediocre:* half-assed, – cocked, Wall Street didn't jump

excl. 4. base!

ATTRIBUTES

29. Weight
n. 1. *something heavy:* gorilla, wodge
adj. 2. gross, nuggety, thumping, whopping

30. Flexibility; Texture; Colour
adj. 1. blue (US black dark-skinned)

31. Temperature
mod. 1. *hot:* hot as a bastard, – a bitch, – buggery, – hell, hotter than hell
2. *cold:* cold as a bastard, – a bitch, – a well-digger's arse, – a brass monkey – witch's tit, cold enough to freeze the hind leg off a donkey

32. Strength
n. 1. get-up-and-go, guts, juice, legs, steam
2. *physical strength:* beef, the doings, elbow grease, jism, meat, muscle, what it takes
3. *directed force:* bang, biff, boot, flash, ginger, guts, jolt, kick, oomph, pep, powie, smackeroo, smacko, snap, sock, sockeroo, swack, wallop, zip
v. 4. *to exert strength:* put beef into, – muscle into, – one's back into, – one's elbow into, strongarm
5. *to be potent:* have a shot in one's locker, – lead in one's pencil
adj. 6. *strong:* ballsy, big ass, built like a brick outhouse, – brick shithouse, bullet-proof, heavy, mean, ruggsy, warry

33. Weakness
v. 1. *to be weak:* can't cut it, – fight one's way out of a paper-bag – get it together, – hack it, – knock the skin off a rice-pudding, – take it, doesn't cut the mustard
2. *to weaken:* bottle out, cave in, chicken out, conk out, crack (up), hit the skids, honk out, lose one's bottle, pull a fadeout, wimp out

3. *make powerless:* bash, bugger up, botch –, do –, do over, do the business on, – up (brown), gum –, put the kibosh on, – out of commission, queer one's pitch, put a spanner in the works, screw up
mod. 4. *weak, flimsy:* weak as catspiss, wet as a dishrag
5. *unsteady:* cockeyed, dotty, groggy, skewiff, wonkey
6. *effeminate:* faggy, he-she, la-de-da, nance, pansy, pantywaist, queer, swish (see also Homosexuals: 404)
adj. 7. *vulnerable:* up for grabs, wide-open
8. *weak:* candy-ass, chickenshit

APPEARANCE

34. Appearance; Looks
n. 1. front, getup, phizog, stackup, turnout
phr. 2. *unhealthy appearance:* looking green about the gills, – like a dog's dinner, you look like I feel

35. Beauty
n. 1. class, dog, spiff
2. *something beautiful:* beaut, cutesie, cutesiepie, dream, dreamboat, corker, daisy, dish, eyeful, hot stuff, looker, nifty, peach, pip, pippin, spanker, stunner, sweetie
3. *ornaments:* fixings
4. *attractive figure:* built, classy chassis, stacked, plenty of what it takes
v. 5. *to look beautiful:* (to be) easy on the eyes, knock dead, – one's eyes out, – out, look a knockout, – fit to kill, – a million bucks, – some, stack up nice
6. *to decorate:* doll up, spiff up, tart up
adj. 7. *beautiful:* beaut, cute, cutesie, dishy, dreamy, dreamboat, fit, foxy, ginchy, hot, keen looking, knockout, neat, no slouch, peach, wow

36. Ugliness
n. 1. *something ugly:* a bag, fit
to stop a clock, no oil painting,
– prize, something the cat dragged
in
adj. 2. *ugly:* bagged out, corroded
(US black), grisly, groaty, grody,
– to the max, gross, grotty, gucky,
hard on the eyes, – to take, hurtin'
for certain, icky, manky, pitty,
ragged out, ratty, rough, rugy,
scrungy, skrungy, scummy, scuzzy,
tacky, white bread
phr. 3. *disregarding ugliness for sex:*
you don't look at the mantlepiece
when you're poking the fire

Space

DIMENSIONS
37. Dimension
adj. 1. *thin:* beanpole, herring-gutted, ribby, skinnymalink, weedy
2. *short:* hammered down, knee high to a grasshopper, – jack rabbit, sawn-off, tee-tee, titchy
3. *fat:* beefy, broad in the beam, built like a brick outhouse, – shithouse, cornfed, double-gutted, fat-assed, pot-bellied, two-dinners
4. *measure of dimension:* wall-to-wall, yea (as in 'yea high', 'yea big')

38. Distance
n. 1. along, chance, piece, ways
2. *long distance:* good way, – piece, long chalk, neat step, tidy –, back of beyond, back of Bourke (Aus.), beyond the rabbit-proof fence (Aus.)
3. *short distance:* close shave, hop and a step, near as dammit, near thing, piece, (in) spitting distance, near squeak
v. 4. *to be near:* be hot, – warm
adv. 5. *far:* back of beyond, cold, to hell and gone, faraways
6. *near, close:* bang up (against), breathing down one's neck, as near as no matter, – dammit, texan rude (backsl. = next door), under one's nose, (by a) nose, up one's daily (rhy.sl. = daily mail = tail = behind), ringside, upside (US black)
7. *measurement:* klick (kilometer), mike-mike (millimeter)

SHAPE
39. Straightness
n. 1. beeline

adv. 2. *straight:* down the alley, in the groove, on the beam

40. Crookedness
adv. ·1. *crooked:* all anyhow, assbackwards, cockeyed, crinched, everywhichway, gimped (in), hell west and crooked, screwy, six ways from Sunday, skewiff

---

PLACE
41. Situation; Location
n. 1. posish, sitch
2. *ground:* deck
3. *small place:* manhole (US black)
v. 4. *to put, place:* dock, park, plant, spot
5. *lay down, put down with force:* bing, blop, bop, chuck, flop, kerplunk, lam, nail, peg, plank, plop, plunk, slap (down), smack, sock, swack, whang
6. *to be in a place, to reside:* (drop) anchor, hang out, – up one's hat, park one's carcase, perch, pitch camp, roost
adv. 7. *where:* anywheres, somewheres, any place, some –, on deck, at (as in 'where are you at?')
8. *everywhere:* all over, – the map, – the shop, from hell to breakfast
9. *in the wrong place:* off one's manor, – patch, – turf, on the flip side, on the Jersey side

42. Town; City
n. 1. big city, burg, met, metrop
2. *small town:* jerkwater (town), one-horse town, sticks, tank town, whistle stop
3. *suffix:* -ville

43. Cities: Nicknames

n. 1. Apple (NYC), Bay City (San Francisco, Calif.), Bean Town (Boston, Mass.), Berdoo (San Bernadino, Calif.), Big A (Amarillo, Tx. or Atlanta, Ga.), Big Smoke (Sydney, Aus.), Big T. (Tucson, Ariz.), Cowboy City (Cheyenne, Wyo.), Dago (San Diego, Calif.), Guz (Devonport, UK), Hip City (black use: Cleveland, Ohio), Jew York (derog: NYC), Nueva York (NYC), Nap Town (Indianapolis), P-Town (Philadelphia), Pompey (Portsmouth, UK), Rubber City (Akron, Ohio), Shaky City (Los Angeles), Sin City (Las Vegas, Nev.), the Smoke (London), Tinseltown (Hollywood, Calif.), TJ (Tijuana, Mexico), Windy City (Chicago, Ill.), Yidney (derog: Sidney, Aus.)
2. *imaginary cities:* Shitkicker, Ohio, Woop Woop (Aus.)
3. *areas:* Bible Belt, Borscht Belt, gin and Jaguar belt, scampi belt

44. Cities: Districts

n. 1. Chocolate City (any black ghetto), the Coathanger (Sydney Harbour Bridge, Aus.), the Drain (the London Underground), Dream Street (47th St, NYC, betw. 6th and 7th Avenues), Foggy Bottom (the State Department, Washington, DC), Forty-Deuce (42nd street, NYC), the Bush (Shepherd's Bush, London W12), the Gate (Notting Hill Gate, London W11), the Grove (Ladbroke Grove, London W10, W11), the Junction (Clapham Jnct, London, SW4), Kangaroo Valley (Earls Court, London, SW10), Rods (Harrods of Knightsbridge), Swone One (London SW11), Silicon Glen, Silicon Valley, up West (the West End of London), the Water (the River Thames, London)
2. *spec. college use:* Big Green (Dartmouth), Big Red (Cornell), Bruno (Brown U.), Crimson (Harvard U.), Eli (Yale U.), Farmington (Miss Porter's School), Old Nassau (Princeton U.), St Grotlesex (a fantasy amalgam of US prep schools)
3. *spec. prisons:* the Island (Parkhurst, IOW), the Scrubs (Wormwood Scrubs, London W14), the Ville (Pentonville, London N1)
4. *spec. homosexual use:* Boystown (the gay area of West Hollywood), Queen's Row (Boston, Mass), Swish Alps (Hollywood Hills), Vaseline Heights (gay centre of Portland, Ore.)

45. Countries: Nicknames

n. 1. Bananaland (Queensland, Aus.), Big Ditch (Atlantic Ocean), Blighty (UK), Down Under (Australia), Honkers (Hong Kong), Jamdung (Jamaica), the World (the USA as seen by troops in Vietnam)

46. Region; Locality

n. 1. boonies, boondocks, manor, nabes, neck of the woods, patch, side (W1), stamping ground, turf
2. *unpleasant place:* armpit, bottoms (US black), craphouse, creepsville, dump, lavatory, Motel Hell, muckhole, nowhere city, shitheap, skid row, toilet, wrong side of the tracks
3. spec. blue feature (water area on a map); civvy street, Cloud 9

47. Thoroughfare

n. 1. *road:* blacktop, double nickel, drag, frog and toad (rhy.sl.), M-way; spec. milit. use: redball (enemy road, in Vietnam)
2. *street:* bricks, drag, field of wheat (rhy.sl.)
3. *main street:* Afro set, fast lane, front line, front street, main drag, – stem, set; spec. bread and butter

(rhy.sl. = gutter), Johnny Horner
(rhy.sl. = corner)
4. *meeting place:* meat market,
– rack; spec. homosexual use:
cottage, tearoom

48. Enclosure
n. 1. bullpen, hootch, shovel and
broom (rhy.sl. = room); spec. office
(any workplace – pilot's cabin,
pimp's bar, etc.)
2. *house:* cat and mouse (rhy.sl.),
gaff, joint, pad; spec. deri, derry
(derelict house), fancy crib,
mahogany flat (US black)
3. *sleeping place:* doss, doss house,
flop, – house, kip, – house
4. *residence:* crib, dorm, fleabag,
padding crib; spec. slaughter house,
whip shack (US black: a place for
sex); animal house (US campus: the
least fashionable fraternity house)
5. *garden:* Dolly Varden (rhy.sl.)
6. *spec. places:* bone yard, silent city
(cemetery); cooler (mortuary); caff,
greasy spoon, takeaway (cafe);
chippy (chip shop); labour (labour
exchange); tekram (backsl. =
market); farm, funny farm,
giggle-house (Aus.), loony bin,
– farm, nut house (mental hospital);
prison: nick; sport: end (of a
football ground); crime: flat joint
(gambling), honky-tonk, slaughter
(a dump for stolen goods); uni
(university); bog, crapper, dike,
john, loo, shitter, snakes house
(lavatory), grubber (Aus.); spike
(vagrants' hostel); trap (club); slide
(transvestite club)
7. *homeless:* on the bricks, – stones,
– street
8. *unpleasant, dirty place:* pisshole,
shithole

MOTION: VELOCITY
49. Speed; Swiftness
n. 1. action, the double, get-up-and-
go, go, hot-foot, hustle, lick, pep,
quick-time, rabbit fever, zip

2. *going fast:* hot-footing, scoot,
scram, skedaddle, spin, whirl; spec.
white line fever (driving fast)
3. *something fast:* bat out of hell,
blue streak, greased lightning,
scorcher, streak of lightning; spec.
wham-bam thank-you ma'am (quick
intercourse)
v. 4. *to go fast:* ace, ball the jack,
barrel (it), belt along, blow ass,
broom, do a fair lick, get one's
skates on, go full blast, – like a bat
out of hell, – a blue streak, – a
bomb, – a house on fire, – a shot
out of hell, – greased lightning,
– like hell, – like nobody's business,
– like the clappers, – through like a
dose of salts, hightail (it), hit it,
– the wind, hoof it, move one's ass,
neckbreak (US black), pour it on,
rattle one's dags (Aus.), rip (along),
scoot off, shoot off, – over,
– through (Aus.), skedaddle, snap it
up, streak (off), take a powder, take
a runout powder, tear ass, – off,
turn it on, up and dust, whizz (off),
zip, zoom (off)
5. *to hurry:* fall (all) over oneself,
get a move on, get one's arse in
gear, get the lead out, get weaving,
look sharp, make it snappy, move
it, – yourself, shake a leg, shift arse,
snap it up, step lively
6. *to run:* beat feet, cut dirt, fan
one's butt, flap the heels, hightail
(it), lay 'em down, pick 'em up
7. *to accelerate:* hop on it, jump to
it, let her rip, put the skids under
8. *to make go faster:* put the skids
under
adj. 9. *fast:* at a rate of knots,
chop-chop, double quick, hot and
strong, hot cross bun, (rhy.sl. = on
the run), lickety-split, like a bat out
of hell, like a dose of salts, like a rat
up a drain, like winking, off like a
bride's nightie, on the double, on
the hop, on the hurry up, on the
trot, toot sweet, zippy
excl. 10. where's the fire!

11. *full speed:* all the way, all out, at full bat, wide open
12. *hurry up!:* snap it up, wake it up

50. Slowness
v. 1. *to be slow:* dog it, drag –, go nowhere fast, leadfoot, mosey (along), slowpoke
2. *not hurry:* hold one's horses, hold one's water, keep one's shirt on, take it easy
3. *to slow down:* put on the anchors
adj. 4. *slow:* doggy, drag-arse, lazy-arse

MOTION: DIRECTION
51. Direction
n. 1. *U-ie* (u-turn)
v. 2. *go straight:* make a beeline (for)
3. *change direction:* flip-flop, hang, hang a Lilly, – a Louie, – a Ralph, – a U-ie
adv. 4. *moving:* back to square one, on the hoof
5. *in all directions:* all over the shop, everywhichway, hell west and crooked, six ways from Sunday
6. *from both directions:* double-doored (Can.)

52. Approach
n. 1. *arrival:* blow in, check-in, drop in
v. 2. *to arrive:* beat (one) to the punch (US Black use = to arrive first), belly up to, blow in, breeze in, drop in, – by, hit, lob in (Aus.), make the scene, roll in, – up, sneaky-pete, tool in; spec. working use: clock in

53. Entrance
v. 1. *to enter:* barge in, blow in, bob up, breeze along, – in, bust in, drop in, – by, duck in, ease in, ooze in, pop in

2. *enter forcibly:* bust in, crash in, gatecrash, muscle in, nose in
excl. 3. emok nye! (backsl. = come in!)

54. Departure
n. 1. blow, bow-out, check-out, the fade, kiss-off, send-off
2. *hasty departure:* bunk, bust (out), hightail, jump, lam, one-two, powder, runout, – powder, scoot, scram, scrambola, scramskie, skedaddle, skip, vamoose
v. 3. *to leave:* amscray, bail (out), beat feet, – it, beetle off, be missing, blow, – out of, boogie-woogie (US black), book (US black), break in, broom, bugger off, bug out, bunk off, buzz off, check out, choof, clear off, cut (out), cut along, – loose, do a bunk, – a powder, – a runner, fade away, flake off, fly the coop, fuck off, get lost, – on one's bike, – the hell out of Dodge, hat up, haul ass, have it away, – on one's dancers, – on one's toes, heel on (US black use), hightail (it), hit the bricks, – the road, – the street, – the trail, – the wind, hive off (Aus.), honk on, hop the wag, iris out, jam (US black), leg it, let's boogie, light out, make it, mug up (US black), nick off, pedal one's dogs, piss off, pop off, pull up stakes, push along, – off, put it in the wind, raise up (US black use), roll out, run out (on), Scapa Flow (rhy.sl. = to go), scarper, scat, scoot (off), scram, shoot off, shoot the coop, shoot through (Aus.), shove off, skedaddle, skip, sky, sky off (US black use), sling one's hook, slope off, sod off, split, take a hike, – a powder, – a runout powder, – it on the lam, – off, – the air, – the wind, tear off, – loose (US black use), toddle off, up and dust (US black use), vamoose, whizz off, zoom (off); spec. move one's belongs at night to avoid rent: shoot

the moon; hand in one's dinner plate (resign from a job)
4. *sneak off:* do a bunk, duck out, ease out, gumshoe, iris out, skip (out), squirrel off, take it on the creep; spec. jump the gun (start off prematurely)
adv. 5. *departing:* ready for the off, off with a bang
excl. 6. *leave!:* be missing!, blow!, break it up!, bugger off! buzz off!, case off! eff off!, fuck off, get lost! – rooted! (Aus.), go pound salt up your arse!, – to hell!, hop it!, kaycuff foe! (backsl.), naff off!, on your bike!, piss off!, push off!, rack off! (Aus.), scram!, shove off!, sod off!, take a hike! vamoose!; spec. lead on, Macduff (exhorting another person to take the initiative)
7. *spec. goodbye:* Abyssinia, catch you later, toodle-pip, TTFN (ta-ta for now)
8. spec. AWOL (milit. absent without leave)

55. Ascent
n. 1. stiff pull
v. 2. *ascend:* shimmy up, skin up, zoom (up)
excl. 3. alley-oop!, upsidaisy!

56. Descent
n. 1. *fall:* bop, brodie, cropper, flop, header, kerplump, nose-dive, plop, plump, purler, spill
v. 2. *to fall:* come a cropper, – a purler, go arse-over-appetite, – arse-over-tit, go kerplunk, hit the deck, take a spill, – a brodie, – a flier
3. *to sit down:* give the dogs a rest, grab a chair, – a flop, park yourself, – your carcase, take it easy, – a log off (your feet), – the weight off your feet
adv. 4. *head-over-heels:* arse-over-appetite, arse-over-tit

57. Irregular Motion
n. 1. bumpity-bump, flitter-flutter, pitapat
v. 2. bobble
3. *to jerk:* yank

MOTION: TRAVEL
58. Travel in General
n. 1. *wanderer:* mumper
v. 2. *to wander:* bat around, (go on the) bum, case (it) around, cat around, knock about, mooch, slap the pavement, swan around, tool around, tromp (around), truck; spec. island-hop: the Grand Tour (campus use); pack (live as a female tramp)
mod. 3. *moving:* on the go, – the trot

59. Walking
n. 1. ball and chalk (rhy.sl.), footslogging, Guy (Fawkes) (rhy.sl.), leg work, yomping; spec. UK royal family: walkabout; US black use: Memphis glide, pimp stride, slidewalk
v. 2. *to walk:* air out, ankle along, bop, diddy-bop, foot it, poke along, ride shanks' pony, walk the dogs

60. Riding
n. 1. *ride:* hitch, spin, whirl; spec. run (Hell's Angels outing)
2. spec. banker (cab-driver's regular route), burn-up (fast riding of a motorcycle), chicken run (teenage virility ritual involving cars), Hollywood swoop (US black use, one vehicle halts the other by passing and then cutting in front of it)
3. *speed of ride:* herbs (Aus.), horses (horsepower)
v. 4. *to drive fast:* ball the jack, belt it, burn rubber, buzz, caravan, deadhead, do a ton, floor, give (it) the gun, – the herbs (Aus.), gun (it), hammer, hit the gas, jam it, lay

rubber, let her go, – her out, peel out, pill out, put the hammer down, rev, romp it, sandbag, screw it on, thrash (Aus.), wind her up
5. *to ride in a car:* spec. ride punk, ride pussy, ride the bitch's seat (US black: a woman seated between two men); ride tough (US black: drive a smart car)
6. spec. hot-wire (to start a car without an ignition key), Kojak (to find a parking place easily), nerf (to collide with another car), put on the anchors (brake), run out of road (to crash, after failing to take a corner), (have a) shunt (to collide), soup up (to improve the car's performance), tailgate (to follow too closely)
7. *to hitchhike:* bum, go on the thumb, hitch, push the thumb, ride one's thumb, thumb it, thumb-trip
8. *spec. surfing:* to ride the planks
phr. 9. *what do you drive?:* what are you pushing (US black)

MOTION: TRANSFERENCE
61. Transference
v. 1. *to transport, haul, carry:* cart, hump, pack, tote
2. *to pull:* schlep (Yid.), snake, yank
3. *to reach for:* make a long arm
4. *to raise:* hike

62. Throwing
n. 1. chuck, shy; spec. cricket use: dollydrop, skier, steepler
2. *hard throw:* bullet, hot one, hotshot, hummer, ripper, scorcher, sizzler, smoker, steamer, streaker, whizzer, zipper
v. 3. *to throw:* bung, chuck, cut loose (with), let go (of), rifle (it in), shy, smoke, uncork

63. Ejection
n. 1. *discharge, dismissal:* the air, the axe, big E, boot, boot-out, bounce, brush (off), bump, bum's rush, chuck, dust, elbow, gate, KB, kiss-off, knock-back, order of the boot, Spanish archer ('El Bow'), walking papers
v. 2. *to dismiss:* blow out, boot (out), bounce, bump, call it a day, chuck, ditch, eighty-six (rhy.sl. = nix), elbow, give the air, – the sack, the belt, – the brown envelope, – the (old) heave-ho, – the elbow, axe etc. (see n. 1), hoof out, put the skids under, – the screws to, sack, see the back off, send away with a flea in one's ear, send packing, show the door, – the gate, sling out, turf out; spec. kick upstairs (move to a senior but less important job)
3. *to be dismissed:* get the chop, – the bullet, – the order of the boot, – the sack, etc. (see n. 1.)
adv. 4. *dismissed:* booted, out on one's ear, – one's arse

Matter

GEOGRAPHIC CONDITIONS
64. World; Earth
n. 1. the great outdoors, Mother Nature

65. Heavens; Space
n. 1. upstairs, up there
2. *the sun:* bath bun, currant bun (rhy.sl.), rays, UVs
v. 3. *to sunbathe:* catch some rays

66. Natural Phenomena; Weather
n. 1. *hot weather:* blazing (down), peas in the pot (rhy.sl. = hot), roaster, scorcher, sizzler, swelterer
2. *cold weather:* brass monkey weather, cold snap, dirty weather, filthy weather, freezer, Naughton and Gold (rhy.sl.), potatoes in the mould (rhy.sl.), taters
3. *wet weather:* bucketing down, pissing down
4. *rain:* Andy Cain (rhy.sl.), pleasure and pain (rhy.sl.); spec. send her down, Hughie (Aus.: an appeal for rain, or good surfing)
5. *fog:* peasouper
6. *winds:* Irish hurricane (dead calm)
v. 7. *to rain:* bucket down, piss down, rain cats and dogs, spit
8. *to be windy:* blow great guns

FLUIDS
67. Liquids
n. 1. *water:* Adam's ale, fisherman's daughter (rhy.sl.)
2. *sea:* big ditch, – lake, briny, Davy Jones' locker, deep, ditch, drink, frog pond, oggin, pond, puddle; spec. surfing use: Big Kahoona (a perfect wave)
3. *waves:* spec. white horses (white caps on choppy waves)
4. *ice:* rocks
5. *petrol:* gas, juice; spec. hot rod use: nitro
6. *oil:* black gold, crude, lube
7. *thick, sticky liquid:* dope, gism, glop, goo, goop, guck, gunk
8. *glue:* dope, goo

MATERIALS; DEVICES
68. Raw Materials
n. 1. *things in general:* stuff
2. *spec. oil rigs:* mud; iron-, glassworks, etc. grog (refractory material)
3. *gold:* red stuff, yellow stuff
4. *silver:* white stuff
5. *stone, brick:* Irish confetti (when thrown at others)
6. *silk:* squeeze
7. *lead:* bluey

69. Devices; Implements
n. 1. *equipment:* fit-up, gear, kludge, lashup, layout, rig, rig-up, set-up, shebang, works
2. *indefinite objects:* bits and bobs, dingbat, dingus, doings, dojigger, do(o)-dad(s), doodah, do(o)-hickey, gitty-gap, gizmo, gubbins, jig, junk, majigger, motherfucker, oojah, shebang, so-and-so, stuff, thingummibob, thingummijig, thingy, whamdoodle, what-d'you-call-it, whatchamacallit, whatnot, whatsit, whodjamaflop, you know, you know what
3. *new object:* wheeze, wrinkle

4. *tool:* April fool (rhy.sl.), ratfucker, (home-made starting handle)

5. *prizing tool:* jemmy, jimmy

6. *hammer:* Birmingham screwdriver, Irish screwdriver

7. *wrench:* knuckle buster, monkey

8. *household equipment:* asswipe (lavatory paper), B-52, church key (can-opener), band of hope, Cape of Good Hope (rhy.sl. = soap), hottie (hot water bottle), jerry, Ted Frazer (rhy.sl. = cut-throat razor); spec. homosexual use: trick towel (used by male prostitute to clean up after a client)

9. *knife:* axe, blade, charming wife (rhy.sl.), chiv, cutter, flick, nigger-flicker, shiv, slicer

10. *scissors:* snips

11. *shovel:* banjo, Lord Lovel (rhy.sl.)

12. *drill:* kanga

13. *keys:* church key (can opener), twister (house key)

14. *saw:* bear's paw (rhy.sl.)

15. *nails:* monkey's tails (rhy.sl.)

16. *matches:* cuts and scratches (rhy.sl.), strikers

17. *clock:* dickery (dock), hickory dock (rhy.sl.), ticker

18. *stationery, etc.:* blotch, (blotting paper), bungy (eraser), nerd pack (holder for pens)

19. *cleaning:* honey cart, – wagon, pooper-scooper

20. *carriers:* cock sparrow (rhy.sl. = barrow), esky, poly bag (polythene)

21. *covering:* Auntie Ella (rhy.sl. = umbrella), brolly, tarp (tarpaulin)

22. *lights:* finsburies (rhy.sl. f. park = arc), glim, Harry Randall (rhy.sl. = candle)

23. *vehicles:* body and soul lashing (sailing use); George (automatic pilot)

24. *musical instruments:* axe, bull-fiddle (double bass), joanna (rhy.sl. = piano), Strat (Stratocaster electric guitar), taps (drums)

25. *record players, etc.:* boofer box, chatter box, ghetto blaster, Third World briefcase, wog box; nigger box (TV); sides (records)

26. *technology:* bug (surveillance device); spaghetti (a mass of wires), stinger (a light socket extension); number-cruncher (large computer)

27. *contraceptive devices:* flying saucer (diaphragm), French letter, – tickler, frenchie, frenchy, rubber, rubber boot, – johnny, safe, scumbag

---

WEAPONS; EXPLOSIVES

70. Weapon

n. 1. *weapon:* enforcer, heat, persuader, piece, tool

2. *clubs:* life preserver, sap, slug

3. *brass knuckles:* brassies, iron mikes, knuckle dusters, knucks, maulers

4. spec. pimp sticks (a whip made of wire coathangers)

5. *pocket knife:* chiv, toothpick

71. Firearm

n. 1. action piece, bad news, barker, belly gun, Betsy, cannon, chopper, chunk, equalizer, gat, grease-gun, heater, hog-leg, iron, peacemaker, piece, poker, pom-pom, rod, roscoe, Saturday Night Special, speaker, tool, zipgun; spec. thirty-eight (.38), forty-five (.45), Mag (Magnum); pump (pump-action shotgun); sawed off (sawn off shotgun)

2. *machine gun:* Chicago piano, – typewriter, chopper

3. *spec. military use:* arty (artillery), Bouncing Betty (a mine that springs into the air), chopper (helicopter), dick gun (a rubber bullet gun), fast mover (F-4 fighter-bomber), flat top (aircraft carrier), frag (fragmentation grenade), Huey (HU-1 helicopter), Leaping Lena (see Bouncing Betty), MA

(mechanical ambush), slicks
(helicopters), the gun (M-60 light
machine gun), thumper (M-79
grenade launcher), tin can (naval
destroyer), toe popper (M-14
anti-personnel mine), willie peter
(white phosphorus)

72. Ammunition; Explosives
n. 1. ammo, buck (buckshot),
hardware, lead, rockets; spec.
pineapple (bomb or grenade)

73. Explosion; Shot
n. 1. bing, boom, bong, bop, bust,
pam, plink, plunk, pow, whoomp,
whomp
2. *gunfire:* Chicago lightning; spec.
lit up (under fire), incoming (hostile
gunfire)
v. 3. *to shoot:* bust caps, hose down,
lead (down), pop (off), turn on the
heat; spec. dry-snap (to fire a
weapon without ammunition)
4. spec. frag (to assassinate a fellow
soldier with a fragmentation
grenade)

74. Armed
n. 1. drop (being able to draw a
weapon before a rival)
v. 2. *to be armed:* pack iron, – a gat,
rod, etc.
adv. 3. *armed:* heeled, loaded for
bear, packing iron, etc., rodded,
tooled up
phr. 4 spec. rock and roll (milit.:
firing an automatic weapon in a
steady burst)

VEHICLES AND MOTORS
75. Vehicle
n. 1. *car:* auto, boat, buggy, flivver,
heap, iron, jam jar (rhy.sl.),
john-john (WI), motor, ride, short,
wheels
2. *large car:* Al Capone ride (US
black use), big boat, brougham (US
black use), cruisemobile, gangster

doors, – ride, gas-guzzler, limo,
pimpmobile, spivmobile; spec. black
taxi (Aus. official limousine)
3. *old car:* banger, bone-shaker,
clunker, jalopy, junker, rust-bucket
4. *specific cars:* Bird (thunderbird),
cad, caddy (Cadillac), Connie
(Lincoln Continental), deuce 25,
deuce and a quarter (Buick 225),
DV (Cadillac de Ville), geetoh
(GTO), Jag (Jaguar), Jew Canoe
(derog: Cadillac in US, Jaguar in
UK), kitty-cat (US black: Cadillac),
LD (Cadillac Eldorado), Masers
(Maserati), Merc (Mercedes), rado
(Cadillac Eldorado), Roller, Woler
(Rolls-Royce), Vette (Corvette);
black and white (US police car thus
painted); crummy (transport in
logging camps); ringer, tweedler
(UK criminal use: illegitimate cars);
passion wagon (car used for
seductions); dump truck (derog: car
full of lesbians); woodie
(wood-panelled station wagon);
ringer (stolen and disguised
second-hand car)
5. *trucks:* rig, ute (Aus. utility
trucks)
6. *motorcycles:* ass hammer,
chopper, garbage wagon, hog,
machine, one-lunger; spec. wheelie
(trick riding on a motorcycle)
7. *aircraft:* coffee grinder (old,
unstable aircraft)
8. *ships:* halfpenny dip (rhy.sl.),
tub, the tubs (transatlantic
liners)
9. *railways:* Bedpan line (BR line
between Bedford and St Pancras)
10. *bicycle:* do as you like (rhy.sl.)
11. *ambulance:* blood wagon
12. *public transport:* drain, rattler
(London underground trains); swear
and cuss (rhy.sl. = bus)
13. *cabs:* fast black, flounder and
dab (rhy.sl.), spin; spec. bill (a
taxidriver's license)
14. *collision:* pile-up, prang,
rear-ender, shunt

v. 15. *to crash:* prang, shunt, total, write off

76. Automotive Parts
n. 1. *engine:* cams (camshaft), carb (carburettor), crank (crankshaft), headers (manifold)
2. *brakes:* anchors
3. *accelerator:* hammer
4. *seats:* buddyseat (pillion on motorbicycle), shotgun seat (next to driver), pimp post (US black: armrest between front seats)
5. *tyres:* gangster walls (whitewalls)
6. *handlebars:* apehangers (high, extra-long motorcycle handlebars)
7. *interior:* black on black (US black: black car with black interior)
8. *exterior:* rag top (soft top)
v. 9. decoke (to clean spark plugs)
adv. 10. dressed (US black: a car with every conceivable accessory)

77. Motor; Engine
n. 1. boiler, kettle, pot, hog, mule, donkey; spec. four-, six-banger, four-, six-lunger, kicker (outboard motor)
adj. 2. *specially engineered:* hopped up

BUILDINGS AND FURNITURE
78. Building
n. 1. dive, dump, hole, joint, layout, shebang, spot
2. *house, home:* back-a-yard (WI), crib, drum, eemosh (backsl. = house), kip, pad; spec. crash-pad (house where one can sleep temporarily); condo (condominium); pseudy Tudy, stockbroker Tudor (fake 'Elizabethan' architecture)
3. *apartment:* shotgun flat, walkup
4. *lodging house:* doss, – house, kip, – house
5. *hotel:* spec. Hojo (Howard Johnson's)

6. *public house:* battle-cruiser (rhy.sl.), boozer, rubbidy, rub-a-dub (Aus.); spec. drinker (after hours club); public (public bar); balloon (rhy.sl. = saloon bar); nineteenth hole (a golf-club bar)
7. *cafe, club, etc.:* caff, carry-out, takeaway, takeout; spec. clip-joint (club that defrauds its customers); slop chute (USMC bar)
8. *place of entertainment:* bughutch, fleapit (inferior cinemas); cherry hogs (rhy.sl. = dogs = greyhound tracks)

79. Parts of Houses
n. 1. *lavatory:* altar, bog, can, crapper, dunnee, dunnigan, flush, jakes, john, karsy, lav, lavvy, little boy's/girl's room, little office, loo, pisshole, pisshouse, shithouse, shit jacket, shitter, snakes' house, throne, thunder-box; spec. head(s) (naval)
2. *outside lavatory:* one-, two-holer
3. *lavatory paper:* asswipe, bumf, bum fodder, wipe
4. *window:* burnt (cinder) (rhy.sl.)
5. *fire:* Anna Maria (rhy.sl.)
6. *stairs:* apples and pears (rhy.sl.), wooden road to Bedfordshire
7. *floor:* Rory (rhy.sl. = Rory O'Moore)

80. Camp
n. 1. spec. jungle (US hobo camp)

81. Furniture
n. 1. fixings, sticks
2. *bed:* kife, kip, sack, Uncle Ned (rhy.sl.)
3. *pillow:* weeping willow (rhy.sl.)
4. *table:* Cain and Abel (rhy.sl.)
5. *chair:* lion's lair (rhy.sl.), ryache (backsl.)
6. *mirror:* snake in the grass (rhy.sl = looking glass)
7. *clock:* dickory dock (rhy.sl.)
8. *style:* Jewy Louis (derog: over-ornate

phr. 9. *shut the door:* put the wood in the hole

DRESS
82. Clothes
n. 1. duds, clobber, doodads, drapes, fronts, pieces, rags, rig, schmutter, threads, togs, traps, wrapping; spec. clear cut (US black use: stylish clothes); night clothes (criminal use: dark clothes used for robberies at night)
2. *suit:* piccolo and flute, whistle and flute (rhy.sl.), vine
3. *formal dress:* d.j., monkey suit, soup and fish, tails, tux
4. *best clothes:* best bib and tucker, glad rags, go to meeting clothes, silks (US black)
5. *old clothes:* grubbies, tat
6. *second-hand clothes:* hand-me-downs, reach-me-downs
7. *uniform:* spec. colours, originals (patches, jeans and jacket worn by Hell's Angels); rabbit skin, sheepskin (academic tippets)
8. *civilian clothes:* civvies, dog-robbers (suits worn by off-duty officers)
9. *skirts:* midi, mini, maxi
10. *underwear:* Alan Whickers (rhy.sl. = knickers), BVDs, didies, east and west (rhy.sl. = vest), fleas and ants (rhy.sl. = pants), Harolds (pants), kecks, long johns, passion killers, skivvies, snuggies, UBs (underbodies); spec. falsies; VPL (visible pantie line)
11. *trousers:* bins, council houses (rhy.sl.), daks, kicksies, loon pants (very baggy), petrols (Aus. rhy.sl. petrol bowsers), round the houses (rhy.sl.), strides (Aus.), trou; spec. baggies (shorts worn for surfing)
12. *coat:* benny, boolhipper (US black: leather), crombie, leather piece, nanny goat (rhy.sl.), rod, smother, weasel (and stoat)
13. *swimming costume:* cossie (Aus.)
14. *pyjamas:* jim-jams, pjs
15. *shoes:* beetle-crushers, boppers, bovver boots, brothel creepers, − stompers, daisy roots (rhy.sl. = boots), dogs, howd'ye dos, reptiles, roach-killers, shit stompers, stomp(ers), waffle-stompers, winkle-pickers; spec. air hose (shoes worn without socks); thousand eyes (US black: heavily perforated leather shoes); wellies (wellingtons)
16. *running shoes:* chucks, daps, quick starts (US black)
17. *hats:* chimney, titfer (rhy.sl. tit for tat); spec. boonie hat (soft military hat for jungle use), skidlid (crash helmet), steel pot (steel helmet)
18. *shirts:* dicky dirt, Uncle Bert (rhy.sl.); spec. fag tag, fruit loop (small loop sewn to back of shirt)
19. *pocket:* bin, Lucy Locket, sky (rocket) (rhy.sl.)
20. *sportswear:* jock, jockstrap (athletic supporter)
21. *tight sweater:* shrink; spec. boob-tube (narrow cylindrical garment, encircling breasts)

83. Accessories
n. 1. *gloves:* turtle (doves), (rhy.sl.); spec. mittens (boxing use)
2. *handkerchief:* bubble duster, snotrag
3. *cane:* whangee
4. *tie:* fourth of July (rhy.sl.), Peckham (rhy.sl. Peckam Rye)
5. *socks:* almond (rocks) (rhy.sl.); spec. pimp socks (US black: socks with thin vertical lines)
6. *spectacles:* cheaters, Lancashire lasses (rhy.sl.), shades (dark glasses)
7. *bag:* diddy-bag
8. *wallet:* dummy, goitre, leather, poggler, poke

9. *watch:* Gordon and Gotch (rhy.sl.)

10. *jewellery:* bobbles, glass, ice, jim, red stuff, rocks, Simple Simon (rhy.sl. = diamond), sparkler(s), tom, tomfoolery (rhy.sl.), tot (WI); spec. patacca (fake, rubbishy jewels)

11. *sanitary towels, etc.:* diaper, do rag, G-string, jam-rag, jelly sandwich (US black), rag, sling shot

12. *contraceptives:* bag, French letter, frog, johnny, rozzer (US black), rubber, rubber johnny

13. *cosmetics:* lippy, slip

14. *braces:* airs and graces (rhy.sl.)

84. Dressing

v. 1. *to dress:* get dolled up, – togged up, pile into

2. *to dress up:* dike down, dog it, doll up, look sharp, put on the dog, spiff (oneself) up, tart (oneself) up, tog (oneself) up

adv. 3. *dressed up:* (in one's) best bib and tucker, buttered (US black), choked down (US black), dap, dressed to the nines, dressed up like a dog's dinner, – like a pox doctor's clerk, dolled up, dyke down, flossed up (of a woman), fonked out heavy (US black), full buf, got up, kitted up, laid out, laid to the bone (US black), piss elegant, pressed (US black), pimped down (US black), pooned (up), ragged down (heavy) (US black), suited (down) (US black), spiffed (up), tabbed (US black), togged to the bricks; spec. drag (dressing in the clothes of the opposite sex)

4. *smart:* clean, clean to the bone, fonky –, mod –, ragged –, silked –, tabbed (US black), neat, nifty

5. *colourful:* jazzy

85. Undress

n. 1. dishabilly

2. *nudity:* the altogether, birthday suit, (stark) bollock naked, (in the) buff, (in the) raw

v. 3. *to undress:* drop the duds, – the gear (Aus.), peel, – down, – off, shuck down, strip (off)

4. *teenage pranks:* drop trou, hambone (Aus.), moon, press ham

5. *to undress someone:* debag, pants

adj. 6. *naked:* bare-ass, peeled, raw, starkers

phr. 7. Charlie's dead (your slip is showing)

8. it's one o'clock at the water-works (your fly is undone)

FOOD
86. Food

n. 1. belly timber, choff, chop, chow, chuck, eats, feed, fixings, fodder, fuel, grease, groceries, grub, hash, munga, munger, nosh, peck(s), scoff, scran, tack, tuck, tucker; spec. junk food (fast food)

2. *bad food:* crap, dog's dinner, dog vomit, garbage, glop, gunge, slop(s), shit, vom; spec. burnt offering (burnt food)

3. *bread:* needle and thread, Uncle Fred (rhy.sl.), tommy

4. *sandwich:* butty, sango (Aus.), sarnie

5. *meat:* beemal (backsl. = lamb), cold (frozen meat), delock (backsl. = cold), feeb (backsl. = beef); kayrop (backsl. = pork), piano (US black, spare ribs), teekay (TK = town killed); spec. Kate and Sidney (rhy.sl. = steak and kidney)

6. *sausages:* snorker, snags, swags; spec. red-hots (frankfurters with chilli)

7. *poultry:* elwoff (backsl. = fowl)

8. *stew:* Mulligan stew (tramp's assembly of available foods)

9. *mince:* shit on a shingle (minced meat on toast)

10. *spreads:* marj (margarine), stammer and stutter (rhy.sl. = butter)

11. *potatoes:* murphies, praties,

spuds, taters; spec. bimps (french fries)

12. *cake:* Joe Blake, Sexton Blake (rhy.sl.); spec. sinker (doughnut)

13. *mayonnaise:* mayo

14. *watermelon:* African golf ball, culture fruit

15. *cheese:* bended knees, stand at ease (rhy.sl.)

16. *sugar:* sand

17. *breakfast cereals:* burgoo, soggies

18. *vegetables:* veggies; spec. prison use: has-beens (rhy.sl. = greens)

19. *kipper:* Jack the Ripper (rhy.sl.)

20. *pizza:* za

21. *pickles:* Harvey Nichols (rhy.sl.)

22. *pasta:* spag bol (spaghetti bolognese)

23. *gravy:* army and navy (rhy.sl.)

24. *salad:* rabbit food

25. *soup:* loop-the-loop (rhy.sl.)

26. *foreign food:* (an) Indian, (a) Chinese, Chink chow

27. *egg dishes:* Adam and Eve, – on a raft (of toast), – on a raft and wreck 'em (scrambled eggs on toast), two looking at you (two fried eggs), sunny side up (eggs fried on one side only), two down, – with their eyes closed, over easy, (eggs turned over), two on a slice of squeal (two eggs on fried ham)

28. *prison tea:* diesel

29. *ice cream:* scream

30. *chilli:* red

87. Beverage: Drink (non-alcoholic)

n. 1. *coffee:* java, joe

2. *tea:* brew, cuppa, Rosy Lea, – Lee (rhy.sl.), splosh, you and me (rhy.sl.)

3. *cocoa:* ki (RN use)

4. *milk:* cow, Grade-A

5. *lemonade, soda, etc.:* pop

v. 6. *to drink:* chugalug, dip the beak, gargle, inhale, knock back, put away, wet the whistle

88. Preparing and Serving

v. 1. chase up, dish up, rustle –, scare –, fix; spec. shackle up (tramp use, cooking lunch), brew up (to make a pot of tea)

2. *to serve food:* hash, jump tables, sling hash

3. spec. spud-bashing (peeling potatoes)

4. *to boil:* Conan Doyle (rhy.sl.)

89. Eating

n. 1. *daily food:* three squares

2. *catered food:* take away, take out

3. *breakfast:* brekker; spec. Mexican breakfast (a cigarette and a glass of water)

4. *dinner:* din-din, Jimmy Skinner, Lilley and Skinner (rhy.sl.), Tommy Tucker (rhy.sl. = supper)

5. *feast:* beano, blow-out, bust-out, gross-out, grubfest, nosh-up, spread, tuck-in; pig heaven (gross over-eating)

v. 6. *to eat:* chow down, feed one's face, get one's eating tackle around, gnaw a bone, grab a bite, grub up, hook down, lower (it), peck, put away (the groceries), put on the feed bag, – the nosebag, spoon, stoke up, stow away, tie on the feed-bag, – nosebag

7. *to eat greedily:* blow (oneself out), cram, dig in, eat like a horse, fill one's face, gross out, go for the groceries, grub it up, guzzle, hog it (down), ibble out, knock (it) back, lay into, mac out, pig out, pitch in, pork out, scarf (up), scoff, shovel (it) down, slop (it) up, stack (it) away, throw (it) down, wade into, whack (it), back; spec. guzzle (choke)

8. *to eat a small meal:* catch a bite, tear off a bite

phr. 9. *calls to eat:* chow down!, come and get it!, dig in!, pitch in!, grub('s) up!

abbrev. 10. FHB (family hold back)

90. Appetite; Thirst
n. 1. inner man
2. *hunger:* spec. munchies
(cannabis-induced cravings for
food)
3. *lack of appetite:* spec. chuck
horrors (loathing of food that
follows withdrawal from heroin)
mod. 4. *hungry:* peckish

91. Cooking and Dining Utensils
n. 1. *eating utensils:* Duke of York
(rhy.sl. = fork), eating irons;
sunbeam (Aus. a clean item of
cutlery on the table); drugstore (the
cutlery trolley in a restaurant)
2. spec. doggie-bag (a bag provided
in some restaurants to take away
leftovers)

LIQUOR: PERSONS
92. Liquor Dealers and Drinkers
n. 1. *alcohol seller:* mine host
2. *barman:* apron, barkeep,
mixologist
3. *drunkard:* barfly, booze artist,
– hound, boozer, bottle baby,
dredge-head, jarhead, jickhead (US
black), jughead, juice-freak, – head,
lush, piss artist, pisspot, plonky,
rum-dum, rummy, rumpot, sauce
hound, soak, souse, tosspot; spec.
bottle-a-day man, two-bottle
man, etc.
phr. 4. *free:* on the house

93. Abstainers and Prohibitionists
v. 1. to go to the wagon
mod. 2. TT (teetotal)
phr. 3. off the bottle, on the wagon

LIQUOR: ALCOHOL
94. Liquor (general)
n. 1. alky, bevvy, booze, the
creature, eel juice, gargle, grog,
hooch, juice, jump steady (US
black), neck-oil, oil, piss, sauce,
shicker, swag (US black), tea; spec.

hard stuff (spirits as opposed to
beer, wine)
2. *superior liquor:* (just) what the
doctor ordered, a little of what you
fancy, the (real) goods, the real
McCoy, – stuff
3. *inferior liquor:* cat's pee, – piss,
dishwater, gnat's pee, – piss, rat's
pee, – piss
4. *illegal liquor:* jungle juice, kong,
moon, moonshine, nigger-pot,
panther piss, potato jack, white
lightning
5. *effects of liquor:* bang, boot,
buzz, jolt, kick, lift, oof, oomph,
pep, powee, punch, smack, sock,
wham, zing, zip, zowie
6. *measure of liquor:* shot

95. Varieties of Liquor
n. 1. *beer:* amber fluid, – liquid,
– nectar, apple fritter (rhy.sl. =
bitter), beevos, brew, brewski,
Crimea (rhy.sl.), greenie, joy juice,
jug, oh my dear (rhy.sl.), reeb
(backsl.), road brew, skimmish,
stage fright (rhy.sl. = light ale),
suds, wallop; spec. Nigerian lager,
photo finish (rhy.sl.), plain
(Guinness stout)
2. *wine:* berries (US black), plonk,
pluck (US black), schoolboy scotch
(US black), smash, vino
3. *cheap wine:* red Biddy, dago red,
muski (muscatel), railroad whisky,
sixteen-year-old after-shave, smoke,
sneaky Pete
4. *champagne:* boy, bubbly,
champers, fizz, poo, pop; spec. the
Widow (Veuve Cliquot)
5. *whisky:* brownie, the creature,
gay and frisky (rhy.sl.), gold watch,
pimple and blotch (rhy.sl. = scotch)
6. *cheap spirits:* dog juice, redeye,
rotgut
7. *brandy:* fine and dandy,
Jack-a-dandy (rhy.sl.)
8. *gin:* mother's ruin, Vera Lynn
(rhy.sl.)
9. *port:* didn't ought (rhy.sl.); spec.

WPLJ, shake-'em down (white port and lemon juice)
10. *rum:* Tom Thumb (rhy.sl.)
11. *abnormal drinks:* blob (Aus. mix of brandy, wine and hot water); corporation cocktail (coalgas in milk), metho, smoke, white lady (Aus. metholated spirits)

96. Mixed or Adulterated Drink
n. 1. spec. bloody (bloody Mary)
phr. 2. on the rocks (with ice), back (on the side, ie: 'soda back')

LIQUOR: DRINKING
97. Drinking (general)
n. 1. boozing, hitting the bottle, lushing (it up), swilling, tying one on, wetting one's whistle
2. *a drink:* bracer, drop (of the creature), gargle, hit, jag, jolt, liquid lunch, night-cap, rosiner (Aus.), shot, slug, snifter, snort, squirt game, tincture, tonic, turps (Aus.), wet; spec. eye-opener, phlegm-cutter (first of the day); leg opener (drink when used for seduction); hair of the dog (an anti-hangover drink); one for the ditch, – for the road (a farewell drink); pick-me-up (invigorating drink)
v. 3. *to drink:* bend one's elbow, booze, – it up, chug, chug-a-lug, crack a bottle, – tube (Aus.), dip the bill, – the snoot, farm, gargle, get a load on, get a snootful, get an edge on, – one's nose painted, – one going, hit the booze, – the bottle, – the jug, – the sauce, hoist one, inhale (a snort), irrigate the tonsils, knock (one) back, lush, – it around, – it up, oil the tonsils, put one/a few back, – down, shicker (Yid.), slop (some) down, sneeze, splice the mainbrace, suck the bottle, swig, swill, take a drop, – a few, – one, – a wet, etc., throw (one, a few, etc.) down, tie one on, tip, wet

one's whistle; spec. brownbag (to drink from a 'hidden' bottle when public drinking is banned); fall off the wagon (to resume drinking after a period of abstinence); wet the baby's head (to celebrate by drinking)
adv. 4. *drinking:* on the bash, on the bottle; D&D (drunk and disorderly)
phr. 5. it's the beer talking (an excuse for breaking wind)

98. Spree; Party
n. 1. bat, batter, bender, binge, blind, booze-up, bout, gig, shitface, shindig, shindy; spec. down to Larkin (free drinks); BYO (Aus. 'Bring Your Own' drink to a party); beer bust, beer fest (beer-drinking only)
v. 2. *to go drinking:* cut up, go on a bat, a bender, etc., hell around, raise hell, paint the town red, pull to a set (US black)
adv. 3. *on a party:* on a bat, – a batter, – a bender, – a bust, – a toot, on the lush, – the piss, – the randan, – the razzle, – the tiles, – the tipple

99. Toasts; Drinking Invitations
phr. 1. best of luck!, bottoms up!, bung-ho!, cheerio!, cheers!, chin-chin!, down the hatch!, good luck!, here's how!, here's looking at you!, here's mud in your eye!, more power to your elbow!
2. *invitations to drink:* get them in, it's your corner, what's your poison?, your shout, you're in the chair

100. Temperance; Abstinence
v. 1. to get straight, go on the wagon

LIQUOR: EFFECTS
101. Drunkenness
n. 1. affliction, blind staggers, edge, glow, skinful, snootful, staggers, thick head

v. 2. *to be drunk:* to be addled, – afflicted, – afloat, – basted, – blasted, – bevvied, – bowsered, – boxed, – canned, etc. (see 101.3), bet one's kettle, burn with a low blue flame, – one's shoulder, get a jag on, – one's shoes full, go Borneo, – for veg, – to Mexico, hang one on, have a buzz on, – a few too many, – a heat on, – a skinful, – one's back teeth afloat, – one's pots on, kill one's dog, lay (US black), lose one's rudder, pepper 'em up (US black), show it, squiff out, tank, walk on one's cap-badge, – on rocky socks, watch the ant races

adj. 3. *drunk:* about right, addled, afflicted, afloat, aled up, alkied, all at sea, all mops and brooms, – wet, arseholed, arse on backwards, awash, awry, back teeth afloat, bagged, basted, belly up, below the mahogany, belted, bevvied, blasted, bleary, blind, blitzed, boiled, bombed, boozed, – up, bottled, bowsered, boxed, Brahms and Lizst (rhy.sl. = pissed), bug-eyed, bullet proofed, bummed, buoyant, buzzed, canned, can't find one's arse with both hands, – hit the ground with one's hat, – see through a ladder, carrying a load, chateaued, clobbered, cock-eyed, comboozelated, commode-hugging (drunk), corked, corned, crocked, crocko, cross-eyed, cut, damaged, damp, decks-awash, dizzy, drunk as a bastard, – a bat, – a beggar, – a besom, – a big owl, – boiled owl, – brewer's fart, – a cook, – a coon, – coot, – a cooter, – a dog, – a fiddler, – a fiddler's bitch, – a fish, – a fly, – a fowl, – a Gosport fiddler, – a hog, – a king, – a little red wagon, – a log, – a lord, – a monkey, – a Perraner, – a pig, – a piper, – a poet, – a rolling fart, – a sailor, – a skunk (in a trunk), – a sow, – a swine, – a tapster, – a tick, – a top, – a wheelbarrow, – to the pulp, elephant's trunk (rhy.sl.), elevated, embalmed, exalted, faced, fallen off the wagon, far gone, feeling funny, – good, – high, – no pain, – right royal, fired (up), flaked, flako, flummoxed, flushed, flying blind, foxed, fractured, fried, full, full as a boot, – a bull, – an egg, – fairy's phonebook, – a fiddler, – a goat, – googy egg, – a lord, – as a pig's ear, – a seaside shithouse on Boxing Day (Aus.), – a state school hatrack, – the family po, – a tick, – two race trains, – to the gills, gaga, gassed, geed (up), giffed (from TGIF: Thank God Its Friday), ginned (up), glad, globular, glowing, goofy, groggy, half-cut, – gone, – seas over, – slewed, – shot, – the bay over, hammered, high (as a kite), hit and missed (rhy.sl. = pissed), iced to the eyebrows, inked (Aus.), in one's cups, – orbit, – the bag, – the tank, – the wrapper, jarred, jiggered, John Bull (Aus. rhy.sl. = full), juiced, laced, laid out, lame, legless, likkered, listing to starboard, lit, – to the gills, lit up, – like Broadway, – a Christmas tree, – Main Street, – a store window, – Times Square, – London, loaded, loaded to the barrel, – the earlobes, – the gills, – the guards, – the gunnels, – the hat, – the muzzle, – the Plimsoll mark, – the tailgate, looped, low in the saddle, lubricated, lushy, maxed (out), melted, mizzled, mulled (up), muzzy, newted, not all there, off nice, oiled, on a brannigan, – a skate – a tipple, on the booze, – the floor, – the fritz, – the grog, – the piss, – the sauce, one over the eight, out of one's head, out of one's mind, out to lunch, over the top, paralytic, petrified, pickled, pie-eyed, pissed, – as a fart, – as a newt, – as a rat, – to the ears, – up, pixillated, plastered, polluted, pop-eyed, potted, primed, putrid, ratted, reeking, rigid, ripe, ripped (to the tits), roaring, rolling, rotten (Aus.), saturated, sauced schizzed, seeing double, – bats, – the bears, – pink elephants, etc., shellacked, shickered, shitfaced, skulled, skunked, skew-whiff, slewed, slopped, sloshed, smashed, snockered, snootered, soaked, sodded, soused, sozzled, spifflicated, squashed, squiffy, stewed, – as a prune, – to the eyebrows, – the gills, stiff, stinking, stinko, stoked, stoned, stonkered, stretched, stung (Aus.), swacked, swacko, tanked (up), teed up, teeth under, three sheets to the wind, tiddly, tipsy, tired, tired and emotional, top heavy, topped up, totalled, trashed, tubed, tweeked, twisted, under the influence, under the table, under the weather, vegetable, wasted, wazzocked, well away, well-oiled, whazood, wollied, woozy, wrecked

102. Hangover
n. 1. DTs, head, Joe Blakes (Aus. rhy.sl. = shakes), morning after (the night before), pink elephants, shakes
v. 2. *to feel ill:* have a mouth like the inside of an Arab's underpants, – the bottom of a bird's cage, – a Turkish wrestler's jockstrap
3. *a drink to recover:* hair of the dog

LIQUOR: MANUFACTURE; SALE
103. Manufacture and Sale
n. 1. spec. wash (WI: mash used in home-distilleries)
v. 2. *to work in a bar:* behind the stick

104. Drinking Establishment
n. 1. battle-cruiser (rhy.sl. = boozer), booze joint, boozer, dive, drinkery, filling station, jack (rhy.sl. = jack tar = bar), jinny, juice house, leeky store, LIQ (US black), rescue station, rubbidy, rub-a-dub (rhy.sl. = pub), scatter, vineyard
2. *illicit establishment:* blind pig, blues (WI), shebeen, slygrog (Aus.)

105. Drink Container
n. 1. *liquor container:* perch (pint), trophy (half a gallon), puppy (small bottle)
2. *wine bottle:* crop (fifth of a gallon), mickey, short dog
3. *beer:* frosty, minnow, stubby, tinnie, tube
4. *empty bottle:* dead, – man, marine, soldier

TOBACCO
106. Tobacco
n. 1. baccy, salmon (and trout) (rhy.sl. = snout), snout
2. *cigarette:* burn, butt, ciggie, coffin nail, dub, dubber, fag, gasper, Harry Wragg (rhy.sl. = fag), oily (rhy.sl. oily rag = fag), rette, straight, weed
3. *end of a cigarette:* bumper, butt, dog-end, fag-end, short, shorts, snipe
4. *hand-made cigarette:* roll-up, roll-your-own
5. *cigarette papers:* papers, skins
6. *cigarette lighter:* flint
7. *cigar:* la-dee-dah (rhy.sl.), stogie; spec. guinea stinker (a cheap cigar)
v. 8. *to pass cigarettes:* flash the ash, toss the squares (US black)
9. spec. defug (to get fresh air into a smokey room)

107. Tobacco Using
n. 1. *a puff of a cigarette:* drag
v. 2. *to smoke:* take a drag, – puff,

– pull, suck on; spec. bog, niggerlip (to wet the end of a cigarette when smoking)

3. *to light a cigarette:* spec. match me!

4. *share a cigarette:* do a twos (WI)

Animate Existence

LIFE

108. Life
n. 1. school of hard knocks, university of life; spec. good run, long innings (long life)

109. Pregnancy
n. 1. pudding club
2. *foetus:* little stranger
v. 3. *to make pregnant:* knock up, put in the family way, – in the club, – up the duff, stork; spec. break an ankle, cheat the starter (to become pregnant out of wedlock)
mod. 4. *pregnant:* a bun in the oven, clucky (Aus.), egg in the nest, fat (US Black), in pig, in the (pudding) club, in the family way, infanticipating, knocked up, on the hill, – the nest, poisoned (US black), preggers, priggling, pu the elop (backsl. = up the pole), the rabbit died, up the creek, – the duff, – the flue (Aus.), – the pole – the spout

110. Birth
n. 1. blessed event

111. Age
n. 1. *old age:* anno domini
v. 2. *to be old:* be over the hill, – past it, have whiskers, make old bones, seen better days; spec. senior out (to abandon the young lifestyle)
adj. 3. *young:* wet behind the ears
4. *old:* no chicken, one foot in the grave, over the hill, past it, seen one's best days; spec. on the shelf (of an ageing woman, still unmarried)

DEATH

112. Death
n. 1. big sleep, (big) chill, (final) curtain, curtains, end of the ball game, fadeout, kickoff, kiss-off, last farewell, – goodbye, – muster, – roundup, long goodbye, (final) pushoff, the (grim) reaper, send off; spec. Roman candle (milit. use: death when a parachute fails to open)
2. *corpse:* cold meat, dead –, goner, rags and bones, stiff, wormbait
3. *cemetery:* bone yard; spec. Davy Jones' locker (a watery grave)
4. *coffin:* six-foot bungalow, pine overcoat, wooden kimono, – overcoat
v. 5. *to die:* answer the last roll-call, – the last muster, – the last round-up, be thrown for a loss, bite the dust, buy the farm, call it a day, – quits, cash in one's chips, check out, come to a sticky end, conk out, crap out, croak, curl up one's toes (and die), cut one's cable, drop off the twig, – the cue, feed the worms, get (as in 'get yours, get his', etc.), get it in the neck, give up the ship, go belly up, – for a Burton, – west, go for one's tea, go to the races, hand in one's dinner pail, hang up one's harness, – one's hat, have one's chips, – one's number come up, join the great majority, jump the last hurdle, keel over, kick off, – the bucket, – up daisies, – up dust, lay down one's knife and fork, pass in one's dinner pail, peg out, push up the daisies, put one's checks in the rack, quit, slam off, snuff it, strike out, take the big jump, throw

in one's cards, – one's hand, – the sponge, turn one's face to the wall, – up one's toes, weigh out

6. *to drown:* go feed the fishes, go to Davy Jones' locker, turn into fish food

7. *kill oneself:* do the Dutch, do oneself in, take a Brodie, – the easy way out; spec. gorge out (leap from a high cliff), bump oneself off, put out one's lights, take a powder, top oneself, turn off one's lights, wipe oneself out

8. *bury:* to plant, put six feet under, send home in a box

9. *to be dying:* on one's last legs, one foot in the grave, (have) one's number come up, pegging out

adv. 10. *dead:* across the river, all bets are off, all up, belly up, checked out, counting worms, croaked, dead as a doornail, done for, gone for a Burton, – west, kicked the bucket, – off, one's hash is settled, – number is up, – race is run, out for the last count, – of the picture, – of one's misery, pegged out, popped off, pushing up daisies, rubbed out, shuffled out of the deck, stiff, through, (all) washed out, – washed up, wasted; spec. KIA (milit. abbrev. killed in action)

113. Killing; Murder
n. 1. the business, – big chill, – kiss-off, the bump (off), the chill, hit, one way ticket, rub-out, wipe out, the works; spec. one-way ride, slay-ride; necktie party (a hanging or lynching); contract (a killing arranged for a fee)

2. *death by shooting:* lead poisoning
v. 3. *to be executed:* spec. burn, fry, sit in the hot seat, take the juice (die in the electric chair); swing (for it) (to be hanged)

4. *to kill:* biff, blast, blow away, brush off, bump (off), cancel one's ticket, chill, clean up, croak, cut loose, erase, do in, do the business on, – the job (on), drop, fog, give the business, – the chop, – the rap, – the works, get shot of, grease, hit, ice, knock (US black), knock off, – out, – over, let one have it, make cold meat of, off, plaster, polish off, put away, put out one's lights, – to sleep, rain on, rip off, rub out, send up the river, snipe (US black), snuff (out), spifflicate, squib off, stop one's clock, take care of, – for an airing, – for a ride, – off the count, – out, top, waste, whack out, zap; spec. DX (milit. euph: direct exchange); make one's bones (Mafia use: perform one's first murder); reimburse (murder some who will not pay debts)

5. *to shoot:* lead down, plug; spec. gutshoot (to shoot in the belly)

6. *to mark for death:* put a notice on, – the cross on, take out a contract on

PLANTS
114. Plants
n. 1. April showers (rhy.sl. = flowers)

2. spec. carnies (carnations, Aus.), glads (gladioli, Aus.)

ANIMALS
115. Animals
n. 1. *dogs:* bow-wow, goddie (backsl.), mutt, pooch, tyke; spec. dachsie, sausage dog (dachshund)

2. *chicken:* chook (Aus.)

3. *birds:* bow and arrow (rhy.sl. = sparrow)

4. *insects:* clinch (bedbug), cooties, creepy crawly, taxi-cabs (rhy.sl = crabs)

5. *dog excrement:* dog, doggy-do, hocky; spec. pooper-scooper (implement for cleaning up after dog)

6. spec. alderman's nail (rhy.sl. = tail)

7. spec. BEM (Bug-Eyed Monster)
8. *donkey:* burro, donk, moke
9. *elephant:* heffalump
10. *horse:* critter, dobbin, dog, gee-gee; spec. screw (an inferior horse); trotter (racehorse)

THE BODY
116. Parts of the Body
n. 1. *the body:* bod, chassis, frame; spec. shaft (the female body considered purely for sex)
2. *hair:* barnet (fair) (rhy.sl.), righteous moss (US black)
3. *mind:* gourd, thinker, upstairs
4. *head:* attic, bean, belfry, biscuit, block, boko, bonce, chump, coco, conk, crust of bread (rhy.sl.), deache (backsl.), dome, loaf, napper, noggin, noodle, nut, pimple, scone (Aus.), swede, topknot, top storey, wig
5. *face:* airs and graces (rhy.sl.), beezer, boat (rhys.sl. boat-race = face), chevy chase (rhy.sl.), clock, dial, esaff (backsl.), frontage, Jem Mace (rhy.sl.), kisser, lug, map, mug, mush, pan, phiz, phizog, puss, smiler
6. *jaw:* jackdaw, rabbit's paw, (rhy.sl.); spec. glass jaw (boxing use: a fragile jaw)
7. *mouth:* bazoo, cakehole, chops, flapper, gob, hole, kisser, maw, north and south (rhy.sl.), puss, smush, trap, yap
8. *teeth:* choppers, eating tackle, Hampsteads (rhy.sl. Hampstead Heath), laughing tackle, pearlies, toothy pegs
9. *nose:* beak, beezer, boko, bugle, conk, honker, hooter, horn, I suppose (rhy.sl.), konk, schnozzle, schnozzola, schnoz (Yid.), snitch, snoot, snout, snoz, snozzle
10. *beard; moustache:* face fungus, fungus, mouser, muff, stache, tash; spec. bum-fluff (light beard of a teenager)

11. *ears:* flaps, lug, lughole; spec. cauliflowers (ears deformed through boxing); tin ear (no ear for music)
12. *eyes:* babyblues, bins, daylights, headlights, minces (rhy.sl. mince pies), optics, peepers; spec. luggage (bags under the eyes); mouse, shiner (a black eye)
13. *stomach:* Auntie Nelly (rhy.sl.), breadbasket, Darby Kelly (rhy.sl.), elly-bay (backsl.), gizzard, kishkes (Yid.), Ned Kelly (rhy.sl.), Newington Butts (rhy.sl. = guts), tum (-tum), tummy, yellib (backsl.)
14. *ribs:* slats
15. *hands:* deenach (backsl.), German bands, hooks, lunch-hooks, Mary Anns (rhy.sl.), maulers, mitt, paw
16. *fist:* bunch of fives, dukes, maulers, meathooks
17. *fingers:* bell ringers (rhy.sl.), forks, lean and lingers (rhy.sl.), lunch hooks; spec. presents (US black: lucky white spots on fingernails)
18. *legs:* bacon and eggs (rhy.sl.), doog gels (backsl. = good legs), drivers, drumsticks, gams, ham hocks, hammers, pegs, pins, Scotch pegs (rhy.sl.), shanks' pony, stumps, timbers
19. *shoulder:* redloch (backsl.)
20. *knees:* biscuits and cheese (rhy.sl.)
21. *neck:* Gregory Peck, bushel and peck (rhy.sl.)
22. *feet:* hoff, mud flaps, plates of meat (rhy.sl.), puppies, trotters
23. *chin:* button, Errol Flynn, Gunga Din (rhy.sl.)
24. *heart:* pump, raspberry tart, ticker
25. *womb:* kidney
26. *skin:* hide, pelt
27. *freckles:* angel kisses
28. *bodily fluids:* claret (blood), axle grease, cream, come, emok (backsl. = come), gissum, gizzum, jam, load, love juice, melted butter,

sugar, water of life (US black), whipped cream (semen); spec. crud (dried semen on sheets or clothes); cheese, crotch cheese, jelly baby (secretions around the penis or vagina)

29. *anus:* arsehole, asshole, backeye, – slice, – slit, blot (Aus.), brown-eye, brownie, bucket, bumhole, bung, – hole, cornhole, date (Aus.), deadeye, dinger (Aus.), dirt chute, – road, freckle, gazoo, gripples (US black), jacksie, jampot, kazoo, keester, keister, leather, poop-chute, quoit, ring, satchel, shit chute, shitter, stank (US black), winker-stinker

30. *buttocks:* arse, ass, batti (WI), bottle and glass (rhy.sl.), BTM, bum, buns, butter (US black), caboose, can, chips, Daily Mail (rhy.sl. = tail), date, dinger (Aus.), elephant and castle (rhy.sl. = arsehole), fanny (US), heinie, kab edis (backsl. = backside), kazoo, keel, keister, Khyber Pass (rhy.sl. = arse), labonza, North Pole (rhy.sl. = arsehole), parking place, poop, pratt, quoit (Aus.), rusty-dusty, seat, sit-me-down, sit-upon, squatter, tail, tooshie, toches, tuches, tushie (Yid.)

31. *female breasts:* apples, balloons, bazoom, bazoomas, brace and bits (rhy.sl. = tits), Bristol City (rhy.sl. = titty), Bristols (rhy.sl. Bristol bits = tits), BSHs (British Standard Handfuls), bumpers, cakes, cats and kitties (rhy.sl. = titties), charlies (Aus. rhy.sl. Charlie Wheeler = Sheila = female, thus breasts), chichi (Mex.), cupcake, dairies, diddies, dubbies, dugs, gazungas, gib tesurbs (backsl. = big breasts), grapes, grapefruits, hangers, headlights, jugs, knobs, knockers, lollies, lungs, mams, maracas, Mary Poppins, milkers, mountains, nay-nays, ninnies, norks, pumps, rack, T and A (tits and ass), tits,

titty, TNT (two nifty tits), top bollocks, tremblers, wallopies; spec. eyes (nipples)

32. *genital area:* down there, genials, naughty bits, rude parts, sweet potato pie (US black), you know where

33. *male genitals:* accoutrements, basket, crown jewels, equipment, family jewels, gear, kit, marriage gear, necessaries, nick-nacks, rig, string and nuggets, three-piece set

34. *penis:* acorn, almond (rhy.sl. almond rock = cock), arm, baby maker, bald headed hermit, bazooka, beef (US black), beef bayonet, big bird, big foot Joe, bird, blue-veined piccolo, – steak, – trumpet, blow stick, box, candy stick, cannon, cherry splitter, chopper, cock, colleen bawn (Irish), creamstick, dagger, dangler, derrick, dibble, dick, dickory dock (rhy.sl.), dingaling, ding-dong, dingus, dinosaur, dirk, do-jigger, dong, doodle, doover, dork, driving post, end, enob (backsl. = bone), ferret, flapper, four-eleven-forty-four (US black), gigglestick, goober, good time, gun, gutstick, hammer, Hampton rock (backsl.= cock), Hampton Wick (backsl. = prick), hog, honker, horn, ice cream machine, ID ('let's see your ID'), inch, Irish root, jigger, jock, joint, JT, John Thomas, joy prong, – stick, kidney wiper, knob, lob, lunch, maggot, member, middle leg, mole, mouse mutton, – dagger, nimrod, nob, one-eyed brother, – trouser snake, peacemaker (US black), pecker, peenie, percy, peter, piece, pillock, pipe, pistol, plonker, pole, pooper, pork sword, prick, prod, prong, pud, putz, rabbit, ramrod, reamer, rod, root, schlong, shitstick, short arm, skinflute, stalk, stick, string, stump, swack, swipe, tadger, thing, third leg, todger, tommy, tool, tubesteak, tummy

banana, Uncle Dick (rhy.sl. = prick), turkey neck, wand, wang, wanger, wang-tang, weapon, weenie, wienie, willy, winkle, wire, wood, woofer, worm, ying-yang, yoyo, yutz; spec. IBM ('itty bitty meat' = small penis); donkey-rigged, hung (having a large penis); puppy (small penis); stringbean (US black: thin penis)
35. *erect penis:* Bethlehem steel (US black), blue vein, bone, colleen bawn, Marquis of Lorne (rhy.sl. = horn), prong, scope; spec. dead rabbit (penis that remains limp)
36. *testicles:* ballocks, balls, bollocks, cobs, cods, cojones (Sp.), eggs in the basket, flowers and frolics (rhy.sl. = bollocks), frick and frack (US black), goolies, grand bag, knackers, nerds, Niagara Falls (rhy.sl = balls), nuts, orchestra stalls (rhy.sl. = balls), pills, rocks, sack o'nuts, slabs (backsl. = balls), tommy rollocks (rhy.sl.)
37. *foreskin:* lace curtains, snapper; spec. blind, cavalier, near-sighted (uncircumcised penis)
38. *circumcised penis:* clipped, low neck and short sleeves, roundhead
39. *pubic hair:* area, brush, bush, cotton, Fort Bushy, garden, grass, lawn, squirrel, wool
40. *vagina:* apple, bacon sandwich, barge, beaver, bite, boat, booty, box, butcher's window, canyon, catty-cat, central cut, chasm, chopped liver, chuff, cock (US South), cono, cooch, coot, cooze, crack, cranny, crevice, cunt, damp, Dead End Street, diddly pout, ditch, down there, drain, fanny (UK), fig, finger pie, fish, fluff, front bum, – door, fud, fur, furburger, furrow, furry hoop, futy, futz, fuzzburger, fuzzy cup, G (goodies), gap, gape, garden, – of Eden (US black), gash, gib teenuck (backsl. = big cunt), ginch, glory hole, golden doughnut (Aus.), groceries, grumble and grunt

(rhy.sl. = cunt), gulf, gully (hole), gutter, hair pie, hatchi, hole, honeypot, Irish fortune, jam, jellybox, jing-jang, joxy, joy trail, kennel, kettle, kitty, kitty-cat, little sister, lucky bag, lunch box, Maggie's pie (US black), magpie's nest (US black), maw, met, middle-cut; minge, mink, monkey, muff, muffin, mutton, nasty, nest, notch, passion pit, PEEP (perfectly elegant eating pussy), penocha (Sp.), placket, pole hole, poon, poontang, poozle, prime cut, pta (US black: pussy, titties and armpits), puss, pussy, pussycat, quiff, quim, rag box, rattlesnake canyon, red lane, rubyfruit, scat, second hole from the back of the neck, sharp and blunt (rhy.sl. = cunt), slice of life, slit, slot, snapper, snapping turtle (puss), snatch, split beaver, stank, stench trench, stink, stinkpot, tail, that there, toolbox, trench, trim, trout, tuna, twat, vag, where the monkey sleeps, you know where; spec. cherry (maidenhead), horse collar (large vagina)
41. *female pudendum:* ace of spades (US black), fern, ha'penny, hide, jelly roll, moneymaker, rubyfruit, you know where; spec. cuffs and collars (pubic hair the same colour as head hair)
42. *clitoris:* boy in the boat, button, clit, clitty, dot, joy buzzer, little man, (little) man in the boat, nuts (US black), taste bud
43. *labia:* beef, curtains, flange, Hottentot apron, piss flaps
44. *throat:* red lane
45. *arm:* Chalk Farm (rhy.sl.)

117. Physical Characteristics
1. *of the weight:* bagels, beer belly, – gut, broad in the beam, fat city, hipsters, love handles, Milwaukee goitre, spare tyre, taff (backsl.), zaftig (Yid.)

2. *skin problems:* Conan Doyle (rhy.sl. = boil), custards, goob (small spot, fr. goober = peanut), zit hickey (love bite)

3. *scars:* glassed (cut in the face), stripe, tram line

4. *of the eyes:* eyes like pissholes in the snow

5. *having a large penis:* hand-reared, straps it to his ankle, well-hung

6. *naked:* bare-ass, (in one's) birthday suit, bollock naked, bollocko, in the altogether, – the buff, – the rude, laid to the natural bone (US black), nuddy, starkers, stripped to the buff

7. *of the fingernails:* in mourning (dirty)

8. *of the face:* fish-faced, poker-faced, sour-pussed; spec. more chins than a Chinese laundry (fat-faced)

9. *of the hair:* bottle blonde (dyed hair)

10. *bald:* chrome-dome

11. *having a good figure:* built, best-built, stacked

12. *large:* built, built like a brick outhouse, built like a brick shithouse, hunky

13. *having good legs:* leggy, legs up to her arse

118. Bodily Functions

n. 1. *menstruation:* beno (Aus. 'be no fun'), curse, monthlies, on the rag, red dog on a white horse, red Mary (US black) wallflower week

2. *breaking wind:* beast, breezer (Aus.), fart, guff, raspberry tart (rhy.sl.), thumper

3. *mucus:* dewdrop, lunger, oyster, snot

4. *an erection:* boner, hard (on), stand, touch-on; spec. piss proud (early morning erection); brewer's droop (impairment of erection by alcohol); muddy waters (US black: loss of erection)

5. *orgasm:* big O, come

6. *vomiting:* school lunch rerun, technicolour rerun, technicolour yawn

v. 7. *to menstruate:* be on the rag, have a little visitor, – the flag out, – the painters in, – the rag on, put the flags out, ride the rag (US black), stub one's toe

8. *to break wind:* backfire, cheese, drop a beast, – a thumper, drop one's guts, fart, repeat; spec. he who smelt it dealt it (cp)

9. *to spit:* gob

10. *to sneeze:* bread and cheese (rhy.sl.)

11. *to achieve erection:* crack a fat (Aus.), flood (US black), get a boner, – a hard (on), etc. (see 118.4)

12. *to achieve orgasm:* cheese, come, get one's gun off, – rocks off, light off, pop one's nuts, shoot (off) one's load, – wad

13. *to vomit:* barf, blow one's cookies, – doughnuts, – groceries, – lunch, boot, buick, call for Hughie, – Ralph, cat, chuck, chuck a dummy, chunder, cry Hughie, – Ralph, – Ruth, drive the big white bus, drive the porcelain bus, dump one's load, feed the kippers, flash, go to instant boot camp, go the big spit, – big split (Aus.), hack, have a liquid laugh, have a technicolour yawn, heave, hug the porcelain, hurl, kak, kiss the porcelain god, kneel before the porcelain throne, lose one's doughnuts, – groceries, – lunch, park a custard, pray to the porcelain god, puke, ralph, shoot a cat, spew, – one's guts, – one's ring, spill one's breakfast, spread a technicolour rainbow (Aus.), throw one's cookies, – one's voice (Aus.), throw up, Tom and Dick (rhy.sl. = to be sick), toss one's cookies, – one's tacos, Uncle Dick (rhy.sl.), upchuck, vom, woof

14. *to masturbate:* beat off, – one's dummy, – one's hog, – one's meat,

bring oneself off, choke the chook (Aus.), get one's nuts off, jerk off, play pocket billiards, play with oneself, pull one's joint, – one's pud, – one's pudding, – one's wire, rub off, – up, sew (US black), stroke one's beef, tickle one's pickle, toss off, twang one's wire, wank, whip off, – one's wire, whack off, whank; spec. catch a buzz (to masturbate with a vibrator) (see also 360:19)
15. spec. Barcoo salute (Aus. = brushing flies away from the face)
phr. 16. spec. looks like a wet weekend (Aus.: menstruation will make sex impossible)

119. Defecation
n. 1. business, call of nature
mod. 2. *urination:* gypsy's, jimmy (riddle), Johnny Bliss (Aus. rhy.sl. = piss), little jobs, slash, wazz
3. *ordure:* big hit (Aus.), – jobs, boom-boom, crap, crash (Aus.), diddley-poo, dookey, dukie (US black), honey, job, kak, ka-ka, lemon (rhy.sl. lemon curd = turd), number twos, pony (rhy.sl. pony and trap = crap), poo, edopie-plops, Richard the Third (rhy.sl. = turd), shit, tomtit (rhy.sl.), turd; spec. dog, horse apples, road apples (animals); dags, clinkers, dingleberries (adherent excrement); skid marks (stains on underwear)
4. *urine:* little jobs, number ones, pee, piddle, piss, Robert E. (rhy.sl. = Robert E. Lee = pee), snake's hiss (Aus. rhy.sl. = piss), wee-wee, widdle; spec. golden shower (urolognia)
5. *diahorrea:* Aztec twostep, Cairo crud, Delhi belly, GIs, Gyppy tummy, Hong Kong dog, Montezuma's revenge, Rangoon runs, ringburner, runs, scoots, shits, toms (Aus. rhy.sl. = tomtits = shits), touristas, trots

v. 6. *to visit the lavatory:* (go and) see a man about a dog, powder one's nose; spec. caught short, taken short (desperate to visit the lavatory)
7. *defecate:* cramber, crap, choke a darkie (Aus.), dump, shit, take a crap, – dump, – shit, sit on the throne; spec. ride the porcelain bus, – porcelain Honda (to have diahorrea)
8. *urinate:* bleed the liver, drain the dragon, get rid of the bladder matter, have a gypsy's (rhy.sl. = gypsy's kiss = piss), – a jimmy (rhy.sl. jimmy riddle = piddle), – a piss, – a slash, make pee-pee, pee, piddle, piss, point percy at the porcelain, see a dog about a man, see a man about a dog, shake hands with an old friend, shake hands with the wife's best friend, shake the dew off the lily, spend a penny, splash the boots, strain the potatoes, strain the spuds, syphon the python, take a leak, – a pee, – a piss, – a slash, tap a keg, tinkle, visit Miss Murphy, wee-wee, widdle
phr. 9. who cut the cheese (who farted?), SBD (silent but deadly)

THE BODY: CARE
120. Toilet; Hygiene; Grooming
n. 1. *hairstyle:* afro, 'fro, DA (duck's arse), duck's arse, cowlick
2. *parts of the hair:* bugger's grips, sidies (sideburns)
3. *straightened black hair:* fried, dyed and swooped to the side, konk, process
4. *comb:* rack pick (a comb for curly black hair)
5. *wig:* Irish jig (rhy.sl.), rug, syrup (rhy.sl. = syrup of figs)
6. *shave:* dig in the grave (rhy.sl.)
7. *cosmetics, etc.:* axle grease (hair oil), BO juice (deodorant)
8. spec. grease (gay use: KY jelly)
v. 9. *to straighten black hair:* conk,

konk, fry one's hair, press one's hair, process, wig bust
10. *dress one's hair:* have a hair-do, rat one's hair (backcomb hair)
11. *to shave:* dad and dave (Aus. rhy.sl.), mow the lawn
12. *apply cosmetics:* put on one's face, – warpaint; spec. flame (homosexual use)
adj. 13. *natural black hair:* nappy
14. *long-haired:* sheepish

121. Physical Exercise
n. 1. *strength and ability:* fire power
2. *exercising:* pumping iron, pushing iron, throwing iron, working out
3. spec. the burn (in aerobics: the pain barrier)

HEALTH
122. Health; Physical Condition
n. 1. feather, fig, form, kilter, shape, way, whack
2. spec. million dollar wound (milit.: wound that does not kill but invalids out of war)
phr. 3. *enquiries as to health:* how are they hanging? how are you doing?, – going?, how's by you?, how's your head?

123. Good Health
n. 1. fine fettle, – feather, – form, – shape, – whack, tiptop form
v. 2. *to feel well:* feel one's oats, go strong, run on all cylinders
adj. 3. *healthy:* aces, alive and kicking, all there, – to the good, A1, bobbish, bully, chipper, clever (Aus.), feeling one's oats, – right (royal), fit as a butcher's dog, fit as a Mallee bull (Aus.), full of beans, – piss and vinegar, hitting on all four/six/eight (cylinders), hotsy-totsy, hunkydory, in fine fettle, – form, – whack, in good shape, – good trim, in the pink, keen, primo, one hundred per cent, ripper (Aus.), rosy about the gills,

sharp, skookum, slap-up, top hole, – notch, topping, the tops, up to par, – scratch, – snuff, – the mark
4. *replying to enquiries as to health:* can't complain, could be worse, fair to middling, not so bad, nothing to brag about, – write home about, still here, – (alive and kicking)

124. Poor Health
v. 1. *to be ill:* feel a bit green, feel bum, – crook (Aus.), – like hell, – lousy, – off colour, – ratshit, – under the weather, have one foot in the grave, not feel like anything, – too hot, not feel up to scratch, – up to snuff, etc. (see 123.3)
2. *to become ill:* break down, conk out, crack up, fold up, go on the blink, get out of commission, – of sorts, – of whack
3. *fake illness:* come the old soldier, pull an act, swing the lead, work one's ticket
adv. 4. *ill:* below par, blah, bunged up, butcher's (Aus. rhy.sl. = crook), crook (Aus.), crummy, down at heel, in bad shape, – the shit, not so dusty, – so hot, off colour, – form, out of commission, – of sorts, peakish, peaky, punk, putrid, ratshit, run down, seedy, sick as a dog, under the weather, wonky, yucky
5. *dying:* bought and sold and done for, done for, on one's last legs, (with) one foot in the grave, seen better days, – one's best days, (all) shot, through
6. *exhausted, run down:* beat, burned out, dead-beat, dead on the vine, frazzled, fucked, gone smash, wrecked
7. *delirious:* bats (in the belfry), batty, cuckoo, dippy, dotty, gaga, loony, loopy, nuts, nutty, off one's bean, – chump, – head, – nut, – onion, out of one's head, – gourd, – chump, etc., screwy

125. Ailments; Diseases
n. 1. *stomach ache:* bellyache, collywobbles, gutache, tummyache
2. *headache:* a head
3. *cold:* snotty nose
4. *cramp:* Charlie horse
5. *bad breath:* jungle mouth
6. *hepatitis:* hep
7. *cough:* strep throat
8. *cancer:* Big C
9. *cystitis:* honeymoon cystitis
10. *venereal disease:* band in the box (rhy.sl. = pox), clap, cold in the dong, dose, drip, dripsy, gleet, horse (rhy.sl. = horse and trap = clap), jack (Aus.), Nervo and Knox (rhy.sl. = pox), pox, syph, sypho (Aus.); spec. full house (both syphilis and gonorrhoea); nine day blues (incubation period for gonorrhoea); blue balls (testicular swelling)
11. *haemorrhoids:* hems, Nuremburgs (rhy.sl. Nuremburg trials = piles)
12. *fit:* wingding, wobbler
13. *backache:* shagger's back (Aus.)
14. *deaf mute:* D & D (deaf and dumb)
v. 15. *to catch venereal disease:* be jacked up (Aus.), be one of the knights, cop a dose, (get) dosed up, piss broken glass, ride the silver steed, take the bayonet course
16. *to catch a cold:* catch one's death
17. *to faint:* throw a seven (Aus.)
18. *body odour:* BO, the pits

126. Physical Injury
n. 1. *scars:* Mars bars (rhy.sl)
adj. 2. *lame:* gammy, gimpy
3. *injured:* buggered up, out of commission, – whack
4. *wounded:* fucked up

127. Physical and Mental Breakdown
v. 1. *to have a nervous breakdown:* blow it, – up, come unglued, – unstuck, crack up, fall apart, go smash, go to pieces, – pot
adj. 2. *mentally unstable:* cracked, off one's hinges, (all) shot, all to fuck; spec. Shrinksville (a state of mind that may require professional aid), (see also 138.3 and 147)
3. *disorientated:* spaced out

128. Recovery
n. 1. comeback
2. *spec. medicine:* op (operation), plastic job (plastic surgery), short-arm inspection (inspection of genitals), scrape (abortion); dust-off (milit: medical evacuation)
3. *pills:* apples, daily-daily (US milit. anti-malaria pills)
v. 4. *improve, recover:* buck up, perk up, on the up (and up)

SENSATION
129. Sensation; Touch
n. 1. *odd feeling:* creeps, jim-jams, shivers, willies
v. 2. *to touch:* goose

130. Taste
mod. 1. *tasty:* scrumptious, scrummy, yummy
2. *distasteful:* icky, yucky

131. Smell
n. 1. niff, phew, pong, whiff
2. *spec. sexual odour:* funk, wolf-pussy (US black)
v. 3. *to smell:* get a noseful, niff, phew, pong, whiff
4. *to be smelly:* pen and ink (rhy.sl. = stink)
adj. 5. *smelly:* loud, niffy, noisy, pongy, sniffy, whiffy

SIGHT
132. Sight; Look; Glance
n. 1. butcher's (rhy.sl. = butcher's hook = look), Captain Cook, Charlie Cooke (rhy.sl.), darry,

decko, dekko, gander, gig (Aus. =
a glance), glaum, glom, look-see,
lookism, measure, once-over, pipe,
shot, shufti, shufty, slant, squizz,
up-and-down; spec. coke stare (US
black = aggressive stare); glad
eye, goo-goo eyes (amorous
glance); hard eyes (unpleasant
look)
2. *view:* spec. flash, flash of light
(rhy.sl. = sight), free show; theatre
use: Mickey Mouse (rhy.sl. = house
= audience)
3. *spectacles:* bins, cheaters,
gig-lamps, glims, goggles,
headlights, -lamps, peepers, specs;
spec. shades (dark glasses)
4. *maps:* comics
5. *assessment:* recce
v. 6. *to look at:* book (the joint),
cast one's optics (at), – peepers (at),
clock, cop a decko, – gander, – sight
(of), eeson (backsl.), eevach a kool
(backsl. = have a look), eyeball,
gander, gawp, geek, get a load of,
get an eyeful, give a going-over,
give the eye (to), – the once-over,
glaum, glom, goggle (at), have a
decko, – a looksee, key in, lamp,
orb, pan, peg, pipe, run the eye
over, size up, take a flash at, – a
gander (at), – a hinge (at), – a
measure (of), – a shot at, – a slant
at, – a squint at, twig; spec. watch
the birdie, – the dickey-bird
(admonition from photographer to
subject); shoot the squirrel (glimpse
a girl's underwear or genitals)
7. *to spy on:* get a line on,
gumshoe, snoop, tail
8. *to stare:* double-o, gander, gawk,
gawp, gig (Aus.), goggle, rubber,
rubberneck, scope, screw, take a
screw at
9. *to disappear:* do a vanishing act,
go disappearo
10. *show, reveal:* exhib, flash, trot
out, uncork
11. *to assess:* case over, check out,
have one mapped, keep tabs on,

orb, pan, peep one's hole card (US
black), pin
12. *to appear before:* front (Aus.)

133. Light
v. 1. *turn off lights:* douse the
Edisons, kill (the lights), pull the
juice

SOUND
134. Hearing
n. 1. earwigging, the Earie, the Erie
v. 2. *to hear:* catch, earhole, get a
load of, get an earful, peg, take in
3. *listen:* be all ears, bend one's ear,
catch a listen, cop –, earwig, get an
earful, grab a listen, give (it) the ear
4. *eavesdrop:* be on the earie, – the
Erie, have big ears, – long ears
adj. 5. *deaf:* Mutt and Jeff
(rhy.sl.)
phr. 6. loud and clear: lumpy
chicken (milit.)

135. Sound
n. 1. *solid noise (of a blow, or
falling object):* bam, bash, biff,
blam, blop, bong, bop, cachunk,
etc., chunk, dab, flop, flump,
kerbam, kerboom, kerchunk, etc.,
pam, phut, pom, pomp, powie,
slam-bam, slambang, smack,
smacko, sock, socko, swack,
swacko, whack, wham, whammo,
whang, zam, zap, zoom, zowie
2. *light, splashing noise:* burble,
guggle, slap, slip, slop, slosh,
squelch, squidge, squish
3. *loud noise:* biff-bang, biff-boom,
racket, slam-bang
4. *sheet music:* maps
5. *records:* discs, plates, platters,
sides, slices, sounds; spec. box (tape
recorder, record player), wheel (of
steel) (record deck)
6. *instrument:* box (guitar)
v. 7. *to play the piano:* tickle the
ivories
8. *play records:* spec. toast (WI: for

a DJ to add his lyrics to a backing track), spin discs

136. Silence
n. 1. shush
vt. 2. *to quieten:* put down the soft pedal, – the lid on, turn off
3. *to be quiet:* hush one's mouth, – up, (be like dad and) keep mum, put a sock in it, put the lid on, stow it, – the gab
excl. 4. *be quiet!:* can it!, chuck it!, enough!, hold it down!, hush up!, lay off (the racket)!, pipe down!, pull in your ears!, stow it!, take it easy!

Personality

CHARACTER

137. Character; Disposition

n. 1. bag, the likes (of), number, (one's) size, (–) speed

2. *personality:* dope, goods, merchandise, oil, (the old) this and that, what it takes

v. 3. *to be characteristic:* be that way, built that way, be one all over, (about) one's speed, (just) one's speed, right in one's bag, – up one's alley, – down one's street

4. *to have charm:* be on the ball, have it (right) down, have (plenty of) what it takes

adj. 5. *charming:* ducky

phr. 6. where one is at, – one is coming from

138. Idiosyncracy; Eccentricity

n. 1. idiosity

2. *eccentricity:* bats in one's belfry, bee(s) in one's bonnet

v. 3. *to be eccentric:* have a bee in the bonnet, – a screw loose, – bats in the belfry, – bugs in the brain

adv. 4. *eccentric:* barmy, bats, batty, bourbon, cracked, crackers, daffy, doofus, doolally, dotty, funny (in the head), half-cracked, – crazy, kinky, loopy, nutty, off-beat, off-brand, off the wall, on the edge, out of left field, potty, queer as a coot, – as a nine-bob note, screwy, weird (see also unintelligence 145–147)

REPUTATION

139. Repute

n. 1. front, rep; spec. it (US black:

the quintessence of Blackness); bell (US black: personal notoriety)

v. 2. *to have a good reputation:* be in, – in good, count, keep one's nose clean, rate

3. *be important:* (see Greatness: 18), be on top of the heap, make a noise in the world

4. *gain importance:* feature, grab one's fifteen minutes (fr. A. Warhol's dictum 'Everyone will be famous for 15 minutes'), headline, hit it big, hit the headlines, make it big, make the front page, pick up brownie points

adv. 5. *reputable:* aces, all wool and a yard wide, kosher, straight, waxed (US black: anyone who is well known), white

6. *eminent:* (see Greatness: 18), big deal, – cheese, stuff, etc., high-up, high muckamuck, swell

7. *famous:* big-named, (a) celeb, having one's name in lights; spec. glitterati (international social-literary circles)

140. Disrepute

n. 1. bad rep, – smell

2. *loss of reputation:* climb-down, nose-dive

v. 3. *to lose reputation:* be brought down a peg (or two), blow up, come down a peg, – a notch, get a black eye, go down the chute, – the tubes, – on the skids, have one's nose put out of joint, hit the skids

4. *to put into disrepute:* smear

adv. 5. *disreputable:* low-down, lowest of the low, low-life, no-hoper, ornery, past praying for, wouldn't tell you the time of day

6. *obscure, insignificant:* (see
Smallness: 19), bottom of the heap,
lightweight, low rent, no great
catch, – shakes, not amounting
to a piss in the ocean, small
beer, – change, – potatoes,
– time

BREEDING
141. Gentility; Culture
adj. **1.** *genteel, well-bred:* aristo,
blue-blood, blue-book, glitzy,
high-hat, high-tone(d), nobby,
posh, ritzy, slick, smooth, swanky,
tony, upper crust, uptown; spec.
Sloane (Ranger), county (UK upper
bourgeoisie)

142. Ungentility; Vulgarity
v. **1.** *to live in squalor:* pig it
adj. **2.** *vulgar:* all dressed up like a
pox-doctor's clerk, brassy, flash, –
as a Chinky's horse, – as a rat with a
gold tooth, jumped up, lairy (Aus.),
not backward in coming forward,
out of order, over the top, poncy,
smart-ass
3. *rustic:* billyjack (US black),
cornball, corny, folksy, jungly
4. *affected:* artsy-crafty, arty-farty
5. *rough:* hard-boiled,
leather-necked, rough-and-ready,
rough-necked, tin-arsed, wild and
woolly
adv. **6.** *living in squalor:* pigging it,
pig style (US black)

Intellect

INTELLIGENCE

143. Intelligence; Intellect
n. 1. brains, (little) grey cells, grey matter, gorm, gumption, horse sense, nous, savvy, smart money, smarts
2. *an intellectual:* long-hair, pointy-head
v. 3. *to be clever:* be on the ball, have all one's marbles, – what it takes, know a hawk from a handsaw, know a shilling from sixpence, know a thing or two, know enough to come in and out of the rain, know how many beans make five, know one's age, know one's anus from one's ankle, – one's arse from a hole in the ground, – one's arse from one's elbow, know one's boxes, know one's eccer (Aus.), know one's kit, – one's onions, know one's stuff, know one's way about, – something, – up from down, – what's what, – what's happening, know what time it is, know where one's arse hangs, know whether one is Arthur or Martha (Aus.), know whether it's pancake Tuesday or half-past breakfast time, – which way is up, use one's loaf; spec. to know where the bodies are buried (to have knowledge which gives leverage over others)
4. *to be wise, shrewd:* be bright as a new pin, – nobody's fool, – not as daft as one looks, – as stupid etc., have a head on one's shoulders, know what time it is, use the old bean, – chump, – noggin, turnip; spec. graduate (US black: to gain knowledge)
adj. 5. *intelligent:* all there, not so dumb, – dusty, on the beam, there with the goods, smart
6. *wise, shrewd, aware:* (be) down (US black), cool, culture, first cab off the rank, fly, half-wide, hardcore, hep, hip, jerry, long-haired, necklaced, (US black), no flies on . . ., quick on the trigger, ready (US black), ready-eyed, savvy, sharp, spunko, streetified, street smart, street wise, swift, switched on, tasty, together, triple hip (US black), turned on, with it
phr. 7. must have swallowed the dictionary, who slept in the knife box? (and is thus 'sharp')

144. Knowledge
n. 1. dope, know-how, nitty-gritty, savvy
2. *identity:* ID; spec. P Check (UK milit. personality check); Wilkie Bard (ID card)
v. 3. *to be aware of, know about:* (be) hep, – hip, – jerry (to), – on the inside track, – posted, – up on (one's stuff), – wise (to), have a line on, – the inside track, – the goods on, – the stuff on, – dead to rights, – down cold, – down pat, – its number, – it pegged, – it straight, – it sussed, know it backwards, – it down to the ground, – one's stuff, – the ropes, – what time it is, what's happening, etc. (see Intelligence 143), sus out
4. *to recognize:* burn, get a line on, – next to, – on to, give (it) a tumble, make (it for), peg, rumble, tumble (to)
5. *see one's own interest:* blow wise, get hep, get smart, – wise, – next to

oneself, – one's head screwed on, – one's mind right, – straight (to oneself), smarten up, wise up
6. *see through:* be jerry (to), – on one's wavelength – wise (to), blow wise (to), have down, – pegged, – cold, – one's measure, – one's number, – one sussed, know what makes one tick, know where one is at, – is coming from, – where one's head is at, – one's wavelength
7. *to ask for identity card:* card
8. *to prophesy:* Kreskin
adv. 9. *intelligent, aware:* down, fly, hep(ped), hip(ped), jerry, next to, on the ball, on to, smart (to), sussed (out), up to, wise (to)

UNINTELLIGENCE
145. Stupidity
n. 1. numbskullery
v. 2. *to be stupid:* be boneheaded, sapbrained, etc. (see adj. 145), to be a dickhead, dorkbrain, dumbo etc. (see Disreputable: 433), couldn't find one's way to first base, – find his arse with both hands, doesn't know a mule's ass from a lemon, – his ass from a double-barrelled shotgun, – his ass from a hole in the ground, – his ass from his elbow, – his ass from third base, – his butt from a gourd, doesn't know – owl-shit from putty without a map, – sheepshit from cherry-seed, doesn't have a clue, – the foggiest, doesn't know enough to come in out of the rain, – to pound sand in a rathole, doesn't know shit from Shinola, – know from Adam, – know from the man in the moon, – know t'other from which, – know up from down, have one's head up one's arse, – shit for brains, isn't ready for people, thinks it's just to pee through
adv. 3. *stupid:* (see 433: Stupid Person); blockheaded, blubberbrained, boneheaded,

bonkers, chuckleheaded, clueless, cuckoo, daffy, daffydown dilly (rhy.sl. = silly), daft, dead between the ears, – from the neck down, dumb, dumbarse, dingy, dopey, dorky, fatheaded, flaky, foggy, goofy, goopy, green as owl-shit, half-baked, jugheaded, King Dick (rhy.sl. = thick), lame, lamebrained, lunchy, lunkheaded, muttonheaded, nitwitted, not all there, – ready for people, off one's trolley, old enough to know better, ossified, out to lunch, pig ignorant, sap-headed, silly as a two-bob watch (Aus.), so dumb he couldn't find his ass with two hands at high noon, – he couldn't piss out of a boat, – he couldn't piss without a button hook, soft (in the head), slow on the trigger, thick, untogether, wet behind the ears, young in the head (US black); spec. addict (one who falls for confidence tricks)
phr. 4. *of the stupid:* some mothers do have 'em
5. *admitting ignorance:* ask a silly question . . ., ask me another, damned if I know, don't ask me, God knows, I haven't the foggiest, I pass, I give up, it's (all) Greek to me, your guess is as good as mine, what's that when it's at home?

146. Foolishness; Nonsense
n. 1. funny business, monkey business, mug's game, shenanigans; spec. scream (ludicrous idea)
2. *nonsense:* ackamaracka, all my eye and Betty Martin, applesauce, apple butter, ballocks, bollocks, bollox, balls, baloney, boloney, bologna, banana oil, bilge, blatherskite, booshwah, borax, bosh, bushwa, bughouse, bull, bullcrap, bullsh, bullshit, bullshine, BS, bunk, bunkum, claptrap, cobblers (rhy.sl. = cobblers awls = balls), cock, cods, codswallop, cowyard confetti, crap, crock (of

shit), duck soup, eyewash,
fiddle-faddle, fiddlesticks, flannel,
flapdoodle, flubdub, gammon,
garbage, guff, hogwash, hokum,
hooey, hoo-ha, horsefeathers,
horseshit, jiggery-pokery, krazin,
(a) load of applesauce, balls, etc.,
load of reg, – (old) madam,
magoozlum, malarkey, mishegaas
(Yid.), mumbo-jumbo,
phonus-balonus, phooey, piffle,
pigshit, poop, poppycock,
rannygazoo, rhubard, rollocks, rot,
strunz, toffee, tommyrot, tosh,
trash, tripe, twaddle
3. *foolish talk:* air, ballyhoo,
baloney, blah, blather, bull, gas,
guff, hooey, hot air, jive, wind
v. 4. *to play the fool:* arse about,
– around, bugger about, fart about,
– around, fuck about, – around,
grab-arse, piss about, – around,
silly-arse about, – around, sod about
5. *do something stupid:* (see 146.4);
do the crazy act, fuck up, make a
bloomer, – a dumb play, – a prick of
oneself, screw up,
6. *to talk nonsense:* blah (on), bull,
bullshit, crap (on), dish the bull,
– the crap, etc. (see 146.2), flannel,
go off at the mouth, run off at the
mouth, hand (out) a line, – of bull,
– of crap, etc., let off hot air,
ratchet-mouth, rot, shoot the bull,
talk balls, crap, guff, etc., talk
through one's arse(hole), – one's
hat, – the back of one's neck, talk
shit, – trash, tommyrot, wank (on)
phr. 7. *stop being stupid:* act your
age, be your age, cut it out, – the
comedy, – the crap, get your arse in
gear, – yourself together, grow up,
stop arsing around, – buggering
about, etc. (see 146.4)
8. *to make a fool of:* make a
monkey of, – a sap of. etc. (see 433:
Stupid Person)
adv. 9. *foolish:* (see 145: Stupid)
phr. 10. GIGO (garbage in, garbage
out)

excl. 11. *that's absurd!, don't be
absurd!:* applesauce!, are you
kidding!, arseholes!, bagpipe it!,
balls!, blooey!, bull!, bullshit!,
coffee and cocoa! (rhy.sl. = I
should cocoa), come off it!, crap!,
cut it out!, – that out!, – the crap!,
did I fuck!, don't be funny!, – fuck
about!, – give me that!, – make me
laugh!, fiddlesticks!, forget it!,
fucking Ada!, fuck that (for a lark)!,
gag me with a spoon!, gertcha!, get
away (with you)!, – along (with
you)!, get wise!, go chase yourself!,
– run up a drain!, – shit in your hat
(pull it over your ears and call it
feathers)!, – take a flying fuck!, I
should cocoa! (rhy.sl. = I should
say so), in a pig's arse!, knickers!,
later (for that)!, leave it out!, leave
off!, – over!, less of it!, like fuck!,
my eye!, my foot!, never happen!,
no way!, nothing doing!, not much
you wouldn't!, pull the other one
(it's got bells on it)!, quit fooling!,
says you!, screw it!, shut your
mouth and give your arse a chance!,
skip it!, stick it!, stroll on!, tell it to
the marines!, – me another!, turn it
up!, up your arse!, – your gazoo!,
– kazoo!, up yours!, walk on!, what
else is new?, who do you think
you're kidding?, you must be
joking!, you've got a nerve!

147. Insanity; Craziness
n. 1. barminess, bats in the belfry,
lame brains, looniness, (a) screw
loose, space case
2. *mental hospital:* bin, booby
hatch, bughouse, crazy house, funny
farm, loony bin, nut hatch, nut
house
v. 3. *to be insane:* be all over the
board, – around the bend,
– bananas, etc. (see 147.5); have a
screw loose, – a tile loose, – one's
wires crossed, – bats in the belfry,
not be all there, – have all one's
marbles

4. *to become insane:* blow a fuse, – one's cork, – lid, – mind, – top, crack up, flip one's lid, – wig, get out of gear, go balmy, – bananas, – batty (see adj. 147.5), go off one's bean, – one's chump, – one's gourd, – one's nut, – one's onion, go out of one's bean, – one's chump, etc., go off one's rocker, – the rails, – over the edge, lose one's marbles, shoot one's marbles (US black), wig out
adj. 5. *insane, crazy:* all over the board, around the bend, asiatic bananas, balmy, barmy, bathouse, batty, bats, batshit, bats in the belfry, boho, bourbon, bughouse, cuckoo, cracked, crackers, cracko, crazy-arse, cruising with one's lights on dim, daffy, dippy, doofus, doolally, dopey, dorky, dotty, freaky, gaga, gone, half-cracked, – gone, – there, harpic ('clean around the bend'), has a few of his pages stuck together, kooky, lakes (of Killarney) (rhy.sl. = barmy), lamebrained, loco, loony, loopy, loose up top, mental, meshugge (Yid.), neuro, non compos, not all there, – quite there, (not having) both oars in the water, not playing with a full deck, not the full quid (Aus.), nuts, nutso, nutty (as a fruitcake), off-beat, off-brand, off one's bean, out of one's box, – cake, – chump, – gourd, – nut, – onion, – rocker, off the beam, – the wall, out of left field, out of one's head, – mind, – onion, – tree, out of whack, out to lunch, plumb loco, potty, only eighty pence in the pound, queer as a coot, – as a nine-bob note, rum, schitzi, screwy, (one) shingle short (Aus.), sicko, squirrelly, stark staring bonkers, troppo (Aus.), two bricks short of the load, two pence short of a bob, toey (Aus.), twisted, unglued, whack-a-doo, whacked out, whacko, whacky, weird, wig city, wigged out, wiggy, wild, wild-arse,

(living in a) worm farm, wired, yarra (Aus.)
phr. 6. keep taking the tablets

ATTENTION
148. Attention; Heed
v. 1. *to be alert:* be all there, – fly, – on the job, get down (US black), keep one's eye on the ball, know what's what, – what the time is, look alive, – sharp, – slippy, not miss a trick, – take any wooden nickels
2. *to become alert:* brace up, buck up, get on the case, – on the job, get with it, jump to it, snap (it) up, snap out of it, stand point
3. *to notice:* catch
4. *to point out:* finger, put the cross on
5. *make an obscene gesture (at):* give the finger, flip the bird, make a V-sign
6. *to be involved:* get in deep
adv. 7. *alert:* alive and kicking, all there (with the goods), chipper, hot to trot, Johnny on the spot, live, (up), on one's toes, on the ball, – the hop, – the job, sharp
8. *engrossed, obsessed:* behind, crazy for, have a ring through one's nose (US black), hot for, head over heels, into, up to the neck (in), right in (it), from soup to nuts, – the ground up

149. Care
n. 1. caginess, leariness
v. 2. *take care of:* keep tabs on, ride herd (on), ride shotgun; *spec.* look out for number one (take care of oneself first)
3. *be careful:* keep one's eyes peeled, – one's head down, not stick one's head out, – stick one's neck out, – take any wooden nickels, watch one's arse
4. *be alert:* be on the job, stay on the job, cock a weather eye, keep

one's eyes peeled, look sharp,
– slippery, watch it
5. *keep watch:* give jiggs, keep cave,
– KV, – chickie, – nit, – one's ear to
the ground, lie doggo
excl. 6. *be careful:* be cool!, don't
take any wooden nickels!, get wise!,
hang tight!, stay loose!, take it
easy!, watch it! – your step!, don't
do anything I wouldn't (do)

INATTENTION
150. Inattention; Neglect
v. 1. *to neglect, ignore:* brush off,
drop (it), fake on (one) (US black),
give (it) the go-by, – (it) a miss, let
(it) go, – (it) ride, – (it) slide,
– it sweat, not to give a damn, – a
fuck, – shit, – a tumble (for), skip
it
adv. 2. *absent-minded:* asleep on the
job, blank, dead from the neck up,
– to the world, not all there, – on
the job, somewhere else

151. Carelessness; Recklessness
n. 1. slapdashery, sloppiness
2. *careless work:* cheap and
cheerful, lick and a promise, quick
and dirty, quickie
v. 3. *to perform carelessly:* bang out,
hack –, knock –, slam –, slap –,
whack –, do any which way,
– everywhichway, knock off, not
give a damn (for), – a fuck (for),
etc. (see 150.1)
4. *to be reckless:* ball the jack, break
a leg, go off half-cocked, – like a bat
out of hell, – like hell on wheels,
– hell-for-leather, – hell('s)-bent
(for), rip, tear arse
adj. 5. *careless:* slapdash,
what-the-hell, who-gives-a-damn,
– a-fuck, etc.
6. *reckless:* chancy, iffy
adv. 7. *carelessly:* all anyhow,
everywhichway, half-arsed,
half-cocked, slam-bang, slap-bang,
slap-dab

8. *recklessly:* harum-scarum,
hell('s)-bent, hell-for-leather, (like)
hell on wheels, like crazy, over the
top
phr. 9. fubis (fuck you buddy I'm
shipping out), I could care, I don't
give fuck

REASON
152. Reason
n. 1. *argument:* argy-bargy,
free-for-all, gabfest, set-to, splang
(US black), tangle
2. *conclusive argument:* knockout
v. 3. *to argue:* argy-bargy, chew the
fat, chinwag, fatmouth, go to the
mat, go head-to-head,
– mano-a-mano, – one-on-one,
scream some heavy lines, slug it out,
weigh in
prep. 4. *why?:* how-come?, why in
the name of hell?, – the hell?
– heck?

153. Thinking
n. 1. brainwork
2. *idea, thought:* brainchild,
brainstorm, brainwave, hot one,
wheeze, wrinkle; spec. skulldrag
(taxing thought)
3. *opinion:* two cents'
worth
v. 4. *to think:* bear down on, beat
the brains, chew the cud, figger,
figure, hammer away at, have
something on one's head beside
one's hat, – one's hair, pound
(one's) brains, put on the thinker,
– thinking cap, run down, skulldrag,
use the (old) bean, – brainbox,
– chump, – noggin, – thinker,
– turnip, use one's loaf, zero in on;
spec. run it up the flagpole (and see
if anyone salutes) (to put forward an
idea)
5. *to think again:* get back (US
black)
adj. 6. crackerbarrel (homespun
philosophy)

7. *intellectually demanding:* thick
(US black)
8. *spontaneous thought:* off the top
of one's head
adv. 9. *lost in thought:* dead to the
world, – the wide, elsewhere, out to
lunch
10. *thinking about:* on one's chest,
on the brain, under one's hat
excl. 11. *think about:* bite on that!,
chew on that!, stick that in your
pipe (and smoke it)!, stick that in
your hat!
12. *what do you think (of that)?:*
how does that grab you?, – do you
like them apples?, like it?

INQUIRY
154. Interrogation
n. 1. *question:* draw, feeler, sounder
2. *cross-examination:* going over,
grilling, hot seat, roasting, third
degree, workover
v. 3. *to interrogate:* give a
going-over, – a roasting, – a
workover, go over, go to town on,
– to work on, grill, open up on,
pump, put in the hot seat, put the
cosh on, put the screws to, – the
squeeze on, – through the grinder,
shake down, sweat, throw the hook
into, turn inside out, work over;
spec. put the feelers out (to pump
for facts)
phr. 4. what's biting you?

155. Inquisitiveness; Curiosity
v. 1. have a stickybeak, – big ears,
– long ears, poke one's nose in, Paul
Pry; spec. study (gay use: to observe
a possible pickup)
adj. 2. long-nosed, nosy,
sticky(beak), snoopy
phr. 3. what's it (all) in aid
of?

156. Investigation; Examination
n. 1. eye, look-see, measure,
once-over, the tape; spec. tale of

the tape (boxing use: rival boxers'
vital statistics)
2. *test, trial:* go, shot, tumble,
workout
v. 3. *to investigate:* check out,
– over, dig into, figure, line up, size
–, give the eye, – the once-over,
have a look-see, take a decko (at),
– a shufti (at), root about – around,
run the tape over, see how the cat
jumps, – the land lies, – the wind
blows, – which way the wind is
blowing; spec. case the joint (cant:
to inspect a place that may be
robbed)
4. *experiment:* fool (with), fuck
around (with), futz around (with),
mess (with), play around (with), try
it on the dog
5. *to study:* hit the books, oil it

157. Search
v. 1. *search for, hunt:* be after, – on
the prowl for, grubble (around), go
gunning for, gun for, look all over
the shop, peel the eyes for, scout
(around), scout out, sniff out, take a
gander (for), turn upside down;
spec. declare open season on (to
hunt with intent to kill or harm)

POSSIBILITY
158. Possibility; Probability
n. 1. hope, shot
2. *Impossibility:* Chinaman's
chance, Chinese chance, dead
pigeon, dog's chance, fat chance,
longshot, no-no, some chance,
– hope, sweet chance
v. 3. *to be possible:* be on the cards,
– in the running, can do, run, stands
fair to, worth a punt
4. *to be impossible:* be out of the
running, not have a hope (in hell),
not have a dog's chance,
– Chinaman's chance, etc. (see
158.2), not stand a cat's chance in
hell, – a snowball's chance in hell
adv. 5. *impossible:* done for

6. *possible:* on the cards
phr. 7. *that's impossible:* forget it, forget you, no dice, not a hope in hell, not an earthly, no soap, no fear, no way I should be so lucky, – I should live so long, not on your Nellie
8. *in emergency:* at a pinch

159. Certainty

n. 1. blue-chip(s), cert, cinch, dead cert, good thing, lead-pipe cinch, monte, a moral, moral certainty, nice one, shoo-in, sure thing
v. 2. *to be certain:* bank on, bet one's life, go bail on, put money on
adj. 3. *certain:* bang to rights, dead sure, dead to rights, (down) cold, in like Flynn, no ifs and buts, no two ways (about it), open-and-shut, stoneginger, sure as eggs is eggs, – God made little green apples
adv. 4. *certainly:* abso-bloody-lutely, abso-fucking-lutely, and how!, as sure as eggs is eggs, – as God made little green apples, def (definitely), fair dinkum (Aus.), for sure, natch, no shit, poz, pozzy (positively), sho' 'nuff

BELIEF
160. Belief; Credence

n. 1. cred, sell, slant, twist, wrinkle
v. 2. *to believe:* Adam and Eve (rhy.sl.), buy, buy the (whole) farm, fall (for), figure, go for, have, swallow
3. *to be credulous:* be an easy mark, – easy, – green (as grass), – raw, bite, go for (it), gobble (it) down, lap (it) up, take the hook, tumble (for), walk into
4. *to be confident:* bank on, bet one's life, – one's bottom dollar, – the lot, – the wad, go bail on
adj. 5. *plausible:* unsus
6. *gullible:* sold, sold on

161. Disbelief; Suspicion

v. 1. *to disbelieve:* not see (it), – go for (it), – swallow (it)
2. *to be suspicious:* be leary, – sus, hawk, rumble, smell a rat, tumble
3. *to act suspiciously:* fancy pants
adj. 4. *suspicious:* fishy, hincty, leary, sus, sussy, wet (US black)
adv. 5. *incredible:* bit steep, – tall, – thick, – thin
excl. 6. *I don't believe it!:* (see Nonsense 146); all kidding aside, are you for real?, are you kidding?, can it, come off it!, the hell you say!, don't give me that!, don't kid yourself!, – make me laugh!, – shit me!, get along (with you)!, – away!, fuck off!, I ask you!, I don't believe this!, I don't buy that!, I'll eat my hat!, in a pig's eye!, – arse!, my (giddy) aunt!, my eye!, my foot!, no kidding!, no shit!, says who?, sez who?, – you!, tell it to the marines!, tell me another!, there (just) ain't such an animal!, you must be joking!, you've got to be joking!

SOLUTION
162. Solution; Discovery

n. 1. *evidence:* dope, goods (on), lowdown (on), nitty-gritty, stuff
v. 2. *to solve:* blow wise, break, crack, crack wise (to), get outside of, – a line on, – a slant on, have taped, – by the tail, – down, knock over, size up
3. *to discover:* catch up with, clap eyes on, cop, get a line on, – next to, – onto, – wise to, give a rumble, – tumble, glaum, glom, make, nab, nail, nick, nip, peg, slap the peepers on, sniff out, rumble, tumble (to), twig
4. *to meet with, happen on:* barge into, bump into, connect, hit up with, knock into, run into
5. *to catch, catch out:* bust, catch bending, – cold, – on the hop, – with one's pants down, – trousers

down, do up (like a kipper), do up
right, have bang to rights, – by the
short and curlies, – by the short
hairs, – the dope on, – the goods on
6. *to be caught:* be bowled out,
– caught bending, – cold, etc. (see
162.5), dead to rights
adv. 7. *solved:* bang to rights,
cinched, cracked, doped out, down
cold, nailed, sussed out, taped

163. Judgement; Conclusion
n. 1. at the death, bottom line,
clincher
2. *result:* come-out, curtain, end of
the line, payoff
3. *estimate:* guesstimate
v. 4. *estimate:* angle, dope (out), get
a line on, – the hang of, – the lay of,
size up
5. *to deal with:* square away
adv. 6. *estimated:* by guess and by
gosh

ACCURACY
164. Accuracy; Truth
n. 1. *facts:* brass tacks (rhy.sl.), nuts
and bolts, nitty-gritty, rodge,
runabout, (US black), score,
strength, ticket
2. *truth:* the goods, gospel, inside
track, legit, straight dope, – goods,
– poop, – shit
3. *essentials:* brass tacks, cases,
name of the game, nuts and bolts,
nitty-gritty, real grit (US black)
4. *real thing:* aces, cheese, goods,
legit, real McCoy, – McKay, stuff,
ticket
v. 5. *to be correct:* be right there,
– (right) on the ball, hit the spot,
have (it) down, – bang to rights,
– dead to rights, hit it, nail
it
6. *tell the truth:* come across,
– clean, lay it on the line, shoot
straight, tell it like it is
7. *promise the truth:* bet one's
boots, – bottom dollar, – life (on it),

cross one's heart (and hope to die),
swear blind, – to God.
adj. 8. *genuine, true:* aces, all wool
and a yard wide, as large as life (and
twice as natural), blowed in the
glass, dinki-di (Aus.), dinkum,
eighteen-carat, for real, – sure,
legit, no ifs or buts, on the level,
– the up and up, pukka, sure
enough, sho' 'nuff, solid, straight up
adv. 9. *precisely:* bang on, – up, in
the groove, on the button, – the
line, – the nail, – the spot
10. *correct:* bang to rights, dead –,
bang on, jake, righteous, rodge,
(just) what the doctor ordered
11. *directly:* bam, bang, blam, blap,
blip, blop, caplump, caplunk,
casmack, dap, slap-bang,
smack-dab, smack, sock, spang,
wham
phr. 12. *you're right:* AOK, ain't
that so, – a fact, – the truth, and no
mistake, back of the net, check and
double check, don't I know it, hole
in one, 'nuff said, I'll say she does,
– you do, no shit, now you're
cooking, – talking, righto, Roger,
seen (WI), that's telling them, that's
the stuff, you ain't just whistling
Dixie, you bet, you can say that
again, you don't know the half of it,
you got it, you know it is, you're
dern tootin', you're telling me,
you've got me there, you've got
something there, you've said it

165. Error; Mistake
n. 1. bad break, balls up, blue
(Aus.), bloomer, boob, boob play,
boo-boo, bum steer, bust, cropper,
dumb play, – trick, fluff, foulup,
fuckup, howler, miscue, misfire,
plumb, rick, ricket, wrong'un
v. 2. *to be wrong:* back the wrong
horse, be all wet, have another
guess coming, not hold together,
– hold water
3. *to make an error:* ball up, blot
one's copybook, boob, bugger (it)

up, cock (it) up, cock up, come a
cropper, drop a brick, fluff, foul up,
fuck (it) up, goof, go off the rails,
louse up, make a bloomer,
– boo-boo, etc. (see 165.1), put
one's foot in it, – in one's mouth,
put on a black, screw up, step on
one's dick, – one's prick, zeke (US
black)
adv. 4. *mistaken, wrong:* barking up
the wrong tree, cuckoo, daffy, (a)
mile wide, off (the) beam, – (the)
line, – the tack, screwed up, way
off, – out
excl. 5. *you're wrong:* (see 146); are
you kidding!, don't kid yourself!,
– make me laugh! in a pig's eye!,
– arse!, like fuck!, – fun!, – hell!,
etc.

UNDERSTANDING
166. Intelligibility
n. 1. savvy
v. 2. *to understand:* blow wise, crack
wise, catch (on), colly (US black),
connect, cop, dig, earwig (rhy.sl. =
twig), figure (out), get a line on,
– next to, – outside of, – the
message, – the picture, – with it,
glaum, glom, grok, have a line on,
– a slant on, – pegged, – it down,
– the goods on, know the score,
– the number, – the ropes, – the
words and music, latch on (to),
make, make the scene, nail, peep
one's hole card, spot one out (US
black), sus out, tumble (to), tune in,
twig; spec. flash on (to have a
sudden moment of comprehension)
3. *to be understood:* talk one's
language
adv. 4. *understanding:* into, onto,
up one's alley
phr. 5. *I understand:* (see 164.12);
AOK, check, – and double check,
gotcha, got it, got you, reet, seen
(WI), you said it
6. *do you understand:* are you with
me?, comprenny? (Fr. comprenez?),

dig?, do you read me? – get me?,
get it?, you get my drift?, – my
meaning?
7. *to read:* crack the books

167. Unintelligibility
n. 1. double Dutch, Greek
v. 2. *cannot understand:* can't
figure, – sus, etc. (see 166), don't
know from, no can see, no savvy,
not have the foggiest, – the first idea
adv. 3. *incomprehensible:* above
one's head, over –, beyond one,
clear as mud, geechie (US black)
excl. 4. *what?:* er?, huh?, says
which?, sorry, what in the hell?
– Sam Hill? etc., what you say?,
whatta whatta, you what?
phr. 5. *I don't understand:* beats
me, – the hell out of me, beyond
me, don't ask me, fucked if I know,
God knows, (I) can't get that
together, it's got me, sod that (for a
lark), you've got me (there), your
guess is as good as mine

168. Bewilderment; Perplexity
n. 1. botheration, backward
thinking (US black)
2. *problem:* bamboozler, curly one,
facer, handful, Harvey Nichol
(rhy.sl. = pickle), headache,
queeb, (bad) shit, shit on a string,
teaser
v. 3. *to confuse:* bamboozle, floor,
flummox, get (one) going, keep
(one) guessing, stump, throw (for a
loop)
4. *to be confused:* don't know one's
arse from one's elbow, – from a
hole in the ground, – whether one is
coming or going, get one's head up
one's arse, go into a flat spin, need a
foghorn, up a gumtree, – a stump
adv. 5. *confused:* all at sea, – at
sixes and sevens, between a rock
and a hard place, hot and bothered,
on one's beam ends, up against it,
up shit creek (without a paddle);
spec. on the fence (undecided)

169. Bewilderment; Confusion; Disconcertion
n. 1. *muddle:* dopiness, dottiness, fuddleheadedness, fuziness, grogginess, muzziness, wonkiness, wooziness
v. 2. *to be disconcerted, muddled:* (all) balled up, be like a chicken with its head cut off, run around in circles, not know whether you're on your head or heels, walk on one's head
3. *to disconcert, muddle:* discombobulate, drive up a pole, – out of one's brain, – gourd, – skull, etc., faze, flabbergast, flummox, jive, make one's head swim, put all at sea, put at sixes and sevens, – in a flat spin, – on the hop, – on a crosstown bus (US black), spifflicate
adj. 4. *bewildered:* all behind like a fat woman, all to shit, cockamamie, discombobulated, dusty (US black), fazed, gimped up, in a (right) two and eight (rhy.sl. = state), in a flat spin, paranoid, up in the air
5. *muddled:* addled, addle-pated, adrift, arsed up, at sixes and sevens (all) at sea, dopey, dotty, frazzled, goofy, in a loop, in a spin, jingled, muzzy, not all there, – with it, screwy, twisted, (having) one's wires crossed, woozy

---

RECOLLECTION
170. Memory
v. 1. *to stay in the mind:* get under one's skin, – in one's hair
2. *to reminisce:* cut up old scores
3. *refresh the memory:* beat the brains, pound the brains, jog the brains, polish up, sharpen, shine up, wise up
4. *to remember:* wake up
5. *to learn:* mug up
6. *to remind:* ring a bell

171. Forgetfulness
v. 1. *to forget:* bury (it), draw a blank, let slide in one ear and out the other, lose the combination, wipe (Aus.)
adj. 2. *forgetful:* foggy, rusty, with a head like a sieve, with a hole in the head

---

EXPECTATION
172. Expectation; Anticipation
n. 1. *presentiment:* hunch
v. 2. *to expect:* feel in one's bones, figure, reckon
adv. 3. *expectant:* (all) hopped up, hot (to trot), raring (to go)
4. *as expected:* nothing to write home about, par for the course

173. Inexpectation; Surprise
n. 1. bombshell, jar, jolt, knockout, turn, turn-up
v. 2. *surprise:* catch asleep at the wheel, – bending, – flat-footed, – off-base, – with one's pants down, – trousers down, give one a (nasty) jolt, – turn, etc., jump
3. *to astonish, amaze:* blindside, blow away, – one away, blow one's mind, knock for six, knock dead, – cold, – down with a feather, – for a loop, make one's hair curl, – head swim, psych out, smoke out (US black), strike all of a heap, – one blind, – dead, – dumb, – pink, wow, zap, zoom one out
4. *to be surprised:* take the knock
adv. 5. *unexpected:* out of the blue; spec. unbuttoned (unprepared)
6. *astonished:* all of a heap, blown away, buggered, flabbergasted, jiggered, on the ropes, reelin' and rockin'
excl. 7. *what a surprise:* are you ready!, are you prepared!, as I live and breathe!, blow me down (with a feather)!, blow my nose!, bugger me!, can you beat it!, can you feature that!, – you hack it!, did

you ever!, for crying out loud!, for a motherfucker! (US black), for days!, heavens to Betsy!, – to Murgatroyd!, hell's bells!, – teeth!, holy smoke!, (well) hush my mouth!, if that doesn't beat the band!, (well) I'll be a monkey's uncle!, (well) I'll be fucked, lumme!, my word!, shit a brick!, shit, eh!, (Aus.), sock it to me!, starve the lizards!, stiffen the lizards! (Aus.), (well) strike me blind!, – me pink!, – a light!, (well) strip my gears!, shiver my timbers!, stone me!, stone the crows!, swipe me!, this'll pin your ears back!, that's news!, that too much!, fuck!, too fucking much!, what a turn-up!, who (the hell) would've thought it!, yikes!, yipes! you could have knocked me down with a feather!, you wouldn't read about it, (see Oaths 194); spec. Mercy Mary! (homosexual use)
8. *imagine!:* fancy!
9. *really!:* do say!, do tell!, don't tell me!, go on!, he/she did!, he/she didn't!, izzatso!, no shit!, say it ain't so!, the hell you say!, you did!

SUPPOSITION

174. Supposition; Conjecture
n. 1. *guess:* potshot, shot (in the dark), stab –; spec. guesstimate (informed guess)
v. 2 *to predict:* call it (right), call one's (best) shot, dope out, figure, hit (it) on the head, – the nose,
3. *to guess:* go it blind, take a shot (at), – stab (at), make a stab (at), whistle in the dark, – in the wind

175. Imagination; Fantasy
n. 1. pie in the sky; spec. thousand-yard stare (the 'lost' look of a combat soldier)
v. 2. *to imagine:* moon around, space out
adv. 3. *fantasising:* moony, spaced (out), sanpaku (fr. Zen), T-zoned (T = transcendental)

Communication

LANGUAGE

176. Language; Speech
n. 1. chat, -ese (language peculiar to a person or profession)
2. *jargon:* gobbledegook, Morkrumbo (journalese)
3. *slang:* slanguage
phr. 4. as she is spoke

177. Word; Letter
n. 1. dickybird (rhy.sl.), peep (as in 'not a peep'), verbals
2. *hard word, big word:* jawbreaker, mouthful, two-dollar word
3. *introductory word:* er, like, look, you know, now, right, say, well
4. *printed character:* dog's cock, – bollocks, screamer (exclamation point)

NAME

178. Name
n. 1. handle, label, monicker, tab, tag, trademark
2. *title:* his nibs, hizzoner
3. *general forms of address:* boyo, boysie, bub, bubby, buddy, buster, cock, cocky, cuz, dad, daddy-o, dearie, digger (Aus.), ducks, ducky, guv, guvnor, hon, honey, Jim (US black), John, Jack, love, lovey, mac, mate, mister, momma, moosh, mush, my man, pal, squire, toots, tosh, wack; spec. Miss (homosexual use)

179. Nickname
n. 1. *UK football team:* Addicks (Charlton Athletic), Brough (Middlesbrough), Canaries (Norwich), Cestrians (Chester), Dons (Wimbledon), Fifers (East Fife), Filberts (Leicester), Forest (Nottingham Forest), Gills (Gillingham), Glaziers (Crystal Palace), Grecians (Exeter City), Gunners (Arsenal), Hammers (West Ham), Imps (Lincoln City), Latics (Oldham), Lions (Colchester), Moorites (Burnley), Orient (Leyton), Owls (Sheffield Wednesday), Paraders (Bradford), Pilgrims (Plymouth), Rangers (Queen's Parks Rangers), Reds (Manchester Utd, Liverpool), Robins (Bristol City), Saddlers (Walsall), Seasiders (Blackpool), Shakers (Bury), Spurs (Tottenham Hotspur), Trotters (Bolton Wanderers), Villains (Aston Villa)
2. *commercial:* Coats and 'Ats (C&A), Freds (Fortnum and Mason), Rods (Harrods), Gucky (Gucci), Moss Bross (Moss Brothers), M&S, Marks (Marks & Spencer), Woolies (Woolworths); spec. Chucks, Cons (Converse basketball boots)
3. *military:* The Andrew (RN), big Deuce (WW2), Kate Karney (rhy.sl. = the army), looey (lieutenant)
4. *US college courses:* blabs in labs (linguistics), shocks for jocks (basic engineering), stones & bones (prehistory), darkness at noon (art history slide show), slums and bums (urban sociology), rocks for jocks (introduction to geology), stars for studs (basic astronomy), chokes and croaks (first aid and safety education), sounds and tunes (campus songs), clapping for credit

(music appreciation), physics for poets (basic physics of arts graduates), jock major (physical education), holes and poles (sex education classes), nuts and sluts (abnormal psychology); spick (Spanish), number-cruncher (involving complex maths), nudes for dudes (art), Plato to NATO (European civilisation), monkeys to junkies (anthropology), gods for clods (comparative religion), Monday Night at the Movies (film school)

5. *UK newspapers:* Daily Excess, – Getsmuchworse (Daily Express), Thunderer (The Times), News of the Screws (News of the World), Grauniad, Garudnia, Grudian, etc. (The Guardian – from its many misprints)

6. *racial:* (see Persons: Nationalities 385); Johnny- (as in Johnny-Chinaman, Johnny-Pathan, etc.)

7. *first names:* Del (Derek), Tel (Terence)

8. *'inevitable' nicknames:* Agony (Paine, Payne), Betsy (Gay), Blanco (White), Bodger (Lees), Bogey (Harris), Bomber (Harris), Brigham (Young), Buck (Taylor), Busky (Smith), Chalkie, Chalky (White), Charlie (Peace), Chats (Harris), Chatty (Mather), Chippy (Carpenter), Cock (Robins, -son), Dan (Coles), Darky (Smith), Dickie (Bird), Dixie (Dean), Dodger (Green), Dolly (Gray), Doughy (Baker), Dusty (Miller, occ. Jordan, Rhodes, Smith), Dutchy (Holland), Edna (May), Fanny (Fields), Flapper (Hughes), Foxy (Reynolds), Ginger (Jones, Smith), Granny (Henderson), Gunboat (Smith), Happy (Day), Hooky (Walker), Iron (Duke), Jack (Sheppard, -erd, -herd), Jesso (Read), Jigger (Lees), Jimmy (Green), Johnny (Walker), Jonah (Jones), Jumper (Collins), Kitty (Wells), Knocker (Walker, Wright), Lackery (Wood), Lefty (Wright), Lottie (Collins), Mouchy (Reeves), Muddy (Waters), Nobby (Clark, -e, occ. Ewart, Hewart, Hewett, Hewitt), Nocky (Knight), Nutty (Cox), Pedlar (Palmer), Peeler (Murphy), Piggy (May), Pills (Holloway), Pincher (Martin), Pony (Moore), Rabbit (Hutchins, -son), Rattler (Morgan), Sandy (Brown), Shiner (Black, Bright, Bryant, Green, White, Wright), Shoey (Smith), Shorty (Wright), Slinger (Woods), Smoky (Holmes), Smudger (Smith), Snip (Parsons, Taylor), Snowy (Baker), Spider (Kelly), Spikey (Sullivan), Spokey (Wheeler, Wheelwright), Spud (Murphy), Taffy (Davis, -ies, Jones, Owen and other Welshmen), Timber (Wood), Tod (Hunter, Sloan), Tom (King), Topper (Brown), Tinkle, Tinker, Tottie (Bell), Tubby (Martin), Tug (Wilson), Wheeler (Johnson), Wiggy (Bennett)

9. *rhyming nicknames:* Charlotte the Harlot, Dennis the Menace, Even Stephen, Flo the Chro (Aus.), Giggling Gertie, Hairy Mary, Harriet the Chariot, Harry the Horse, Merv the Perv, Myrtle the Turtle, Nola the Bowler (Aus.), Peter the Poof (Aus.), Phil the Dill (Aus.), Randy Mandy, Roger the Lodger, Terry the Ferry (Aus.), Dizzie, Tizzie Lizzy

10. *of strong men:* Buck, Bull, Butch, Spike

11. *of hair:* Darky; Blondie; Bricktop, Carrots, Ginger, Red; Curly; Baldy

12. *of a slim person:* Daddylonglegs, Lanky, Lofty, Spider

13. *of a fat person:* Chubby, Chubs, Fats, Fatso, Fatty, Jumbo, Tiny, Tub, Tubby, Tubs

14. *of a short person:* Half-Pint,
Pee-Wee, Shorty, Tiny, Titch
15. *of one who wears glasses:*
Four-eyes
16. *of a foolish person:* Dizzy,
Dopey, Goofy, Sappy, Simp
17. *of a conceited person:* (Mr, Mrs,
etc.) Knowitall, – Smartarse,
– Smartypants
18. *BBC:* Auntie, Beeb, Corp
19. *popular black use:* T-bone

180. Pet Name
n. 1. *names of affection,*
endearment: angel, -face,
apple-dumpling, babe, baby,
babycakes, birdie, blossom, booful,
buggins, buggle, bunny, buttercup,
chick, -adee, chicken, chicky,
cutems, cutesie, -pie, dear heart,
diddums, duck, ducks, ducky, fruit
pie, honey, – bunny, -child, -pie,
-suckle, izzum, -kins (general
suffix), lamb, -chop, -pie, little one,
– thing, love, lovey, lovey-dovey,
oodlum, oozit, peach, pearl, pet,
– lamb, piggy, poopsy, precious,
– heart, pretty, pudding, pussums,
rabbit, snooks, snookums,
squidlums, sugar, -bun, -pie, -plum,
sweet, sweetie, – pie, sweetness,
sweets, toots, tootsie, – wootsie,
turtle-dove, ums, wootsie

SIGN
181. Sign; Symbol
n. 1. *badge:* buzzer, potsy; spec.
pips, stripes (milit. use)
2. *certificate, etc.:* union card (US
certificate of one's degree)
3. *medal, award:* gong, ruptured
duck; spec. leather medal, wooden
spoon (metaphorical award for
coming last)

182. Signal
n. 1. flash, high sign, nod, office,
tipoff, wink
2. spec. Maggie's drawers (US milit:

on a firing range, the flag that
denotes a miss)
v. 3. *to signal:* flash, give the high
sign, slip the ink, tip the nod,
– wink

SPEECH
183. Speech; Talk
n. 1. blab, broadcasting, bunny,
crack, gab, gaff, gas, guff, jaw,
jaw-jaw, kaylack (backsl.), (mouth)
music, noise, patter, rabbit, (rhy.sl.
= rabbit and pork), rap,
tongue-wagging, wind, yap; spec.
ji-jibe (US black: unimportant
chatter); fat lip (US black:
unpleasant talk); blooper
(embarrasing public verbal error);
beef (complaint)
2. *smooth talk:* applesauce, banana
oil, blarney, bull, bullshit, BS,
bunk, bunkum, chat, (the) con,
come-on, eyewash, flannel,
gammon, line, (old) oil, riff, soap,
spiel, snow (job), speeching (WI),
spit-bit (US black); spec. sob stuff,
– story (stories intended to persuade
through pity)
3. *complaining:* beating the gums,
going on (at), wanking (on)
4. *remark:* capper, crack, whammy,
zinger; spec. (the) liquor's talking
(to talk unrestrainedly or
embarrassingly)
5. *articulacy:* gift of the gab
6. *voice:* pipes
v. 7. *to talk:* beat the gums, bat the
breeze, blab, blow, break one's
chops, bunny (= rabbit), burble,
cackle, chew (the fat), dish, gab,
gas, go (as in 'I go . . . and he goes
. . .'), jaw, jib (US black), rabbit,
rap, shoot a line, – the breeze,
sound off, spiel, spill a line, warble,
yap
8. *whisper:* blow down one's ear,
talk out of the side of one's neck;
spec. deadpan (to speak without
expression)

9. *talk loudly:* ballyhoo, blart, blat, bloviate, blow hard, blow off (at the mouth), broadcast, loudmouth, sound off, talk big

10. *to remark:* crack, cut loose (with) dish, let loose (with), out with, shoot (one's wad), sing one's song, spew (it out)

11. *to become abusive:* curse out, get down dirty (US black), slag off; spec. rub in (to emphasise maliciously)

12. *to talk sincerely:* be one hundred per cent, come flat out (with), get down to brass tacks, let oneself go, pull no punches, make no bones (about), put one's cards on the table, rap on the real (US black), shoot straight (from the shoulder), show one's (hole-) card, take no prisoners, take the gloves off, talk turkey, touch base with; spec. on one's say-so (on trust); put the bee on (air one's obsessions)

13. *to talk cleverly:* come the smart arse, crack wise, deliver the goods, say one's stuff, spritz (Yid.), talk like a book

14. *to start talking:* fire away, out with (it), shoot; spec. break squelch (milit: break radio silence)

15. *interrupt:* butt in, chip in, pick up fag ends; spec. pull one's coat (to draw attention)

16. *to talk aptly:* hit the button, say a mouthful, strike home, touch base

17. *offer an opinion:* cop an attitude, put in one's two cents, say one's piece, sound off (about)

18. *speak foolishly:* go off half-cocked, put one's foot in it, – in one's mouth, shovel (the) shit; spec. foot in mouth disease (constant stupidities)

19. *to talk smoothly:* apply the oil, blarney, bull, bullshit, BS, feed a line, hand (out) a line, pour on the oil, soft soap, schmooze, shoot the bull, snow (under)

184. Talkativeness
n. 1. *chatter:* babble, blarney, blather, bosh, burble, cackle, dribble, gas, gift of the gab, guff, gush, hot air, jabber, jive, natter, schmoose, tosh, wind, yackety-yak
v. 2. *to chatter, talk idly:* bang on, beat one's chops, – one's gums, bend one's ear, blow (off), blow off steam, break one's chops, burble, chew the rag, flap at the jibs (US black), gab, gabble, gas, go off (at the mouth), go on, jaw, jawbone, natter, pop off (at), run off at the mouth, schpritz, shoot blanks (US black), shoot off (at one's mouth), spout (off), spruik (Aus.), talk a blue streak, – the hind leg off a donkey, waffle, woof (US black), yackety-yak, yak, yawp; spec. work the room (chatter at a party)
3. *to tell a secret:* blow the gaff, let the cat out of the bag (see also 202)
adj. 4. *talkative:* full of it, gabby, gassy, gobby, mouthy, yappy

185. Grandiloquence
n. 1. blah, gas, hot air, jazz, wind
v. 2. blah, lay it on, pile it on, splash it on, swallow the dictionary, swank; spec. do a Melba (announce one's retirement, glean the publicity, then continue working)
3. *to boast:* sell a wolf ticket (US black)

186. Conversation; Discussion
n. 1. bull sesh, – session, chinwag, confab, dialogue, gabfest, frank and fearless, pow-pow, rap, sound; spec. commo (US milit: communication); stiffin' and jivin' (US black: an unreal, false conversation); spec. bad talk (US black: politically unsound talk)
2. *'line', 'pitch':* mack (US black), riff, snow job, spiel, stuff (as in 'do your stuff')
3. *conference:* confab, huddle, pow-wow

4. *explanation:* rundown
5. *response:* comeback, feedback
v. 6. *to discuss:* bat (it) around, chew the fat, – the rag, kick (it) around, pow-wow, run down some lines (US black), splish and splash (US black); spec. say something (US black: to make a profound statement)
7. *to 'shoot a line':* come on (to), crack (something) up, give one a song and dance, give (one) the old boracic, run down some lines (US black), scream some heavy lines (US black)
8. *to communicate:* keep the lines open
9. *to discuss again:* rehash
phr. 10. talk to the engineer, not the oily rag (talk to the boss)
excl. 11. get this!, what's it to you?

187. Public Speaking
n. 1. bitch box (US milit: Tannoy), PA (public address system)
2. *publicity:* ballyhoo, hype, promo
v. 3. spec. belt (it) out (to sing loudly)

188. Call; Cry; Shout
n. 1. bleat, boola-boola, hog-caller, holler, squawk, whoop, yawp, yip
v. 2. barrack, bleat, holler, squawk, whoop, yawp, yell blue murder, yip
3. *summon:* bell (by telephone), hoy (Aus.)

189. Cursing; Profanity
n. 1. effing and blinding, four-letter words, toilet talk
2. *curse:* hex
v. 3. *to swear:* cuss, Lord Mayor, rip and tear (rhy.sl.); spec. excuse my French, pardon my French (apologies for swearing)
adj. 4. *cursed:* all-fire(d), blame(d), blankety, blasted, bleeding, blessed, blinking, blithering, bloody, blooming, blowed, buggering, cocksucking,

consarn(ed), corksacking, cussed, dad-blasted, dad-gasted, dadgummed, damnation, dang(ed), dashed, dern, deuced, doggone, dratted, effing, fizzing, flipping, freaking, frigging, fucking, God-blasted, gd, goddam, goldarn(ed), goldurn(ed), gosh-damned, – danged, – dern, hell-fired, mammy-jamming, mammy-ramming, mammy-tapping, mollyfocking, motherflunking, motherfouling, motherfucking, mothergrabbing, motherhugging, mother-jiving, mother-jumping, motherless, motherloving, mother-raping, pissing, plaguey, shitting, sodding, stinking
excl. 5. *damn!:* balls!, barf!, barf me out!, begorra!, bejabers!, bejazus!, bless me!, – my heart!, – my soul!, blimey!, blow (it)!, botheration!, bugger!, bugger me!, by George!, – golly!, – gosh!, – gorry!, – gum!, – jimminy!, – jingo!, – jove!, – the great horn spoon!, Christ!, – Almighty!, – on a crutch!, Christmas!, Christopher Columbus!, chuck you Farley!, cor!, cracky!, crikey!, criminy!, cripes!, crumbs!, damnit!, – to hell (and back)!, damn my stars!, – sakes!, darn!, dash!, dash it (all)!, dern!, doggone!, drat!, ferchrissakes!, for Christ's sake!, – crap's sake, – cripes' sake, for crying out loud!, – a mother-fucker! (US black), – gosh sake!, etc., – God's sake!, – heaven's sake!, – landsakes!, – the love of Mike!, – of Peter!, fuck a duck!, – this for a lark!, – for a game of soldiers!, fudge!, gee whillikins!, – whillikers!, – whiz!, glory (be)!, goddam!, goldarn!, goldern!, etc., golly!, gor blimey!, Gordon Bennett!, gosh!, gosh-almighty, gosh-darn!, etc., great Caesar's ghost!, great Scott!, – snakes!, etc., heavens to Betsy!, – to Murgatroyd, heck!, hell!, hell's bells!, Hogan's ghost! (Aus.), holy

cats!, – cow!, – cripes!, – mackerel!,
– Moses!, – smoke!, Jesus!, – H.
Christ!, Jiminy Cricket!, Judas
Priest!, jumping Jehosaphat!,
landsakes, Lawd(y)!, lawks!, Lord
love a duck!, Mary!, mercy!,
motherfuck!, mollyfock!, etc., my
(holy) aunt!, my sainted aunt,
– eyes!, – gosh!, – hat!, – stars (and
garters), nerts!, nuts!, pigs!,
pigshit!, radishes!, rats!, sheet!,
shit!, shit and derision!, shoot!,
shucks!, strewth!, suffering cats!,
sugar!, sweet (bleeding) Jesus,
tarnation!, the hell with it!, to hell
with it!, what the hell!, – the fuck!,
– shit!, ye gods! – and little fishes!,
your mother!

6. *I'll be . . .!:* I'll be a Chinaman!,
– a Dutchman!, – a dirty word!, – a
monkey's uncle!, – a (lowdown) son
of a bitch!, etc.; I'll be blowed,
– consarned!, – darned!, – jiggered!,
etc. (see 194.5); I'll be hanged,
– shot

7. *curses:* bugger you!, fuck –!, sod
–!, damn your hide, go to hell!, rot
your bones, the hell with you,
– fuck with you, get fucked,
– knotted, (go), take a flying
fuck!, – a run up yourself!, you
piece of crap!, – of shit!, you
SOB!, you son-of-a-bitch!, you
whoreson bastard!, you
scumsucking shit-for-brains!, etc.,
etc.

WRITING
190. Writing
n. 1. hacking (it out), inkslinging,
knocking it out, pen-pushing,
pencil-pushing, whacking it out
2. *ticket:* bat and wicket (rhy.sl.),
ducat, ducket; spec. Annie Oakley,
chinee, Chinese ducket (free,
complimentary ticket)
3. *signature:* handle, John Hancock,
mauley
4. *handwriting:* fist; spec. chicken
scratchings, poultry –, pothooks and
hangers (bad writing)
5. *typewriter:* typer
6. *paper:* repap (backsl.)
7. *book:* Captain Cook (rhy.sl.)
v. 8. *to write:* crank it out, hack (it
out), knock it out, sling (some) ink,
whack it out
9. *to study:* book it, book up, bone
up (on), hack (it)

191. Correspondence
n. 1. *letter:* line (as in 'drop a line'),
pc (post-card)
2. *invitation:* stiff, stiffie
3. *thanks:* bread and butter letter,
thank-you letter, – note
4. *bureaucracy:* bumf, red tape
5. *lovers' codes on envelopes:*
SWALK (sealed with a loving kiss),
SWAK (sealed with a kiss),
SWANK (– a nice kiss),
NORWICH (knickers off ready
when I come home),
SWALCAKWS (sealed with a lick
'cos a kiss won't stick), BOLTOP
(better on lips than on paper – next
to an X for a kiss), ILUVM (I love
U very much), ITALY (I trust and
love you), BURMA (be undressed,
ready, my angel), HOLLAND
(here our love lives and never dies),
EGYPT (eager to grab your pretty
tits)
6. *love letter:* mash note; spec. Dear
John (ending an affair)
v. 7. *to send a letter:* drop a line

INFORMATION
192. Information (inside)
n. 1. dope, goods, hot poop, – stuff,
info, line (up), lowdown; spec. beat,
scoop (exclusive newspaper story);
2. *inside information:* buzz, hot
poop, – steer, – stuff, – tip, inside
dope, – stuff, – tip, lowdown, etc.
(see 192.1)
3. *reliable information:* cinch, good
thing, (the) goods, lead-pipe cinch,

real thing, straight goods, – poop,
sure bet, – thing; Mister Ed
(unimpeachable inside source),
deep throat
4. *false information:* bum steer
v. 5. *to inform:* dish (the lowdown),
– the dirt, dope up, give the dope
on, – the goods on, etc. (see 192.1),
let (one) in, – on the ground floor,
put a word in one's ear, put in the
know, put next to, put on to
something good, – something hot,
smarten (up), wise (up); spec. kibitz
(to offer unwanted information,
esp. to a card-player)
6. *to teach:* larn, learn, show the
ropes, – a thing or two, smarten up,
wise up
7. *to give false information:* bum
steer
8. *to become informed:* get a line
on, get alongside, get behind, get
the hang of, get into, get next to,
get onto, get on the inside (track),
get wise to, get with (it), sus out
9. *to be uninformed:* not know the
score
adj. 10. *of inside information:* hot
off the presses
11. *reliable:* blue-chip, gilt-edged

193. Disclosure
n. 1. finger-pointing, (dead)
giveaway, let-on, top-off (Aus.),
whistle-blowing
2. *rumour:* sniff
v. 3. *to disclose, reveal:* blab, come
across (with), come clean, cough,
ding, get (it) off one's chest, – (it)
out of one's system, give, – (it) a
name, go the hang-out route, lay
(something) on, loosen up, make a
clean breast (of it), open up, put up
one's hand, put out, show one's
cards, sing, – like a canary, sneeze
(it out), spill (one's guts) – the
beans, – the works, spit (it out),
stand up, unbutton (one's lip),
unload
4. *to betray, inform on:* blab, blow

the gaff, – the whistle (on), bubble
(rhy.sl. = bubble and squeak =
speak), deep throat, dob in (Aus.),
finger, fink (on), grass (up), nark
(on), pin on, put a name up, put
one in (Aus.), put the whisper on,
rat on, rat one out, shop, snitch,
squeal, stool, tip in, tom out (US
black), top-off (Aus.)
5. *to expose:* blow the whistle (on),
muckrake, stir up
6. *to reveal one's intentions:* stand
up, stick one's chin out, – neck out,
tip one's hand, – hole-card
7. *to disillusion:* knock the props
from under, pull the rug from
under, let down easy, puncture
one's balloon
adv. 8. *betrayed:* bubbled, fingered,
grassed (up)

194. News; Newspapers
n. 1. dope, gen, griff, info, (hot)
poop, SP (starting price); spec.
kicker (problematical information)
2. *privileged information:* beat,
lowdown, scoop
3. *spec. newspapers, etc.:* bladder,
book, funnies, funny pages,
– papers, glossy, heavy (serious
paper), linen, scream sheet, tab
(tabloid), sheet; spec. hatched,
matched and dispatched (births,
marriages and deaths columns in
The Times); bread and butter
column (column based on rewritten
PR handouts); bulldog (first edition)
4. *'men's magazines':* one-hand
magazine, stroke book, tit mag;
spec. eight-pager, Tijuana bible
(small pornographic comic book)
5. *pin-ups:* beefcake, cheesecake,
leg art
6. *journalistic technique:*
baby-sitting, body-snatching (hiding
away the human source of a big
story); door-stepping (waiting
outside the house of a possible
interviewee); spoiling (ruining a
rival paper's story)

v. 7. *to appear in a paper:* get some ink
8. *for a story to happen:* break

195 Television; Telephony, etc.
n. 1. *television:* boob-tube, box, custard and jelly (rhy.sl. = telly), gobble box, goggle box, idiot box, Nervo and Knox (rhy.sl.), tube; spec. God slot (religious programmes), sit. com. (situation comedy), soap opera (very long-running drama series); idiot board (cue board), idiot girl (cue board operator)
2. *film:* flicks
3. *porno film:* cock movie, snuff movie (spec. death), trick flick
4. *still picture:* Beecham's (rhy.sl. Beecham's pill), X-ray
5. *telephone:* blower, dog and bone (rhy.sl.), hook, Molly Malone (rhy.sl.), seven digits (US black)
6. *rehearsals, etc.:* Acton Hilton (BBC rehearsal studios); mug book (casting directory)
7. *film types:* ear-jerker (featuring the score); weepie (sentimental/ romantic); oater (Western)
8. *film director:* lenser, megger
9. *photographer:* shutterbug; spec. blinker (camera)
10. spec. sleeper (media use: slowly developing success)
v. 11. *to telephone:* bell, buzz, give (one) a bell, – (one) a buzz, tinkle, tootle
12. *to watch TV:* tube it
13. *to direct a film:* lens, meg

196. Gossip
n. 1. buzz, Daily Mail (rhy.sl. = tale), dirt, dish, furphy (Aus.), jazz, scuttlebutt, whisper
2. *collective gossip:* bull session, bush telegraph, (the) dirt farm, galah session (Aus.), grapevine
v. 3. *to gossip:* bad-mouth, bad-rap, barber, bat the breeze, bum-rap, clean up the walls (US black), dish the dirt, get down dirty, – shitty (US black), hardmouth, put it on the street, put (one's business) on front street (US black), put in the poison, set mouth (US black), shoot the breeze, – the bull, – the regular, – the shit, shovel shit, slay, smartmouth (US black), stir (it up), talk out of school, – that talk, – trash, throw some dirt (on)
adv. 4. *gossiping:* on the wire

197. Description; Explanation
v. 1. *to explain:* break down (US black), clue (one) in, daylight (US black), dope out, fill (one) in, fold one's ears, give, hip (to), lay (the scene) on, light (US black), mark one's card, run (it) down, school (US black), whip it on (one), wire up (US black); spec. kick apart (analyse); knock into (one's skull), – through (one's skull) (to explain to the dull)

198. Story
n. 1. Daily Mail (rhy.sl. = tale), spiel, tell, yarn
2. *unlikely story:* cock-and-bull story, con, fairy story, fish story, song-and-dance, tall story, wind-up; (see Lie 312)
3. *depressing story:* hard-luck story, Newgate gaol (rhy.sl. = tale), sob story, tearjerker
4. *exciting story:* chiller, cliffhanger, shocker, snorter, spine-tingler, thriller; spec. potboiler (story written purely for cash, not art)
5. *romantic story:* bodice-ripper, gay gothic, hysterical historical, sweet savagery; spec. confessional (religious romance)
v. 6. *to tell a story:* spin a yarn, yarn
7. *to tell an unlikely story:* feed (one) the bull, hand a (cock-and-bull) story, – a line, shoot a line, spin a line

8. *to exchange stories:* cut up touches (with)

AFFIRMATION AND DENIAL
199. Assertion
v. 1. *to assert:* lay down the law, – it on the line, take no shit, tell it like it is

2. *to believe absolutely:* eat one's hat, – one's head, hope to die, swear till one's blue in the face, bet one's bottom dollar, etc. (see 160)

excl. 3. A!, ain't that a fact!, – so!, – it the truth!, all kidding aside!, all reet!, all right!, and don't you forget it!, and that's a fact!, AOK!, awright!, believe me!, betcha!, bet your boots!, blood oath! (Aus.), Bob's your uncle!, check!, – and double check!, damn right!, darn right!, dern right!, etc. (see 164), did I ever!, does a bear shit in the woods?, – the Pope shit in the woods?, fucking A!, go on twist my arm, harbour light! (rhy.sl. = all right), honest injun!, I ain't just whistling (Dixie)!, I don't mean maybe!, I hear you!, I'll say!, I'll eat my hat!, – my head!, etc., I mean!, I should say so!, Isle of Wight (rhy.sl. = all right), is that ... or is that? (insert subject as to context), is a bear a Catholic?, is the Pope a Catholic?, lahteeache (backsl. = all right), left off!, lovely grub!, naked!, natch!, no kid(ding)!, no risk! (Aus.), no shit!, OK, okey-dokey, on the level!, right arm!, righto!, right on!, scotia! (US black), see (backsl. = yes), seen! (WI), (you can) take it from me!, that's the shot! (Aus.), – the ticket!, way to go!, word!, word up!, would I shit you! (you're my favourite turd!), you bet!, you can say that again!, you don't know the half of it!, you('ve) got it!, you know it (is)!, you're dern tootin'

200. Negation
n. 1. blank, KB, knock-back, nix, no-no

v. 2. blank, give the thumbs-down (to), KB, knock-back, nix, no-no

excl. 3. don't make me laugh!, fat chance!, fuck off!, I don't think!, I'll be damned if!, – fucked if!, like fuck!, – fun!, – hell!, nerts!, nix!, no dice!, – sale!, – soap!, – way!, not bleeding likely!, not on your Nellie!, not on your tintype!, nothing doing!, no siree (Bob)!, nope!, not fucking likely!, nuts!, on! (backsl.), some chance!, – hope!, you must be joking!

UNCOMMUNICATIVENESS
201. Muteness
v. 1. *to be quiet, silent:* button one's lip, – up, clam up, dry up, dummy up, freeze, hold one's noise, – water, keep mum, – stum(m), – the cap on the bottle, put a sock in it, shut one's cakehole, – face, – gob, – hole, – trap, zip one's lip

2. *to make quiet:* choke off

3. *to withhold information:* clam up, dummy up, freeze up, hold one's breath, – out (on), keep the cap on the bottle, – the lid on, – them guessing, – it on one's chest, – under one's hat, keep stum(m), save one's breath, stonewall

adj. 4. mum, stum(m)

excl. 5. *stop talking!:* bag your face!, belt up!, button your lip!, button up!, can it!, cheese it!, cut the chat!, – the crap!, – gas!, – the noise!, drop it!, dry up!, dummy up!, enough said!, forget it!, get back in the knife box!, give your face a rest!, hit me and cut the crap!, hold it!, hold it down!, hold your noise!, hush your mouth!, keep mum!, – stum(m)!, knock it off!, nark it!, nit-nit, 'nuff sed!, put a sock in it!, – the stopper in it!, save it!, – your breath!, shut it!, – your face!,

– gob!, – hole!, – trap!, shut your mouth and give your arse a chance!, stow it!, wrap up!, zip it up!
6. *don't interrupt!:* butt out!, who pulled your chain!

202. Secret
n. 1. cover-up, family jewels, hole card, whitewash
v. 2. *to keep a secret:* clam up, close up, dummy up, hush up, keep it dark, – it down, keep a stiff lip (US black), – mum, – on the strict q.t., – under one's hat, not let the cat out of the bag, not peep, not spill the beans, play the dummy, put the lid on, tell no tales (out of school)
3. *to suppress:* blue-pencil, put the lid on
4. *to confide in:* blow in one's ear, pull one's coat, put wise (to), wise up
adj. 5. *secret:* closet, hole and corner, hush-hush, inside, on the quiet, – the q.t., stum(m) and crumm, under the table, – one's hat, under wraps
adv. 6. *secretly:* on the quiet, – the q.t.

203. Concealment
n. 1. cover-up, smoke screen, whitewash
2. *hiding place:* funk-hole
3. *cache:* drop, slaughter (burglar's storeroom), stash
4. *disguise:* front
v. 5. *to hide* **vt:** bag, drop, dump, law away, plant, stash
6. *to hide* **vi:** dive, duck-out, hole up, keep on the q.t., lay low, lie doggo, – low, lie dead, play dead, – possum, sit quiet, – tight
7. *disguise* **vt:** cook up, doctor (up), fake (up), ring
adv. 8. *in hiding:* holed up, lying low, on the lam, playing possum etc.
9. *disguised:* cooked up, doctored (up), etc., incog

Volition

RESOLUTION; DETERMINATION

204. Resolution

n. 1. balls, guts, stones

v. 2. *to be determined:* barrelass, be out for blood, – for business, do the full sesh, get behind, – down, – into, – (it) on, – one's head down, – some respect (US black), – stuck in, give one's best shot, go for broke, – (for) the whole shot, – nap on, – overboard, – the limit, mean business, play hardball, put one's head on the block, – foot down, run with the ball, shit or bust, shoot one's bolt, shoot to kill, stand pat, step fast (US black), stick one's neck out, take care of business, TCB, take no prisoners, take one's best shot, wade in

3. *to make determined:* psych (oneself) up

4. *to determine:* allow, figure, fix (to), reckon

adj. 5. *determined:* ballsy

adv. 6 *determined:* behind, dead set, hell-bent, hells-bent, hot for, into, psyched up, set

excl. 7. *I mean it:* honest (injun)! I ain't just whistling Dixie!, no kidding!, no shit!, would I shit you? (you're my favourite turd)

205. Perseverance

n. 1. stick-to-itiveness

v. 2. *to persevere:* bang away (at), buck (for), bust a gut, bust one's arse, go down the road (for), hammer away (at), hang in (there), – tight, hit for six, keep the ball rolling, – the show on the road, make the fist (US black), not give up the ship, plug away at, run down one's best game (US black), shag ass, shoot from the hip, – one's best mack (US black), show the flag, sit tight, steam in, stick one's neck out, stick to (it), sweat (it) out, throw one's hat in the ring, tough it out

adv. 3. *persevering:* shovin' and pushin' (US black)

205. Obstinacy

v. 1. *to be obstinate:* have one's head up one's arse, put one's foot down, run into the ground, take no shit

adj. 2. *uncompromising:* bloody-minded, bullnecked, cussed, dog in the manger, hard-assed, hard-nosed, mulish, pig-headed

adv. 3. spec. accidentally on purpose

phr. 4. it's my story and I'm sticking with it

IRRESOLUTION; EVASION

207. Irresolution

n. 1. fence-sitting; spec. touch of the seconds (second thoughts)

v. 2. *to be irresolute:* beat about the bush, – around the bush, fart around, fuck about, hum and haw, piss about, – around, pussyfoot, seesaw, shilly-shally, stall

adj. 3. *irresolute:* betwixt and between, half and half, ho-hum, on the fence

208. Caprice

n. 1. *whim:* bee in the bonnet, wheeze

v. 2. *to act madly:* rally
adv. 3. *acting irresponsibly:* triflin'
(US black)

209. Abandonment; Relinquishment
n. 1. chuck, heave-ho, push, shove
v. 2. *to relinquish, abandon:* axe,
call it a day (give up), chuck (it)
(up), cut loose, ditch, dump, fold,
give (it) the (old) heave-ho, – it the
chuck, – the elbow, – the E, – the
toss, give up the store, hang (it) up,
jack (it) in, junk, kiss goodbye,
– one's arse goodbye, knock on the
head, knuckle down, – under, pack
(it) in, put on ice, sack it up, (US
black), scrub (it), throw in one's
hand, – the sponge, – the towel, top
up, wash out, wind up; (see also:
Discard 25.4)
3. *to retract one's words:* back down,
– out, bow out, call all bets off,
chicken out, clam up, crawfish, eat
dirt
4. *to alter an opinion:* change one's
tune, draw in one's horns, pull in
one's horns
5. *to desert, abandon:* break it off
(with), cut (out), ditch, do a fade
(on), give the brush-off, – the
go-around, go bent (on), kiss
goodbye, – off, lay down on,
leave flat, play the chill (for),
take a powder, – a runout
powder on, throw overboard, toss
overboard (see also **v.** 2)

210. Evasion
n. 1. dodge, duck, E, elbow,
go-around, run-around; spec.
AWOL, French leave (absence
without leave)
v. 2. *to evade:* back off, bob and
weave, buck, cock a deaf 'un, duck
(out), get cold feet, give the go-by,
– the runaround, go AWOL, go
cold on, lose one's bottle, oil out,
play the duck, – hide-and-seek
(with), plead the Fifth, punt off,

shake; spec. beat the rap (avoid
punishment)
3. *to play truant:* flick (US black),
hop the wag, play hookey, wag off
4. *to avoid:* fight shy (of), give a
wide berth, give the go-by, – the
runaround, – the miss, steer clear
(of)
5. *to avoid work:* come the old
soldier, – the tin soldier, dodge the
column, flick (US black), goldbrick,
goof off, lay down on the job,
soldier, swing the lead
6. *to absent oneself:* go AWOL, take
French leave

211. Flight; Escape
n. 1. bunk, disappearing act,
vanishing act, el disappearo,
powder, skip
2. *narrow escape:* close call,
– shave, narrow squeak, near
squeak, – go
v. 3. *to escape:* amscray (backsl. =
scram), beat it, blow, bunk, buzz
the nab, cheese it, cop out, crash
out, cut out, do a runner, – a fade,
– the disappearing act, – the
vanishing act, duck out, fade, fly the
coop, fuck off, get out, – the fuck
out, – the hell out, go on the lam,
go walkabout, have it away, head
for the hills, – the tall timber, – the
tall trees, – the woods, hightail it,
make a break, pull a runner, save
one's bacon, Scapa (rhy.sl. = Scapa
Flow = go), scarper (= Scapa
Flow), show one's heels, skip (it),
sod off, take a (runout) powder,
– the air, take it on one's toes, take
it on the lam, vamoose; spec. flick
(US black: to play truant, to avoid
work)

CHOICE
212. Choice; Option
n. 1. bag, bet, cup of tea, cuppa,
druthers, fave, – rave, scene, thing
2. *alternative:* any old, between hell

and high water, betwixt and between, or else, no two ways about it

v. 3. *to choose:* do one's thing, go for; spec. you pays your money and you takes your choice

phr. 4. *after a decision:* when the chips are down

213. Freedom; Independence

n. 1. open slather (unlimited situation, Aus.), Rafferty's rules (Aus.); spec. indie (entertainment use: an independent TV/film/record company)

v. 2. *to be free, independent:* cut one's own throat, do as one damn well pleases, – one's own thing, footloose and fancy-free, go it alone, go one's own (sweet) way, hoe one's own row, keep oneself to oneself, look after number one, – out for number one, paddle one's own canoe, roll one's own, take care of number one, write one's own ticket

3. *to give freedom:* cut loose, get off one's case, give enough rope, let off the hook

adv. 4. *free:* footloose and fancy-free, on the loose

5. *without rules:* anything goes, no holds barred, no punches pulled, no strings (attached), the sky's the limit

6. *solo:* (all) on one's lonesome, on one's Jack (rhy.sl. = Jack Jones = alone), – one's Pat (Aus. rhy.sl. = Pat Malone = alone), – one's Tod (rhy.sl. = Tod Sloan = alone), under one's own steam

---

CHANCE
214. Chance; Opportunity

n. 1. breaks, fling, go, hope, main chance, shot, show, slant

2. *good chance:* aces, cinch, clean shot, fair go, fair pop, good thing, natch, runner

3. *poor chance:* crapshoot, longshot

4. *no chance:* on a hiding to nothing, not a Chinaman's chance, – a dog's chance, – an earthly (chance), – a hope in hell, – cat's chance in hell, – a hope, – a snowball's chance in hell

v. 5. *to take a chance, to risk:* chance one's arm, – one's luck, give it a go, have a fling (at), – a shot (at), lead with one's chin, odds (it), play a hunch, punt (around), punt it (up), sail close to the wind, stick one's neck out, take a stab (at), wing it

6. *to bet:* bet one's bottom dollar, go the whole bundle, – the whole pile, – the whole wad, put one's shirt on

7. *to have a good chance:* have a look-in, – a hope, stand pat

8. *to have little or no chance:* to be on a hiding to nothing, to have a Chinaman's chance, etc. (see 214.4)

9. *to use one's chances:* not to miss a trick, play one's hand

adv. 10. *at risk:* on spec

excl. 11. *no chance!:* don't make me laugh!, you must be joking!

215. Luck

n. 1. beads, breaks, Dame Fortune, dice, ins and outs, joss, Lady Luck, ups and downs

2. *good luck:* break, mazel (Yid), mozzle, muzzle, turnup (for the book)

3. *bad luck:* tough break, – shit, – titties, tzuris (Yid. = problem)

4. *a bad luck totem:* hoodoo, Jonah

v. 5. *to be lucky:* be in clover, – in fat, – on a roll, – on a winner, break the bank, get the breaks, get hot, luck into, luck out, turn up trumps; spec. born with a silver spoon in one's mouth (to be born to riches)

6. *to be unlucky:* be down on one's luck, be fucked, screwed, etc., crap out, draw a blank, on the outs, not to have the breaks; spec. sizzle (US black = to be unusually prone to arrest)

7. *to cause bad luck:* hoodoo, jinx, Jonah
adv. 8. *lucky:* hot, in clover, in the fat, on a roll, on a winner
9. *unlucky:* behind the eightball, born under a bad sign, cold, jinxed, hoodooed, fucked, screwed, etc.
10. *destined:* in the cards, – the dice, – the stars

CONTROL
216. Authority
n. 1. clout, final cut, juice
2. *order:* say-so
v. 3. *to have authority:* to be in the chair, – in the driving seat, etc. (see 216.4), call the punches, – the shots, come on strong, crack the whip, have (it) covered (US black), – one's act together, – one's act down, – one's game uptight, – shit together, – shit down, – it knocked, hold the can, keep ahead of the game, ramrod, ride herd (on), run a tight ship, sit down, toughen (up) one's game (US black), wear the trousers; spec. go under one's neck (Aus. to usurp another's position)
4. *to give orders:* lay down the law, put one's foot down
5. *to lose control:* blow it, jump the rails
adv. 6. *in authority:* ahead of the game, in the box seat (Aus.), in the chair, in the driving seat, in the saddle, on one's game (US black)
7. *strict:* death on
phr. 8. don't just stand there, do something, if it moves salute it, if it doesn't, paint it

217. Force; Compulsion
n. 1. screws, squeeze, third degree; spec. habe (abbr. habeas corpus)
v. 2. *to compel:* blackjack, clobber one with, dump on, put the screws to, – the squeeze on, scare up, strongarm, twist one's arm

3. *to be forced:* like it or lump it, toe the line, walk the plank

218. Restraint; Curb
n. 1. clamp, crimp, damper, freeze, lid, squelch
v. 2. *to restrain:* bottle (up), clamp (down) (on), crimp, put the clamp on, – a crimp into, sit on; spec. dock (to cut wages)
3. *to subdue:* buffalo, bust, take down a peg (or two), take the frills out of
4. *to restrain oneself:* hold one's horses, pull one's punches, slow one's row (US black), soft pedal
adv. 5. *restrained:* in bondage (US black), over a barrel

INFLUENCE; INDUCEMENT
219. Influence
n. 1. clout, drag, fluence, juice, mojo, pull, strings, wires
v. 2. *to use influence:* pull strings, pull wires, railroad, tickle palms
3. *to have influence:* draw (a lot of) water, have clout, drag, etc., know where the bodies are buried
4. *to persuade:* do a number (on), get around, grind down, hassle, hook in, pressure, put something over, sell (on), sell a bill
5. *to deceive:* ballyhoo, bamboozle, bullshit, con, get at, get one's hooks on, – one's hooks into, pull the wool over one's eyes, set up, take to the cleaners, three-sheet, wind up
6. *to urge:* ding, drum up, egg on, kack up, kid (along), talk (something) up
7. *to influence emotionally:* get to, put through changes

220. Enticement; Allurement
n. 1. come-on, draw, sucker bait
v. 2. *to entice:* give the come-on (to), pull, smoke out, throw out a line, work (on)
3. *to attract:* bring down

adj. 4. *enticing:* come hither

WILLINGNESS
221. Willingness
adj. 1. *willing:* game
adv. 2. *willingly:* at the drop of a
hat, like a shot
phr. 3. I don't mind if I do

222. Consent; Assent
n. 1. go-ahead, green light, OK,
thumbs-up
v. 2. *to consent:* give a nod (to), give
the go-ahead, – the green light (to),
– the OK, – the thumbs up (to), go
with, – the flow, hang loose, lay
down (for), roll with the punches,
stand still (for), stand up, tip the
wink (to); spec. swallow (it) (to
accept – often knowingly – lies);
choke (it) down (accept reluctantly)
excl. 3. spec. bags I! (schoolboy: yes
please!)

UNWILLINGNESS
223. Unwillingness
excl. 1. *I refuse!:* the hell you say!,
the hell I will!, the fuck I will!, don't
make me laugh!, you must be
joking!, in a pig's arse I will!, I'll be
damned, – danged!, – dashed!,
– hanged!, – shot (if I will)!, I'll see
you in hell first!, like fuck I will!,
– fun I will!, – shit I will!, etc.,
include me out!, kiss my arse!, ring
the other one (it's got bells on it)!,
get fucked!, on your bike!, no deal!,
– dice!, – go!, – soap!, – not on your
life!, not on your tintype!, try and
make me!, you've got another think
coming!; spec. bags I (baggy) no
par! (schoolboy: not me!)

224. Refusal; Rejection
n. 1. big E, elbow, nix, red light,
thumbs-down
2. *dismissal:* boot, brown envelope,
sack

v. 3. *to reject:* blank, blow out, ding,
give the E, – the elbow, – the hard
word, give the thumbs-down, – the
red light (to), kiss, kiss goodbye,
kiss off, turn one's nose up at
4. *to chase away:* hunt (Aus.)
5. *to dismiss:* give the boot, give the
brown envelope, give the sack

225. Prohibition
v. 1. *to prohibit:* nix, thumbs-down,
zero
adv. 2. *forbidden:* verboten
excl. 3. *no!:* (see 'Stop it' 11.10);
forget it!, ixnay!, nix!, – on that
(stuff)!, no way!

CUSTOM
226. Habit
n. 1. (daily) grind, nine-to-five,
same old same old
adj. 2. *habituated:* hooked, hung up
(on) (see also Drugs 510)

227. Convention
n. 1. done thing
v. 2. *to be conventional:* follow
one's nose (US black), get in line,
mind one's Ps and Qs, toe the line,
watch one's lip, – step
adj. 3. *conventional:* burbed out,
button-down, grey

228. Unconventionality
n. 1. spec. the Revo (Revolution)
v. 2. *to behave oddly:* to get away
with murder
adj. 3. *bizarre:* craze-o, out of
left field, OTT, over the top, way
out, weird (see also Insanity 152.5)

229. Fashion
n. 1. *glamour:* pizzazz, Tate and
Lyle (rhy.sl. = style)
2. spec. nigger fronts (US black,
very smart clothes)
v. 3. *to be unfashionable:* have
whiskers
adj. 4. *fashionable:* glitzy, happening,

high-tone, keen, mod, ritzy, sharp,
snazzy; spec. early (US black)
5. *unfashionable:* dead as a dodo,
joanie, lunchy, the pits
6. *ostentatious:* flash as a Chinky's
horse, – as a rat with a gold tooth
(Aus.)

BEHAVIOUR
230. Behaviour; Conduct
n. 1. (where one is) at, bag, (where
one is) coming from, doings, goings
on, (one's own) thing
v. 2. *to conduct one's life:* do one's
own thing, keep one's end up,
– one's nose clean, – one's pants
zipped, – on the straight and
narrow, set to rights, shape up,
stack up, wise up; spec. CYA,
cover your arse (look after
yourself)
3. *behave yourself!:* act your age!,
be yourself!, cut the comedy!, – the
crap!, – the funny business!, don't
fuck about!, – muck about!, – piss
about!, get yourself together!,
– your act together!, – your shit
together!, – your arse in gear!, lay
off!, quit fooling (around)!

231. Misbehaviour
n. 1. carry-on, cold shot (US black),
ego trip, shenanigans, to-do
2. *set-to:* big how-de-do, randan,
razzle-dazzle, ruckus, shindy; spec.
knock-down-drag-out (extremely
rough)
3. *social error:* floater
v. 4. *to misbehave:* carry on, come
it, – the old acid, – the raw prawn
(Aus.), create, cut up rough, – up
rusty, draw the crabs (Aus.), hell
around, jump bad, kick up hell,
raise Cain, – hell, – a racket, – a
ruckus, – sand (US black), throw
one's weight about, turn the set out
(US black), trash around, whoop it
up; spec. tart about (for a female to
act like a tart)

adj. 5. *unpleasant:* boldacious (US
black), bucko
adv. 6. *misbehaving:* all over the
board, off the track, out of pocket
(US black), out of order, over the
top, OTT

PLAN
232. Plan; Method
n. 1. angle, big idea, gag, hustle,
lay, moves, racket, ropes, scam,
schmeer, wangle, wheeze
2. *schedule:* layout, lineup, sked,
set-up
v. 3. *to plan:* angle, figure, honcho,
hustle, plot up, promote, wangle
4. *to plot:* be up to (something) (US
black), cook up, fake up
adv. 5. *anyhow:* all ways to hell,
– to shit, anywhichway,
everywhichway
excl. 6. *how?:* how (in) the devil?,
– (in) the fuck?, – (in) the heck?,
– (in) the hell?, – the deuce? the
blazes? the shit? etc.
7. *what's happening?:* how about
it?, how's about it?, what do you
(whaddya) say?, what's the deal?,
what's up?, where do we go from
here?

233. Prearrangement
v. 1. *to prearrange:* fake (up), fix,
put in the bag, – on ice, ready up,
set up, sew up, tie-up, wrap up
2. *to reveal a plan:* spring (it)
3. *to succeed in a plan:* click
4. *to go wrong:* blow (it), duff (up),
gum things up, – up the works;
spec. go in the tank, take a dive (to
lose deliberately)
5. spec. back to the drawing board
(to replan after a failure)
adv. 6. *arranged:* bagged, boxed,
fixed, in the bag, in one's pocket, in
the tank, on ice, open-and-shut,
sewed up, sewn up, stacked up, tied
up, wrapped up; spec. accidentally
on purpose

UTILITY
234. Use
n. 1. *useful part:* business end
v. 2. *to use:* cash in (on), keep on tap, play (it) for all its worth
3. *to make useful:* doctor (up), rejig, rev, revamp
adv. 4. *available:* on tap, up for grabs

235. Uselessness
n. 1. *useless object, idea:* crock (of shit), dead duck, – rabbit, washout, write-off
2. *rubbish:* crap, drack (Aus.), junk, leavings, schlock, tripe; spec. honey (human extrement); round file (waste paper basket); airmail (rubbish tossed out the window)
3. *waste of time:* boondoggle, undertaker job
4. *to waste:* blow, fiddle-faddle away, fool away, footle (away), piddle away, piss away
5. *to waste time:* hack around, piss around
6. *to be worthless:* suck
adj. 7. *spare:* gash
adv. 8. *useless:* crook (Aus.), crude (US black), down the drain, duff, 4-F, gonzo, no account, on doog (backsl. = no good), sunk, washed up; spec. rumour (irrelevant)
9. *third-rate:* crappy, half-arsed, icky, junky, tacky
phr. 10. ain't worth wiping your ass on, don't amount to a fart in a whirlwind, don't amount to a pisspot full of crab-apples, (as useless as) a spare prick at a wedding, – tits on a bull, not worth a fart in a noisemaker, – a light, – a pisshole in the snow

---

ACTIVITY
236. Activity; Liveliness
n. 1. game (US black), goings-on, hustle, jump, lark, play (US black), -tripping, trot

2. *spirit, energy:* bang, bounce, flash, ginger, go, hotcha, hustle, kick, oof, oomph, pep, piss and vinegar, pizzazz, punch, snap, socko, steam, zap, zing, zip, zowie
3. *enthusiasm:* get-up-and-go, hustle, push, spunk, what it takes
v. 4. *to rush around:* bang around, buzz around (like a blue-arsed fly), – like a one-armed paper-hanger, come on (like gangbusters), shazzam
5. *to enliven:* crank (up), hop up, jazz up, pep up, punch up, put some pep, punch, etc. into (it), snap (it) up, stir the possum (Aus.), stoke the fires, zip (it) up
6. *to draw attention:* draw the heat
adv. 7. *lively:* chipper, chirpy, feeling one's oats, feisty, full of beans, – of go, – piss and vinegar, hopped up, on one's toes, offish, on the go, peppy, zappy, zingy, zippy
8. *ambitious, enthusiastic:* full of go, – of pep, – of what it takes, go-ahead, hard-charging, hungry, Johnny on the spot, not backward in coming forward, on the make, pushy, spunky

237. Preparation
n. 1. once-over
v. 2. *to prepare:* clear the decks, gear up, get set, pepper 'em up (US black), prep, ready (up)
3. *to train:* lick into shape, sharpen up, wise up
4. *to rear:* drag up
adv. 5. *prepared:* armed for bear, fired up, good and ready, hot to trot, loaded for bear, up to scratch
6. *unprepared:* half-cock(ed), not cut out for, not up to scratch

238. Undertaking
n. 1. (tall) order
2. *attempt:* crack, dab, fist, fling, go, hack, jab, lick, shot, shy, smack, stab, try-on, whack; spec. good shot

(best, if useless effort), darnedest,
Sunday punch (best effort)
v. 3. *to try:* balloon, give it a burl,
– it a fling, – it a fly (Aus.), – it a
go, – it a tumble, – it a whirl, go for
it, have a see who salutes, take a
pop (at), – a shot (at), etc., try it on
4. *to undertake:* bog in (Aus.), get
into, get one's arse in gear, go out
for, go to bat, motivate, put on the
front burner, take the plunge
5. *to try hard:* be in there pitching,
– slugging, break a blood-vessel,
– one's neck, buck for, bust a grape
(US black), – a gut, – one's arse,
– one's hump, – one's nuts, get
cracking, get down (US black), get
one's act together, – one's finger
out, – one's shit together, lean over
backwards, pull one's socks up, turn
on the heat
6. *to do one's best:* do one's level
best, – one's darnedest, give (it) all
one's got, go for broke, – the limit,
shit or bust
7. *to go to excess:* come it, – on
strong, run (it) into the ground

239. Performance; Accomplishment
n. 1. schtick, shtick, shtik (Yid.),
stunt
v. 2. *to do:* cut loose with, hit, pull,
talk talk and walk walk (US black);
spec. go ahead up (US black: to do
something together); do it like
Mommy (act domestically)
3. *to do roughly:* bang out, knock
out, toss off
4. *to do well:* blow fire (US black),
deliver, – the goods, fire on all
cylinders, do it up (right), do one's
stuff, do the works, – the whole bit,
go great guns, go the route, have
(it) knocked, hit for six, fire on all
cylinders
5. *to accomplish:* bring home the
bacon, come through (with), cut it,
cut the mustard, get away with, get
it together, get outside of, hack it,
lift one's game (US black), play past

(US black), pull a stroke, pull it off,
pull one's finger out, put (it) across,
– (it) over, put one's money where
one's mouth is, score, swing (it),
turn a trick
6. *to complete, finish:* be through
(with), call it a day, – it quits, drop
the curtain, hang up one's tools,
knock it on the head, pack (it) in,
polish (it) off, put (it) away, – (it) in
cold storage, – (it) on ice, – the lid
down, – the lid on it, top (it) off,
wash up, wind up
7. *to work out:* crack (it), lick (it)
8. *to entertain:* do a bit
phr. 9. *completion:* when all's said
and done

240. Production
v. 1. *to creat, concoct:* bodge (up),
– together, cook up, hammer out,
hash up, kludge, lash up, rustle up,
toss off, whip up
adv. 2. *spontaneous:* off the cuff,
– the top of one's head
phr. 3. damned clever these Chinese

241. Work; Employment
n. 1. fag, graft, grind, hang (US
black), nine-to-five, racket, slave
(US black), yakka (Aus.); spec. shit
detail, shitwork (unpleasant work)
2. *a job:* meal ticket, spot; spec.
chump job (US pimp: any 'straight'
work); undertaker job (a hopeless
job); foreigner (an illegal second
job)
3. *work shift:* swing (4pm–12
midnight), graveyard (midnight to
4am), lobster (early morning),
golden hours (overtime)
v. 4. *to work:* be in harness, graft,
punch the clock, sock the clock;
spec. go around the block (gain
work experience); moonlight (to
work two jobs, one at night); stooge
(to work as an assistant)
5. *to start work:* dig in, fire away,
get cracking, – going, – moving,
– off one's arse, – the lead out, – the

show on the road, hit it, hop to (it), jump to (it), knuckle down (to), lay into, let rip, light into, pile in, pitch in, plough into, rip into, sail into, snap (in)to, turn it up, up and at 'em, wade into

6. *to work hard, keenly:* bat (it) out, battle (Aus.), break one's arse, – one's neck, bust a grape (US black), bust one's arse, – one's hump, – one's nuts, fire, go at it hot and heavy, hammer ass, pour it on, root hog or die, shake a leg, sweat it out, work like a black (derog.), work like anything, – like billy-o, work one's arse off, – one's butt off, – one's tail off; spec. gut it (US college: to work all night); spec. nigger-driving (US black: white exploitation of black workers)

7. *to endure tedious work:* bang away, grind, hammer away, peg away, whack (it) out

8. *to end work:* call it a day, – it quits, clock off, down tools, hang (it) up, knock off, punch out; spec. chuck (it) up, go south, jack (it) in (leave a job)

9. *to defy union rules:* blackleg, fink, rat, scab, scissorbill

adj. 10. *busy:* at it, at bat, busy as a one-armed paper-hanger (with the itch), hard at it, on the ball, – the hop, – the jump, – the trot, snowed under, tied up, up to one's eyes, – one's ears, – one's elbows, – one's neck, etc.

phr. 11. *work hard or don't waste time:* fish, or cut bait, piss, or get off the pot, shit, or get off the pot

12. spec. no rest for the wicked; spec. why keep a dog and bark yourself (use the available labour force); illegitimis non carborundum ('Latin': don't let the bastards grind you down)

242. Hiring
n. 1. *employment bonuses:* golden handshake (payoff at dismissal or retirement), golden hello (financial inducement to a new recruit), golden parachute (a long-term contract that must be paid in full even if one is fired)

2. *dismissal:* boot, elbow, heave-ho, sack, tin-tack (rhy.sl. = sack)

v. 3. *to hire:* sign up

4. *to promote:* spec. kick upstairs (to promote into inactivity)

5. *to demote:* bump, bust, kick downstairs

6. *to fire:* can, give the bullet

7. *to be fired:* get one's cards, – the boot, – the slingers

adj. 8. retired: spec. bowler-hatted (retired from the Services)

excl. 9. *I want work!:* gissa job!

243. Fatigue
v. 1. *to collapse:* blow up, burn out, – down, crap out, curl up (and die), drag one's arse, keel over, peg out, peter out, poop out, rock out (US black), tucker out

2. *to work to excess:* have too much on one's plate

3. *to tire out, exhaust:* beat, blow one out, burn out, do in, do over, fag (out), run ragged, tucker out

adj. 4. *exhausted:* all in, – shot, at the end of one's rope, beat, blown out, burned out, – down, bushed, crapped out, creased, dead, dead to the wide, done in, – up, euchred (Aus.), fagged (out), fit, flaked out, flat (Aus.), fuckfaced, jiggered, kerried (rhy.sl. = Kerry Packered = knackered), knackered, muzzy, one's get-up-and-go got up and went, on one's last legs, out of it, out like a light, – on one's feet, played out, pooped, racked, rooted (Aus.), rusty, shagged out, shot, stoked out, stroked (out), sparkers, tuckered, washed up, zoned

INACTIVITY
244. Inactivity; Idleness
n. 1. *to idle, waste time:* arse

around, bum around, dog around, – it, duff around, fart about, – around, – off, fartarse around, fiddlefart around, footle about, freeload, fuck off, futz about, ghost (US milit.), goldbrick, goof off, half step (US black), horse around, jerk off, keep banker's hours, layin' and playin' (US black), let one's game slip (US black), lollygag, mess about, muck about, piddle about, – around, play ring a rosie, ponce around, razzle-dazzle (US black), screw around, scrimshank, shuck and jive, skive (off), sod about, swing the lead, veg out, work one's ticket; spec. punt (US campus: to abandon work)

2. *to remain:* hang about, – around, satellite, stay put, stick around

adj. 3. *inactive:* dead as a doornail, – as a dodo

adv. 4. *unemployed:* at liberty, in dock, on the beach, – the loose, pattin' leather, resting (esp. theatrical)

phr. 5. *you're idle:* don't strain yourself; you'll be a long time dead

245. Laziness
adj. 1. *lazy:* bone idle, born tired, doggy, drag-assed, niggerish (derog.), rum-dum

246. Rest
n. 1. lay-off, lay up; spec. five, ten (as in 'take five' or 'take ten' minutes break)

v. 2. *to rest:* ease it, hole up, lay back, – dead, – up, take five, take ten

3. *to lie or sit down:* flop, park one's carcass, – one's frame, plant oneself, take a pew

247. Sleep
n. 1. beddy-bye, Bo Peep (rhy.sl.), horizontal exercise, kip, rack monster, sack time, shuteye, winks; spec. rack attack (desire to sleep)

2. *nap:* forty winks, zizz

v. 3. *to go to bed:* bunk down, crash, doss down, fall out, flop, get one's head down, go beddy-bye, – bye-bye, – nighty-night, hit the hay, – the sack, hop in the hay, – in the sack, spark out, turn in

4. *to sleep:* bag (some) Zs, cop (some) Zs, crash (out), get some shuteye, kip, pound one's ear, rack, rack out, sack out, pile up some Zs, Z; spec. do skippers, skipper (sleep in derelict houses, etc.)

5. *to take a nap:* catch forty winks, cop a snooze, grab a little shuteye

6. *to get up:* hit the deck, rise and shine, show a leg

adj. 7. *asleep:* crapped out, flaked (out), on flake, sacked out, Z'd out; (see also Tired: 243)

excl. 8. *get up!:* hands off your cocks and on your socks!, let's be having you!, rise and shine!, shake a leg!, show a leg!

248. Delay; Postponement
n. 1. hang-up, stand-off

v. 2. *to delay* **vi**: hold the phone, put on the back burner, take a rain check, – the scenic route, wag (US black)

3. *to delay* **vt**: let (it) ride, put on hold, – on ice, stall

4. *to be impatient:* bite the carpet, chomp at the bit, foam at the mouth, froth at the mouth, sweat it out

excl. 5. *wait:* half a mo!, hang about!, hold everything!, – it, – the phone!, keep your hair on!

6. *stop it:* ock it

INTERFERENCE
249. Interference; Meddling
n. 1. back-seat driving, flak, horning in, kibitzing, nosing around

v. 2. *to interfere:* barge in, cut off at the pass, dip in one's business (US black), horn in, mess with, monkey with, muscle in, nose around, play one too close (US black), poke one's nose in, shove one's oar in, – one's nose in, stick one's bib in (Aus.), stick one's nose into, snoop 3. *intrude in a conversation:* breeze in, put in one's two cent's worth, – two pennorth, mouth in, -off **excl.** 4. *don't interfere!:* butt out!, fuck off!, go bark up another tree!, – blow you own nose!, – chase yourself!, – fish!, – fly a kite!, – fry an egg!, – bag your head!, – join the navy!, – jump in a lake!, – jump off a cliff!, – lay an egg!, – peddle your fish!, – roll your hoop!, – soak your head!, – stick your head in a bucket!, – take a running jump (at yourself)!, – take a walk!, keep stum(m)!, – your nose out!, m.y.o.b.!, pull in your neck!, sit on it and rotate!, slip it where the monkey slipped the nuts!, shove it where the rhino got the javelin!, shove it where Moby Dick got the old harpoon!, what's it to you?

250. Hindrance; Obstacle

v. 1. *to hinder, cause trouble:* ball up, cook one's goose, crab (one's act), cramp one's style, dish, fuck around, – over, gum up, – the works, knock the bottom out of, lumber, put the bag on, – the block on, – the freeze on, – the kibosh on, – the mockers on, – the mozz on (Aus.), – the screws to, queer the pitch, shanghai, throw a spanner in the works; spec. corpse (theatre use: to cause another actor to forget lines)
adv. 2. *hindered, in trouble:* (all) balled up, (all) gummed up, (all) screwed up, up against the wall

FACILITY

251. Facility; Ease

n. 1. blow off, breeze, (dead) cert, cinch, cushy number, doddle, duck shoot, – soup, easy game, – ride, – stuff, free ride, gravy train, gut, money for jam, – for old rope, picnic, piece of cake, – of piss, pushover, snap, snip, soft number, tit, tough stuff (US black), velvet; spec. featherbedding (giving 'jobs to the boys'); sitter (sporting use: an easy catch – cricket; an easy target – hunting)
v. 2. *to make easy:* grease the wheels
3. *to have an easy life:* have it soft, sit pretty
4. *to do easily:* do (it) on one's dick, – on one's head, – on one's prick, have a field day (with), piss it, waltz it
adv. 5. *easy:* as easy as ABC, – as cake and ice cream, – as falling off a log, – as kiss my arse, – as one-two-three, – as pie, – as shooting fish in a barrel, – as taking candy from a baby, – as taking money from a child, – as winking, cheesecake, cushy, easy-peasy, in the bag, pie, pimpsy, plain sailing, right up (down) one's alley, skate, sweet (as a nut), under the odds
6. *easily:* hands down, in a walk, on one's dick, – one's prick, like a house on fire, no sweat, right off the bat
7. *out of trouble:* off the hook

252. Difficulty; Trouble

n. 1. *problem:* bad news, bind, bother, facer, hang-up, hassle, headache, hot potato, hot seat, jam, kick in the pants, Queer Street, screamer, sharp end, skulldrag (US black), sweat, Tom Mix (rhy.sl. = a fix), TS, tough shit; spec. bear (hard college work)
2. *unpleasant situation:* can of worms, drag, (the) devil to pay, – hell to pay, holy mess, – muddle, jive hand (US black), (a) nice how-d'you-do, pain in the arse, pretty mess, – muddle, – pickle,

rainy days (US black), (a) right how-d'you-do, shit city, shithouse, (a right) two and eight (rhy.sl. = state), when the shit hits the fan, when the solids hit the air conditioning

3. *unfair treatment:* bumps, hard lines, iron cross (US black), jack job, more kicks than ha'pence, raw deal, rough end of the pineapple (Aus.), shaft, short end of the stick, static, tough tits, – titty

4. *something difficult:* bastard, bitch, bother, brute, bugger, pain (in the arse), SOB, sod, son of a bitch, tall order, tough nut to crack

v. 5. *to be in trouble:* (be) for it, – in for it, – in the shit, – in the soup, – in shtuck (Yid.), – up shit creek etc. (see: adj. 11 below), catch a cold, catch one's (big fat) tit in a wringer, get one's arse in a sling, go a million (Aus.), have one's cock caught in a zipper, hit some shit, scoff fishheads, scramble for the gills

6. *to cause trouble:* mix (it), put the mozz on (Aus.), shit on from a great height, signify (US black), stir (it up)

7. *to get into trouble:* get in a hole, – in the shit, – in shtuck, – one's arse in a sling; (be) in a pickle, – a holy mess, etc. (see n. 2 above); spec. it's your little hip pocket (US black = you're in bad trouble)

8. *to get into trouble:* dob in (Aus.), hit the shit

9. *to avoid, escape from trouble:* beat the rap, crawl out from under, hang tough, land on one's (own) two feet, play it cool, save one's bacon, slide out (of)

10. *to make trouble for:* crap around, do over, fuck around, – over, – with, have against the ropes, put (up) against the wall, – in shtuck, – on the spot, etc. (see 7 above), screw

adj. 11. *difficult:* bread and lard

(rhy.sl. = hard), no picnic, no laughs (laffs), shitty, sketch, tough

adv. 12. *in trouble:* between the devil and the deep blue sea, – the rock and the hard place, buggered, caught by the short and curlies, cruising for a bruising, done up (like a kipper), floored, fucked, in bother, – a bind, – a jam, – a pickle, – a spot, – a tight hole, – Dutch, – it (for fair), – it (for real), – Queer Street, – Shit Street, – shtuck, – the doghouse, – the shit, – the soup, on offer, on the chopping block, – one's beam end, – the ropes, – the spot, out on a limb, riding for a fall, screwed, shafted, sunk, stymied, under the cosh, – the gun, up against it, up a gum tree, up shit creek (without a paddle), up the creek, up to one's neck, up against the wall, well fucked and far from home

excl. 13. *what's the matter?:* what's eating you?, what's biting you?, what's got into you?, what's the bitch?, what's the beef?, what's up, Doc?, what's with you (him, her, etc.)?

253. Skill; Ability

n. 1. goods, gumption, naus, savvy, smarts, street smarts, what it takes; spec. mileage (experience)

2. *cunning:* curves, fast one, good one, nifty

v. 3. *to be able, skilful:* be all there, – on the ball, – up to snuff, – wised up, come up to snuff, cut it, cut the mustard, hack, have it knocked, – something on the ball, – what it takes, know all the answers, – how many beans make five, – one's arse from one's elbow, – one's onions, – one's stuff, – the ropes, – what time it is, – what's happening, know where it's at

4. *to do well:* be death on, be the berries (at), have a (good) head for,

have its number, – it knocked, piss it, stride (US black), waltz (it)

5. *to be suitable:* hit (it) on the head, – on the nose, – between the eyes, – the bull's eye, fill the bill

6. *to take care of, to deal with:* square, swing (it), TCB, take care of business; spec. hold the baby (to be left to deal with a problem)

adj. 7. *experienced, efficient:* bonified (US black), fly, hip, hot stuff, keen, keeno, no flies on (him, her, etc.), plugged in, sharp, slick, snappy, up to snuff, wicked

8. *suitable:* about one's speed, just one's speed, right up (down) one's alley, right up one's street, etc.

254. Unskilfulness; Awkwardness
n. 1. butterfingers, muffishness
v. 2. *to be unskilful, make a mess of:* arse about, – around, – up, bollix up, bollocks up, bitch up, bugger up, cack-hand, cock (it) up, cods up, foul up, fuck up, gum up, gum up the deal, – the play, – the works, etc., make a cods of, – a cobblers of, – a hash of, put one's foot in, screw up, stub one's toe

adj. 3. *incapable:* can't cut it, – cut the mustard, – hack it (see Facility 253) half-arsed, lame, no can do, not all there: playing with a full deck, etc. (see Unintelligence: 145ff), – up to snuff, out of one's (own) league, playing with the big boys (now)

4. *unsophisticated:* down-home, on fire, square, – to the wood

5. *inexperienced:* amateur hour, green (as grass), half-baked, uncool, unhip, wet behind the ears

6. *clumsy, gauche:* all thumbs, – fingers and thumbs, arsy-versy, gimpsy

phr. 7. *of incompetence:* couldn't run a piss-up in a brewery; couldn't organise a fuck in a brothel

SECURITY
255. Safety; Protection
n. 1. twirl (skeleton key)
2. *to protect:* mind
v. 3. *to protect oneself:* cover your ass, CYA, look after number one, save one's bacon
4. *to stand watch:* give jiggs, keep cave, keep decko, – KV, – jiggers, play chick, – chicken
adj. 5. *safe:* copasetic, in the clear
adv. 6. *secure:* dry land (US black = all clear), home and dry, on a good wicket

256. Danger
n. 1. bad news, – scene, heat, heavy scene, hassle; spec. trick bag (US black = unpleasant situation)
2. *warning:* high sign, tip-off, whisper, (the) word
v. 3. *to warn:* tip (off), put the word about, – out
4. *to endanger:* put in the middle, – on the spot; spec. put in the frame (to frame up)
adj. 5. *dangerous:* heavy, iffy, sus, uncool
excl. 6. *look out!:* heads up!, Hey Rube!, nonnus! (backsl. = someone!), kool toul (backsl. = look out) there'll be blue murder if, watch it!
7. *be careful:* don't do anything I wouldn't do, – take any wooden nickels

ATTAINMENT
257. Success
n. 1. fat city, gorilla, hole in one, killing, numero uno, result, score, smash, smasherino, smasheroo, smashola, sock, sockeroo, sockerino, socko, sockola, three-bagger
v. 2. *to succeed:* ace, beat the game, box clever, break the bank, bring down the house, bring home the bacon, click, come through,

connect, cop a packet, – the lot, crack it, cream, cut the mustard, do (it) up right, get across, get a guernsey (Aus.), get a result, get clear, get it together, get it to the T, get over (US black), get places, go over (big), go over like a house on fire, – like a ton of bricks, go great guns, go to town, hack it, have it dicked, – it taped, – it knocked, hit it (off), knock dead, – cold, KO, make a go (of), make a killing, make (it), – it big, – the grade, make out, mop up, play one's cards right, put it all together, register, score, – big, – heavy, sew up, strike it rich, – paydirt, – oil, take the biscuit, – the cake, turn up trumps, whup the game (US black)

3. *to do successfully:* clean up on, come through, cut it, – the mustard, deliver (the goods), fill the bill, get away (with it), get down, go to town with, hack it, knock for a loop, make a go of, – it stick, – the grade, put (it) across, – (it) over, – over big, wrap (it) up, have it big, wrap (it) up

4. *to be successful:* be there, – the guvnor, – the boss, – number one, get to the top of the heap, – the top of the tree, have it big, wrap (it) up, have it dicked, set the world on fire

adv. 5. *successful:* ahead of the game, doing a hundred (US black), going full blast, – great, great guns, – over big, on the make, – the up and up, on top of the heap, – of the tree, on – velvet, quids in

258. Failure

n. 1. bad job, blow-out, blow-up, brodie, bum deal, – trip, bummer, bust, crackup, crapout, crash, croak, cropper, dive, dud, fadeout, fall, fizzle, flash in the pan, flat tyre, flop, floperoo, flopola, flunk, fold, fold-up, frost, fuck-up, goner, lemon, let-down, mess, miss, muff, no dice, – go, – soap, – sale,

nose-dive, not a bite, – a hope, – a nibble, poop, raw deal, smash, turkey, washout, wipe-out

v. 2. *to fail:* be all up (with), – all washed up, bite the dust, bomb, – off, – out, cave in, cock off, come to grief, come undone, – unstuck, – a cropper, conk out, crap out, crash (out), die, – on the vine, draw a blank, fall down on the job, fall flat, fizzle out, flop, flunk (out), fold (up), fuck up, go all to shit, – all to hell, – all to smash, – all to fuck, – all to buggery, – bluey, – bung, – flooey, – down in flames, – down the pan, – the plug (hole), – down for the third time, – down like a lead balloon, – the drain, – down the tubes, – hang, – phut, – sour, go to pieces, – to the dogs, – to the pack (Aus.), – under, – up the spout, have two left shoes (US black), lay an egg, lose out, lose the ball, miss the boat, – the bus, not cut it, – hack it, etc. (see Success: 257), not get past first base, not hit a lick (US black), peg out, poop out, pull a brodie, score an own goal, shovel shit against the tide, strike out, stub one's toe, suck wind, take a bath, – a fall, – a header, – a nose-dive, – it on the button, – it on the chin, take the count, tube, wipe out; spec. go in the tank, – in the water, take a dive (to fail deliberately)

adv. 3. *failing:* at the end of one's rope, – one's tether, on one's last legs, on the fritz, – kibosh, – skids, riding for a fall

4. *failed:* at the bottom of the heap, blooey, buggered, cold, cooked, cracked, done for, done up, down the pan, – the plug, fizzled out, gone phut, – under, – to hell, – to the dogs, – down the drain, etc., on the rocks, thrown for a loss, upgefucked, up shit creek, up the spout, washed up, wiped out

phr. 5. *resignation:* can't win them all

259. Advantage
n. 1. ace in the hole, – up one's sleeve, beat, card up one's sleeve, drop, edge, hook, inside track, long suit, pull, scoop, set-up, something on one
v. 2. *to have an advantage:* be in on the ground floor, – on the inside, have an ace up one's sleeve, – the inside track, hold all the cards
3. *to put at a disadvantage:* catch bending, come (it) over, do like a dinner, – to a turn (Aus.), fade, have by the short and curlies, – by the short hair, – by the balls, – the edge over, – the drop on, – the jump on, – it over, – cold, – dead to right, – bang to rights, – on toast, – on the run, – one over a barrel, – the drop on
4. *take advantage of:* come something over, give the double-shuffle, put something across, – something past (one), put something over (on), sting, work
adv. 5. *at a disadvantage:* naked

Emotion

FEELINGS
260. Emotion
n. 1. attitude, groove, soul; spec. tude, vibes (one's emotional 'style')
2. *spec. black sensibility:* ebony (US), soul
v. 3. *to undergo emotions:* feel funny, go through changes

261. Sentimentality
n. 1. flapdoodle, goo, gush, hearts and flowers, milk and water, schmaltz (Yid.), slop, slush, sob stuff, sweetness and light, tear-jerking
2. *sentimental talk:* dribble, drool, goo, gush, slobber
v. 3. *to become sentimental:* dribble, drool, gush (over), moon over, slobber
4. *to become mawkish:* give a sob story, go ga-ga, moon about, turn on the water-works
adj. 5. *sentimental:* ga-ga, icky, moony, mushy, sappy, schmaltzy, soppy

EXCITABILITY
262. Excitement
n. 1. fireworks, flap, heat, hoopla, kerfuffle, lather, panic stations, shemozzle, stew, stink, streak, sweat, tizzy, to-do, two and eight (rhy.sl. = state), wind-up
2. *a stimulant:* bang, shot in the arm, turn-on
v. 3. *to be excited:* come in one's pants, cream one's jeans, get a bee in one's bonnet, – one's bowels in an uproar, – one's knickers in a twist, – one's shit hot, – steamed up, go hog-wild, hit the ceiling, – the roof, make a Federal case (out of), run around like a chicken with its head off, wail, work up a circulation, – up a lather, zeek out; spec. let it all hang out (to abandon inhibitions)
4. *to live excitingly:* pace (US black)
5. *to shock:* blow one out, – one's mind, freak one out
adj. 6. *exciting:* hairy, hairy-assed, smoking (US black)
7. *excited:* (all) fired up, (all) hot and bothered, all of a doodah, – of a tiswas, – of a tizzy, hepped up, het up, hopped up, in a lather, – a sweat, – a tizzy, – a twitter, on the hop, psyched (to death), rattled, (all) steamed up, up in the air
excl. 8. tonight's the night! (excited expectation)

263. Nervousness
n. 1. ants in (one's) pants, collywobbles, creeps, edge, heeby-jeebies, jimmies, Jimmy Britts (Aus. rhy.sl. = the shits), jitters, jumps, needle, screaming abdabs, shakes, shim-sham, West Hams (rhy.sl. = West Ham reserves = nerves), willies, wim-wams, yikes; spec. flopsweat (stage-fright); yips (golfer's nerves)
v. 2. *to be nervous:* climb the walls, get the jitters, – shakes, – willies etc., get the wind up, have the breeze up, shizzout
3. *to make a fuss:* do a number, throw a moody, – a wobbler
adj. 4. *nervous:* antsy, busting, edgy, froggy (US black), hyper, jittery, screaming blue murder,

spare, under house, under the cosh,
– the gun, windy
5. *unnerved:* climbing the walls,
cracked up, frazzled, in a frazzle, on
the edge, shattered, shot (to hell, to
pieces), up in the air, uptight
6. *intense:* heavy

264. Impatience
n. 1. lather, stew, sweat
v. 2. *to be impatient:* (to be)
champing at the bit, – hot to trot,
hurt to, in a lather, – sweat, raring
to go, etc. (see adv.)
adv. 3. busting, champing at the bit,
hot to trot, hurting, in a lather, – a
stew, – a sweat, on tiptoe, raring to
go

INEXCITABILITY
265. Calmness
n. 1. cool
2. *emotional freedom:* slack, space
v. 3. *to remain calm:* bite the bullet,
chill out, cool down, – it, hang
loose, keep a tight asshole, – one's
cool, – one's hair on, – the cork on,
lay tight (US black), not turn a hair,
stay cool, taken one's best hold (US
black), track
4. *calm down:* cool, – down, – it,
– off, – the rock, get one's head
together, go off the boil, lighten up,
mellow (out), pull in one's horns,
simmer down
5. *to calm one down:* cool (off), get
someone's head together, mellow
out, tune off
adj. 6. *calm:* laid back, mellow, off
the boil, on a tight leash, Swiss
excl. 7. *calm down!:* cool it!, don't
get your bowels in an uproar!, – get
your knickers in a twist!, – get your
shit hot!, – make a Federal case (of
it)!, keep your hair on!, – your shirt
on!, lighten up!, no muss no fuss!,
pull in your horns! quit racing your
motor!, simmer down!, steady the
buffs!

266. Patience
v. 1. *to be patient:* cool it, hold one's
horses, – one's water, – it down
2. *to endure, tolerate:* go (for), hang
in (there), keep a stiff upper lip,
– one's pecker up, like (it) or lump
(it), not let it get to one, – get one
down, stand still for, stay the pace,
stick with it, take, – it, – it on the
chin, – the nose, etc., tough it out
3. *not tolerate:* take no guff, – no
shit
excl. 4. *be patient:* hang on!, hold
your horses!, hold your water!,
don't shoot the pianist he's doing his
best!

INTEREST
267. Interest
n. 1. hots
v. 2. *to be interested:* fall for, flop
for, go for, give a tumble, – the time
of day, have big eyes for, make a
dead set for, rush, tumble for
3. *to interest.* grab, tick (one)
off
adv. 4. *interested:* all for, hot for,
into, strong on, struck on

268. Desire
n. 1. itch, yen
v. 2. *to want:* choose, do with, go
for, have a yen for, hurt for, spoil
for, want the worst way
3. *to be selfish:* look after number
one, pig it
adj. 4. *desirous:* bursting (for),
crazy (for, to), hopped up, hot
(for), hung for, hurting (for), itchy,
nuts about, nutty, raring (to),
screaming (for), sold on, spoiling
for, steaming, wild (for, to)
5. *greedy:* grabby, piggy
phr. 6. what's in it for me?

269. Ambition
n. 1. get-up-and-go, pizzazz,
stick-to-it-iveness, what it takes (see
Initiative: 236)

v. 2. *to be ambitious:* to have what it takes
adj. 3. *ambitious:* (see Enterprising: 236)

270. Enthusiasm
n. 1. full scream (US black), go, hotcha, oomph, pep, zap, zing, zip, zowie
2. *craze, fad:* bee in the bonnet, bug, -itis, -mania
v. 3. *to be enthusiastic:* be bugs about, carry on (about), crack on (about), flip for, get it up (for), get stuck into, give a shit, go for, – nap on, – on about, – overboard, – to town (on), max out
adj. 4. *enthusiastic:* cooking, full of beans, gung-ho, hung up, jumping, overboard, skied
adv. 5. *enthusiastic about:* as a (Aus.), as a bean (Aus.), bats about, batty about, crazy for, daffy about, gone on, het up over, hot for, – on, hung up on, (all) in a lather about, – a sweat about, etc. (see Excitement: 262), like a good 'un, like crazy, nuts about, rapt (Aus.), shook on (Aus.), stuck on, tiger (for) (Aus.), up in the air over, wild about, worked up (about), wrapped (Aus.)
6. *fanatically:* bugs about, nuts about

DISINTEREST
271. Indifference
n. 1. what-the-hell
v. 2. *to be indifferent:* go off the boil, not give a damn, – a darn, – flying fuck, – a shit, – a tuppenny fuck, – a good goddam, – a hoot, – a monkey's, – give a rap (for), – a stuff, – a tinker's cuss
3. *to act indifferently:* play it cool, sit on the fence
4. *to make no difference:* cut no ice
adj. 5. *indifferent:* deadpan, on the fence, sniffy, stoneface

6. *nonchalant:* flip
excl. 7. *I don't care:* big deal, break my heart, FIGMO (fuck it, got my orders), fuck you Jack I'm all right, I should care, – worry, it's not my funeral, no skin off my arse, – off my nose, see if I care, so what? that's your bad luck, – funeral, – problem, tough tits, what's the percentage?, who gives a damn?, – a fuck?, etc. (see v. 2), what do I do now, cry? beats me, don't ask me, I don't know, – dunno, – wouldn't know, no biggie, three tears and a bucket (US black), your guess is as good as mine, you reckon

272. Dullness; Tedium
n. 1. drag, full tour, snooze job, three-hour tour
2. *something tedious:* corn, fag, history, old hat, – stuff, pain (in the arse), yawn
v. 3. *to bore:* bore stiff, – to tears, – the pants off, have a stick up one's arse
4. *to be bored:* cool off, get jack of (Aus.), (see Disinterest: 271)
adj. 5. *boring:* dead as a doornail, – as a dodo, – from the neck up, – on the vine, dopey, drag-ass, gutty, ho-hum, tired
adv. 6. *bored:* bored stiff, – to tears, drug, fed up with, to have a bellyful of, – skinful, – snootful, jack of (Aus.), sick and tired (of), up to here
excl. 7. *I'm bored:* here we go again, ho-hum, that finishes me, what a life, – a pain

PLEASURE
273. Pleasure; Delight
n. 1. bang, buzz, charge, kick, knockout, thrill, turn-on, wallop
2. *pleasant situation:* bee's knees, hot stuff, humdinger, lollapaloosa; spec. sight for sore eyes (a welcome appearance)

v. 3. *to please:* be up one's alley, click with, go down, go over (good), hit the (right) spot, make a hit, score, turn on, turns one's crank
4. *to thrill:* bowl over, give a bang, – buzz, charge, etc. (see n. 1), go over strong, – in a big way, – like a house on fire, – like a million dollars, hit for six, knock dead, – out, – the pants off, lay one out, mow one down, send out of this world, slaughter, slay, throw, tickle (pink), tickle to death, wow
adj. 5. *pleased:* all over oneself, fit to bust, happy as a dog with two tails, – as Larry, – as a sandboy, (see also 274), over the moon, pleased as the devil, – as heck, – as hell, – as punch, stoked, tickled, – pink, – to death, – to pieces
adv. 6. *pleasant:* ace, bully, cute, daisy, darling, divine, ducky, fantabulous, fucking-A, hotsy, jammy, keen, peachy-keen, the tops, too-too, TF much
excl. 7. *I feel happy:* ain't love grand, – that something, – we got fun, and how, baby, boy, boy-oh-boy, (oh) brother, cowabunga!, daddy, diggety damn, – dog, fucking-A, hey, hotcha, hot-cha-cha, hot damn, – diggety, – diggety dog, – shit, love it to death, man, man oh man, oh mama

274. Happiness; Cheerfulness
n. 1. hoopla, hoot, whoopee
2. *a laugh:* boff, gag, yok, yuk
3. *smile:* spec. shit-eating grin (smug smile)
v. 4. *to laugh:* be in stitches, break up, burst, crack one's face, – up, crease up, fall about, – out, goof on, haw-haw, hee-hee, hoot, laff, piss oneself, roll in the aisles
5. *to make laugh:* bowl over, break up, bring the house down, convulse, get a laugh, hand a laugh, kill, knock them in the aisles, paralyze, put away, put in stitches,

slaughter, slay, tickle the funny bone
6. *to become happy:* brace up, buck up, chirp up, come out of it, drop it, pep up, pull oneself together, snap out of it
7. *to cheer one up:* brace up, buck up, pep up, perk up, pull together
8. *to be happy:* be full of beans, – full of pep, – Mr Laffs, pop
adj. 9. *happy:* bobbish, breezy, chipper, chuffed, grooved, happy as a pig in shit, – as a king, – as Larry, – as you-know-what, high wide and handsome, in the pink, lunchy, nice (US black), one hundred per cent, over the moon, perky, rorty, wrapped tight; spec. slap-happy (slightly eccentric); spec. paralytic, spastic (convulsed with laughter)
10. *merry:* feeling one's oats, feisty, full of beans, larky, on the razzle

275. Contentment; Satisfaction
n. 1. *comfort:* easy street, velvet
v. 2. *satisfy:* cut the mustard, fill the bill, go down one's alley, hold (one's), keep (one's) cool, – sweet, play one's tune, sing one's song, talk one's language, walk on one's side of the street
3. *to be satisfied:* have no beef, – no kick, – no squawk
adj. 4. *satisfactory:* ace(s), all reet, AOK, bang on, can't complain, hunky-dory, (right) in there, jake, jerry, kosher, OK, OK by me, – for my dough, okey-doke(y), okay, a (little) bit of all right, no kick, no squawk, no sweat, on the ball, – the beam, – the button, slap-up, solid, up to snuff
5. *comfortable:* cushy, soft
6. *contented:* all the way live, joint-joint (US black)
phr. 7. *that's satisfactory:* AOK, everything's cool, – hotsy-totsy, – jake, – OK, etc. (see adj. 4), righto, roger, that's affirmative, – a big ten-four, we have lift-off

276. Enjoyment; Fun

n. 1. barrels of fun, barrels of laffs, juice, loads of fun, – of laffs, (a) laugh a line, more fun than a barrel of monkeys

2. *a good time:* (see also Party: 361) action, ball, goof bender, high old time, hot time, shit stopper; spec. the life of Riley (an easy, enjoyable life)

3. *a celebration:* (see also Spree: 98) bat, beano, bender, binge, blast, blow-out, Bushey Park (rhy.sl. = lark), bust, cutup, hi-de-hi, let-go, shindig, shindy, tear, toot, whoopee

v. 4. *to enjoy:* dig, eat up, gas, get down with (US black), – one's thing off (US black), – a bang out of, – a kick out of, etc. (see Thrill: 273), get off on, groove (on), – behind, have a high old time, – a hot time, live it up, – the life of Riley, love it to death, party, rally, swing with, tear up (US black), wig out

5. *to have a good time, celebrate:* bat around, boogaloo, boogie, break loose, cut loose, get one's rocks off, – one's jollies, go bananas, go on a bust, – a shindy, – the razzle, hell around, high-step (it), hit the high spots, jive and juke (US black), kick ass, – up one's heels, let her rip, – one's hair down, make whoopee, paint the town red, raise a hullaballoo, – a racket, – a ruckus, – Cain, – (merry) hell, – sand (US black), skylark, step high wide and handsome, swing, whoop it up

6. *to play the fool:* act up, carry on, clown around, cut up, horse around, kick up one's heels, loon about, play funny buggers, play silly buggers; spec. score yoks (to get laughs); mug (make funny faces)

adj. 7. *playful:* feeling one's oats, feisty, full of beans, etc. (see Animation, Lively: 236)

8. *enjoyable:* hot

adv. 9. *for fun:* for kicks, – laughs, – the hell of it, – trips

phr. 10. *it's been fun:* it's been a slice

277. Wit and Humour

n. 1. *joke:* boff, boffola, crack, fast one, gag, good one, hoot, laff, laff riot, nifty, scream, shit stopper, shriek, yell, yok, yuks; spec. horse laugh (a bad joke); pisser (a very funny joke)

v. 2. *to amuse:* cop the laughs (laffs), crack (one) up, crease (one) up, tickle one's funny bone

3. *to tease:* hack around, josh

4. *to tell jokes:* crack (wise), gag, pull a fast one, – a nifty, etc. (see n. 1)

5. *to play practical jokes:* come it over, horse around with, put over a fast one (on), send for a left-handed monkey wrench, whip the cat

6. *to pull funny faces:* mug

adj. 7. *funny:* killing, rich, ripe wacky

phr. 8. *that's funny:* that's a good one, that's a laugh; spec. funny peculiar or funny ha-ha? (do you mean humorous or not?)

DISPLEASURE

278. Displeasure; Disagreeableness

n. 1. *something unpleasant:* barf city, damper, downer, Motel Hell, nowhere, – city, outers, pain (in the arse), – in the neck, piece of crap, – of shit, pit city, pits, puke, stinker, stinkeroo, tack city

2. *unpleasant time:* dog's life, thin time, tough tittie

v. 3. *to act unpleasantly:* play the heel

4. *to displease:* be hard to take, curdle one's guts, get in one's hair, – up one's arse, – up one's nose, give one a headache, – a pain, – a pain in the arse, – in the neck, stick on one's craw, turn one's stomach, – one's tum

adj. 5. *unpleasant:* bit thick, creepy,

crumby, crummy, deadly,
gut-wrenching, heavy-duty, icky,
icky-poo, jive-ass, low-life,
low-rent, no-hope, on the nose
(Aus.), outers, out of order, putrid,
ratshit, ratty, stinking, stinko,
tacky, ucky, vomitous
adv. 6. *displeased with:* had it
(with), out with, pissed off (with),
up to there with
excl. 7. *of displeasure:* bugger off!,
can you stand for that!, don't give
me that!, drop dead!, fiddlesticks!,
fooey!, fuck off! (out of it), fuck
that for a bowl of cherries!, – for a
lark!, how do you like them
apples?, how does that grab you?, it
shouldn't happen to a dog, nuts!, of
all the . . . !, on your bike!, piss off!,
pull the other one it's got bells on
it!, shit!, shoot!, shucks!, sod off!,
that's just too bad!, the hell with it,
tough shit!, ts, up your arse!, – your
brown!, what's the big idea?, who're
you screwing!, you and who's army,
you would!

279. Sullenness; Depression
v. 1. long face, misery-guts,
sourpuss
2. *depression, misery:* black dog,
blues, dumps, Edgar Britts (Aus.),
glooms, grumps, hump, jimjams,
jimmies, Jimmy Britts (Aus.),
mulligrubs, pits, the pip, red arse
v. 3. *to be sullen, depressed:*
bellyache, come the old moody,
drag one's tail, feel like death
warmed up, gripe, grizzle, grump,
gutache, shit and wish (US black
– 'shit in one hand, wish in another,
see which fills up first'), throw a
moody, wear the dog (US black)
4. *to feel miserable:* be down in the
dumps, – among the wines and
spirits, – in a bad shape, – in the
cellar, feel blue, – ratshit, – sick, get
the hump, get up on the wrong side
of the bed, have (a fit of) the blues,
– the glooms, – the jimmies, etc.

(see n. 1), have one's heart in one's
boots
5. *to depress:* bring down
adj. 6. *sullen:* grouchy, grumpy,
long-faced, mopey, root-faced,
sourpussed, strung out, tight-assed
7. *depressed:* black, blue, brought
down, bummed out, cheesed off,
choked, down, down in the mouth,
drug, fit to bust, hurting, in the
dumps, lower than a snake's belly,
off one's feed, shafted, shot down,
sick as a parrot, torn down (US
black), with one's tail between one's
legs; spec. solitary as a bastard on
Father's Day (Aus. use: lonely)
8. *depressing:* depresso, pit city

280. Temper; Anger
n. 1. bate, peeve, red ass, red pants;
spec. slow burn (gradually rising
temper)
2. *explosion of rage:* blow-up,
carry-on, conniption fit, fireworks,
flare-up, lather, stew, sweat, tizzy
3. *to lose one's temper:* boil over,
blow a fuse, – a gasket, – off steam,
– one's cool, – one's cookies,
– one's cork, – one's gasket, – one's
stack, – one's top, blow it, blow off,
blow up, bust a blood vessel, – a
gut, climb the rigging, – the walls,
create, do one's block, – one's nut,
– the lolly (Aus.), flip, – one's lid,
– one's wig, – out, fly off the
handle, foam at the mouth, get a
hair up one's arse, – hot under the
collar, – mad, – sore, etc. (see adv.
6), – one's dander up, – one's
knickers in a twist, – one's shit hot,
– one's bowels in an uproar, etc.
(see Excitement: 262), – one's back
up, – one's nose out of joint, – the
ass, – the red ass, – the mohawk,
get up on one's hind legs, go ape,
– apeshit, – bananas, – haywire,
– off one's chump, – off one's nut,
– off the deep end, – spare, – up in
the air, – up the wall, grow horns,
have a bellyful (of), – it up to here,

– kittens, – the (dead) needle, – the rag on, hit the roof, kick up a racket, jump down one's throat, jump salty, jump the rails, lose one's cool, – one's hair, – one's marbles, – one's rag, make a (great) to-do, – carry-on, make the fur fly, – the sparks fly, nut up, poke one's mouth off (US black), pop off, – one's cork, raise a ruckus, – (merry) hell, – Cain, – the roof, reach boiling point, run around like a chicken with its head off, see red, simmer, sizzle, smoke, steam (up), throw a fit, – a wingding, trip out, work up (a head of) steam, zeek out, zoon out

4. *to make angry:* burn, get a rise out of, get one's dander up, – one's back up, – one's nose out of joint, – one's mad up, – one going, needle, piss off, rub up the wrong way, ruffle one's feathers, team up

5. *ill-tempered:* crusty, feisty, gritchy, grouchy, in a snit, mean, niggly, ornery, out of sorts, peevish, salty, snappy, sour

adv. 6. *angry:* apeshit, burned (at), fighting mad, (all) fired up, fit to be tied, gutted, hacked, het up, hopping (mad), hot, (all) hot and bothered, in a lather, – a pet, – a peeve, – sweat, jacked (Aus.), leery, loaded for bear, mad, – as a cut snake (Aus.), – as a wet hen, miffed, on one's hind legs, on the muscle, peeved, pissed off, POed, pushed out of shape, raving (mad), sore, steamed (up), uptight, wild

281. Grief
n. 1. hurting dance, pit city, sob stuff
2. *crying:* jag, weeps
v. 3. *to cry:* blub, boohoo, pipe one's eye, squawk, turn on the waterworks

282. Disappointment
n. 1. bring-down, choker, dud, false alarm, frost, lemon, let-down, misfire, no dice, – joy, – soap, sickener

v. 2. *to disappoint:* bring down, burn, dish, fall down on, let down, puncture one's balloon, piss on one's parade, stand up, sting; spec. let down easy (to soften the blow)
3. *to be disappointed:* draw a blank, get left, land with a (dull) thud, lose out, miss the boat, take it on the chin

adj. 4. *disappointed:* burnt, dished, let down, screwed, stood up, stung, taken for a ride

phr. 5. *disappointed:* all dressed up and nowhere to go, looks like he/she lost a pound and found sixpence

283. Anxiety; Worry
n. 1. butterflies (in one's stomach), freak-out, joes (Aus.); spec. all points bulletin (plea for help)

v. 2. *to be worried:* be in a lather, – a stew, – a sweat, drop one's bundle (Aus.), fall apart, freak, give a shit, have a bee in one's bonnet, have kittens, – one's heart in one's boots, piss blood, sweat; spec. feel a draught (US black: to sense racism)
3. *to reveal one's worries:* get it off one's chest, – out of one's system, let down one's hair, spill the beans, take the load off one's mind, unload
4. *to worry:* discombobulate, give one the creeps, mess one's mind, throw one for a loop
5. *to worry about:* have a hard-on for

adj. 6. *worried:* (all) hot and bothered, at the end of one's tether, bitched, buggered and bewildered, blue around the gills, charlie, down, fucked up and far from home, hot pants, in a mucksweat, – a sweat, – stew, – the pits, jacked up, jumpy, sick, uptight, wired

adv. 7. *worrying:* eating (someone), heavy

phr. 8. I can't handle this

284. Annoyance; Vexation

n. 1. bitch, burn, needle, pain, pain in the arse, – the neck, (the) pip; spec. slow burn (increasing rage); aggravation (UK: mutual grievances between police/criminals)

v. 2. *to annoy, vex:* be on one's arse, bitch off, bite, brass off, brown off, bug, burn, burn up, cheese off, drive one nuts, – around the bend, – through the roof, – up the wall, get across, – in one's hair, – one's back up, – on one's wick, – on one's goat, – on one's tits, – one going, – under one's skin, – up one's nose, give one a pain (in the neck, arse), give the needle, – the pip, grief, jerk around, – one's chain, make ignorant, miff, nark, needle, peeve, piss off, put one's back up, – one's nose out of joint, rub (up) the wrong way

3. *to be annoyed:* get the hump, – the needle (with), have a mad on with, – ants in one's pants, – a flea in one's ear, – something biting one, – something eating one, jump salty, steam

4. *to be offended:* get on one's high horse

adj. 5. *irritated:* brassed off, browned off, cheesed off, fed up, had it (with), jacked out, miffed, narked, nettled, on the rag, peeved, pissed (off), ratty, salty, stroppy, teed off, twisted, up a tree; spec. OT&E ('over-tired and emotional' – of an irritable child)

6. *sensitive:* tetchy

7. *perfectionist:* finicky

excl. 8. *of annoyance:* buggeration!, come off it!, don't get funny!, – get smart!, don't mind me I only live/work here!, forget it!

APPROBATION
285. Approval

n. 1. the all-clear, the go-ahead,

the nod, the OK, nod and a wink, thumbs-up

2. *recommendation:* blurb, boost, build-up, plug, write-up

v. 3. *approve:* be (all) for, – behind, give the all-clear, – go ahead etc. (see n. 1), have a soft spot for, OK

4. *to recommend:* front for, go to bat for, – to the mat for, go for, – overboard for, put in a (good) word for, stand up for

excl. 5. *of approval:* all the way!, attaboy!, attagirl!, beaut! (Aus.), (God) bless you!, bully (for you)!, dandy!, death!, fair dos! (Aus.), fair enough!, fairy snuff!, for sure!, fucking-A!, good on you! (Aus.), great!, hubba! hubba!, I should be so lucky!, is that good or is that good!, keen, keeno, nice one Cyril!, no sweat!, not half!, not to be sniffed at!, – to be sneezed at!, now you're cooking!, – you're talking!, solid!, swell!, tasty!, that's it!, that's the stuff (to give the troops)!, – telling them!, – the way!, too Irish stew! (rhy.sl. = too true), too right!, what a boy!, – a man!, – a star!, wicked!, you're a pal!, – a peach!, – a prince!, you're darn tootin'!, – singing my song!, you tell them!, you wrote the book!

286. Praise

n. 1. boost, plug, puff, push, rap (Aus.), rave; spec. log-rolling (mutual praise)

v. 2. *to support, enthuse:* beat the drum for, bang the drum for, boost, come on strong (for), crack on, go on about, hype, lay it on (heavy/thick), pile it on (heavy/thick), puff, push, root (for), sell (up), talk (it) up

phr. 3. *spec. praise of a passing woman:* I could do that a favour, whap that thing! (US black), whacko the diddle-a (Aus.)

287. Flattery
n. 1. applesauce, banana oil, blarney, build-up, bull, eyewash, flannel, grease job, guyver (Aus.), hokum, oil, soft soap; SEG (abbr. shit-eating grin)
v. 2. *to flatter:* blarney, bull, bullshit, butter up, con (along), dish out the applesauce, – the oil, – a line, feed a line, grease, hand a line (of bull), jolly (along), kid (along), kiss the blarney stone, lay it on (thick), – with a trowel, pat on the back, plaster, pour it on (heavy/thick), shmeer (Ger. = grease), shoot the bull, – the shit, – a line, soft soap, spread it on (thick)
3. *to toady:* arse-lick, back-slap, bootlick, brown-nose, creep, get in (solid) with, – next to, kiss-arse, make up to, pal up to, play up to, polish the apple, roll over for, schmooze (Yid.), stooge for, suck around, suck-arse, suck hind tit, suck up to, wax up, wipe one's arse, – one's nose, yes, yessir

---

DISAPPROBATION
288. Disapproval
n. 1. frost, nix, the no, thumbs-down
2. *disapproving look:* dirty look, old-fashioned look
v. 3. *to disapprove:* be down on, corrode, give the no, – the thumbs-down, nix, not go for, put the thumbs down, turn up one's nose at
adv. 4. *disapproving:* down on, on the coat (Aus.)
phr. 5. *of disapproval:* all yours!, bobkhes! (Yid. anything absurd or insulting), count me out!, no way!, perish the thought!, that's so ill!, you've got to be joking!, yuck!
6. *spec. disapproval of passing girl(s):* don't fancy yours, I wouldn't touch it with a (ten-foot)

barge-pole, I wouldn't touch it with yours

289. Objection; Complaint
n. 1. beef, bellyache, bitch, crab, kick, kvetch (Yid.), moody, squawk, yip
v. 2. *to complain:* ballsache, bellyache, beef, beat the gums, bitch, bleat, blow great guns, buck (against), crab (about), go on (about), gritch, grizzle, howl, kick (about), kick up a fuss, – a racket, kvetch, made a Federal case (out) of, – a great how-do-you-do (out of), pitch a bitch, pull one's joint, raise Cain, – a racket, rattle one's beads (gay use), sound off (about/over), squawk, yell blue murder
adv. 3. *complaining:* crooked on (Aus.), on at, po-faced, snippy

290. Censure; Criticism
n. 1. knock, putdown, roasting, slam, slash; spec. hatchet job (journalism); sledging (cricket: on-field barracking)
v. 2. *to criticise:* come down on, come down fonky (US black), come down hard, come down heavy, crab, cut up, go for, go to town on, hack up, hammer, haul over the coals, knock, pull to pieces, put down, roast, rub (US black), savage, slam, slash (up), slice up, take a swipe at, – to pieces; spec. give the duke (to slow handclap)
phr. 3. some people!

291. Scolding
n. 1. bawling out, bit of one's mind, bollocking, calling down, cussing out, dressing down, earful, flea in one's ear, going over, jaw, kick in/up the arse, piece of one's mind, roasting, rocket, rucking, scorcher, serve (Aus.), shakeup, stick, talking-to, toco, what-for, wigging
v. 2. *to scold:* bawl out, – the

(living) hell out of, bear down (on), blow the daylights out of, – sky-high, bollick, bring one up (US black), carpet, chew one's balls off, chew out, climb all over, come down on, cuss out, cut down to size, dress down, drop on, eat one's arse off, get down dirty, – fonky (US black), give (one) a piece of one's mind, – a (good) talking to, etc. (see n.1.), – one some curry (Aus.), – one some stick, give it hot and heavy, – one the business, – it the works, go after (right and left), go for, go to town on, haul over the coals, jump all over, – up and down on, – on with both feet, lay down the law, lay into, let (one) have it, light into, lower the boom on, make it hot for, pin one's ears back, pull one's coat, put a flea in one's ear, – one through it, – the fear of God into, – through the mill, – the blast on, raise hell with, – the dickens with, – the devil with, etc., read the riot act, – the Rocks and Shoals, ride ragged, roast, rollick, say a mouthful, sit on, slag (off), smack down, take a jab at, – a smack at, talk to like a Dutch uncle, tear off a strip, – a piece (or two), tear one's arse, tell a thing (or two), – what is what, – one where to get off, – where to go, throw the book at, vamp on, wade into; spec. read one's beads (gay use)

3. *to be in trouble:* be on the carpet, – on the mat, catch hell, catch it (hot), get it in the neck

4. *to nag:* break one's balls, go on at, hassle, henpeck, stay on one's case

adv. 5. *nagging:* at the micks, on one's case

292. Disparagement

n. 1. knocking, panning, razzing, (big) razoo

2. *sarcastic remark:* crack, dig, raspberry, razz, shot, shy, slam, slant, slap, sock, swipe

v. 3. *to disparage:* bag, base, blow a raspberry, fire on (US black), give the big razoo, – the finger, knock, pan, pin one's ears back, put the hammer on, razz, shoot down, slam, slap, slash (US black), take a shot, shy etc. (see n. 2), vamp on, weigh into

4. *scorn:* bucket (Aus.), chump off (US black), need like a hole in the head

adj. 5. *sarcastic:* sarky

adv. 6. *scorned:* stuffed

excl. 7. *sarcastic comment:* and you!, (the) answer is a lemon!, back in the knifebox!, be your age!, – yourself!, big deal!, bite the ice!, blow it out (your arse)!, bully for you!, butt out!, cost ya!, does your mother know you're out?, don't ask me, I only work here!, drop dead!, eat it!, eat my shorts!, – shit!, fag your face!, famous last words!, get!, get fucked!, – her!, – him!, – knotted!, – onto yourself!, – out of my way!, – stuffed!, give over!, go (and) bark at the moon!, – boil your head!, – jump in a lake!, – take a long walk off a short pier!, go fuck a dead horse!, – fuck yourself!, – fuck yourself in the ass and get some brains!, – fuck yourself with a rubber wienie!, – piss up a rope (and play with the steam)!, – shit in a pot and duck your head!, – to blazes!, – shit in your hat pull it over your head and call it curls!, go to buggery!, half your luck! (Aus.), stick it up your jumper!, stop moing me!, suck it and see!, sucks to you!, take a flying fuck!, – a running jump!, thanks a bunch, – a million, TS!, tough shit!, up your arse, – your brown, – your jacksie, – yours!, with knobs on!, you'll be sorry!, you slay me!, your mama!; spec. shall I put a bit of hair on it? (to an inept workman); were you

born in a barn? – in a tent? (to someone who has left a door open)
8. *contempt:* be hanged, blah!, fuck you!, huh!, nuts to you!, phooey!, pooh!, screw you!, the hell with it!, – with you!

293. Ridicule; Banter
n. 1. Bronx cheer, hee-haw, horse laugh, panning, raspberry, razz, rib, roast
2. *teasing:* codology, kidology, joshing, kidding, ragging, taking the Michael, – the piss
3. *gesture of derision:* the finger, two fingers of scorn, V-sign
v. 4. *to ridicule:* cast nasturtiums, give the bird, needle, pan, razz, rib, roast
5. *to tease:* bull, extract the Michael, get gay with, get one at it, – going, give one the business, – the leg, haze, howl, jack around, josh, kid, move one, piss-take, pull one's leg, – one's pisser, put on, rag, rib, send up, shoot on, sling off (Aus.), sound, stick it to, take the Michael, – the mickey, – the piss, wind up
6. *to make a rude gesture or noise:* flip the bird, give a Bronx cheer, – a raspberry, – the finger
phr. 7. *you silly fool:* (now you've) been and gone and done it

294. Vilification; Slander
n. 1. spec. dozens, dirty dozens, momma's game (US black: ritual 'games' of insult)
2. *slander:* dirt, muck, mud, mudslinging, poison, shit-stirring, smear
3. *abuse:* bullyrag, (the) hard word, rough edge of the tongue, verbals
v. 4. *to vilify:* slag off, talk trash; spec. play the dozens, shoot the dozens (see n. 1)
5. *to slander:* bad-mouth, crap on, dish the dirt (about), poormouth, put the bad word on, – the hard word on, – out the poison, rank,

sling dirt, – mud, – shit, smear, stir shit, stab in the back
6. *to abuse:* bullyrag, call (one) out, chew out, curse out, give the hard word, – rough edge of one's tongue, lay into, let loose on (see Scold: 291), put down, rubbish, schpritz (Yid.), snipe on (US black)

COURAGE
295. Courage; Confidence
n. 1. Aristotle (rhy.sl. = bottle), arry, balls, bottle (rhy.sl. = bottle and glass = arse = 'bottom'), brass balls, cojones, face, grit, guts, hair, heart, intestinal fortitude, moxie, rocks, rooks (US black), spunk, stiff upper lip, stones, what it takes; spec. Dutch courage (liquor-induced bravery)
v. 2. *to be brave:* be a man, have (plenty of) what it takes
3. *to encourage:* brace up, buck up
4. *to encourage oneself:* keep a stiff upper lip, – one's chin up, – one's pecker up
adj. 5. *brave:* ballsy, game (for anything), gutsy, nervy, spunky
excl. 6. *of encouragement:* buck up, it will all come out in the wash, don't make a production out of it, worse things happen at sea, (keep your) chin up!, don't let the bastards grind you down, keep your pecker up, the first hundred years are the hardest, cheer up – the worst is yet to come!, it's a great life if you don't weaken!, be a devil!, go for it!, snap out of it!, stay with it!, hang in there!, up there Cazaly! (Aus.); spec. break a leg! (theatrical)

296. Cowardice
n. 1. dog, funk, yellow streak; spec. edge city (at one's emotional limits)
2. *fear.* blue funk, cold feet, creeps, horrors, white-knuckler
v. 3. *to be a coward:* bottle out,

chicken out, cop out, get cold feet, have a yellow streak (right down one's back), lose one's bottle, punk out; spec. can dish it out but can't take it (usually of a weak bully)
4. *to be afraid:* get the wind up, have one's heart in one's mouth, pack 'em (Aus.), piss (in) one's pants, shit a brick, – bricks, – oneself, wear brown trousers, wet one's pants
5. *to frighten:* freak out, give a bad moment, – a turn, make one's hair curl, psych out, put the fear of God into, – the frighteners on, rattle, scare stiff, – the bejazaus out of, – the pants off, – the shit out of, spook, throw a scare into, wierd out
adv. 6. *cowardly:* chicken, CS, chickenshit, chicken-hearted, dripping, gutless, nervy, weedy, wet, wimpy, yellow, yellow-bellied
7. *afraid:* freaked (out), in a blue funk, packing 'em (Aus.), pissing oneself, scared shitless, – stiff, shit-scared, shitting bricks, – oneself, spooked, white about the gills

---

PRIDE
297. Pride; Conceit
n. 1. high-hatting, (old) acid, snippiness
v. 2. *to be conceited, arrogant:* be too big for one's britches, come it, get a swelled head, – above oneself, have one's nose in the air, high-hat, put on dog, strong it, think one is 'it', throw one's weight around, upstage
adj. 3. *arrogant:* all over oneself, boasie (WI), cocky, dickty (US black), flash, Flash Gordon (US black), highfalutin', high-toned, hincty, hoity-toity, la-de-dah, on one's high horse, smart-ass, smartypants, snobby, snooty, snotty, stuck-up, stuck on oneself,

stuffy, toffee-nosed, too big for one's britches, uppish, uppity
adv. 4. *arrogant:* on one's high horse
excl. 5. *don't be so conceited:* come down off your high horse, – off your perch, come off it, who do you think you're fooling?
phr. 6. more front than Brighton beach, more hide than Jessie (Aus.)

298. Ostentation
n. 1. dog, frills, high-sidin' (US black), high-steppin' (US black), side, splash, splurge, swank
v. 2. *show off:* act the nigger (US black), come on strong, cut a swath, fan, flame (gay use), flash (it about), grandstand, lay it on (thick), peddle one's wares, ponce about, put on (the) dog, put on jam (Aus.), spread it about, strut one's stuff, tart about, show boat, style, throw one's weight around; spec. put on the guiver (to affect a smart accent)
3. *to ornament:* ponce up, tart up
4. *to put on airs:* high-side, high-step (US black), get on one's high horse, put on the ritz, put on frills, – one's high hat, put on the dog, put on jam (Aus.), swank
adj. 5. *ostentatious:* flash, – as a rat with a gold tooth, flossy, jazzy, nouveau, piss elegant, saddity, screaming, sidity, swanky, tarty

299. Boasting
n. 1. ballyhoo, blatherskite, bosh, BS, bull, bullshit, flapdoodle, gas, hot air, six-sheeting, three-sheeting, tall talk, wind
v. 2. *to boast:* advertise, ballyhoo, blow black (US black), blow hard, blow heavy, blah, blow one's own trumpet, broadcast, BS, bull, bullshit, come on like gangbusters, come the big note (Aus.), crack on, crap on, fiend on (US black), gam (US black), gas, give it all that,

grand (US black), high-side (US black), lairize (Aus.), let off some hot air, loudmouth, loudtalk, mouth off, lip off, pop off (at the mouth), put the bee on, run a line, scream some heavy lines (US black), sell a wolf ticket (US black), shoot off at the mouth, shoot the bull, shovel shit, skite (Aus.), spread the bull, swank, talk shit (US black), three-sheet,

adj. 3. *boastful:* all mouth and trousers, – piss and wind, mouthy, smart-arse

excl. 4. *boasting:* did I ever!, is the Pope a Catholic!, does the bear shit in the woods!, is the bear a Catholic, does the Pope shit in the woods, watch my dust!

HUMILITY
300. Humility; Meekness
n. 1. back seat
2. *humiliation:* bring-down, climb-down, come-down, crow, putdown, take-down
v. 3. *to be humble:* be on the (strict) QT, eat crow, fly low, keep a low profile, lie low, take a back seat
4. *to humiliate:* bring down, burst one's bubble, come down on, jump on (with both feet), knock (down), – off one's perch, knock the bottom out of, – the stuffing out of, – the kibosh out of, – off one's high horse, puncture one's balloon, put (one) down, put one where they belong, – the skids under, – one's nose out of joint, settle one's hash, squash, squelch, take the wind out of one's sails, – down a peg, – a few pegs, – the starch out of, tell where to get off

5. *to be humiliated:* come down to earth, – a peg, – a few pegs, land on one's arse, lower one's flag, take a fall, tuck in one's tail

301. Embarrassment
v. 1. *to embarrass:* burn, get, put in the hot seat, – on the spot
2. *to be embarrassed:* be in the hot seat, – on the spot, feel like a horse's arse, – like nothing on earth, – like hell, – like two cents, wilt
3. *to hurt one's feelings:* get one (where it hurts), get one where they live, step on one's corns, touch a soft spot
excl. 4. *of embarrassment:* I could have died!, I didn't know where to put myself!, was my face red!

302. Submissiveness
n. 1. back seat, cave-in, climb-down, second fiddle
v. 2. *to give in:* back down, break, break it down (Aus.), call all bets off, – it a day, – it quits, chuck it (in), chuck up the sponge, crack, cry uncle!, give up as a bad job, give it a miss, go under the table!, – in the tank, knuckle under, take the count, throw in the towel, – the sponge, – one's cards, – one's hand
3. *to be subservient:* crawfish, dep (act as deputy), eat crow, kiss arse, play second fiddle, play the Tom (US black), take a back seat, Tom (US black)
adj. 4. *subservient:* whipped; spec. hincty (US black derog. ref. to blacks who ape whites)
excl. 5. *of resignation:* if you can't beat 'em join 'em, that's the ball game, that's the way the cookie crumbles

Morality and Religion

INTEGRITY
303. Morality
n. 1. straight and narrow; spec. Brownie point (an award for 'goodness')
adj. 2. *moral:* tallawah (WI), white
3. *self-righteous:* pi, prissy, stuffy

304. Obligation
n. 1. *responsibility:* load
2. *to be responsible:* pay one's dues, pick up the tab, put one's money where one's mouth is, stand up, stick one's neck out
3. *to make responsible:* wish on, – upon
4. *to deserve:* be in line for, get one's come-uppance, have it coming
adv. 5. *due:* down to

305. Honesty
n. 1. fair go (Aus.), fair shake (Aus.), the handsome thing, no stuff (US black), square shake, straight poop, – goods, – shit, – shooting
2. *blamelessness:* clean nose, – sheet
v. 3. *to be honest:* act on the square, be on the level, – on the legit, – on the up-and-up, etc. (see adj. 6), lay (it) on the line, – one's cards on the table, play it square, – with a clean deck, shoot straight, – square, toe the line, walk the line
4. *to treat fairly:* be one hundred per cent with, do the handsome thing, give a fair crack of the whip, – a fair shake, – a square shake, play it straight (down the line), – the game, – the white man
5. *to be blameless:* have a clean nose, – a clean sheet, keep one's

nose clean, – in the clear, stay kosher
adj. 6. *honest:* clean, dinkum (Aus.), for real, kosher, (on the) legit, on the level, outfront, ridgie-didgie (Aus.), righteous, straight, up and up, upfront, white
7. *frank:* straight from the shoulder, – down the line
8. *trustworthy:* A1, aces, all wool and a yard wide, blowed in the glass, dinkum (Aus.), kosher, the (real) McCoy, the (real) McKay, on the level, – the legit, – the square, one hundred per cent, regular, right, solid, sure-fire, sure-as-shit
excl. 9. *honest!:* fair crack of the whip!, fair dinkum! (Aus.), fair shake of the dice!, on my life!, stand on me!, straight up!, strictly!, you know me Al!

IMPROBITY
306. Immorality; Evil
n. 1. bad news, backmark (US black), no-no
v. 2. *to become immoral:* crack up, go blooey, – downhill, – down the chute, – down the tubes, – haywire, – smash, – to the dogs, – to the bow-wows, – to hell (on a rocket), – to pot, – to shit, – to the devil, hit the rocks, – the skids, smash up
adj. 3. *immoral:* alias (WI), as bad as they come, – as they make them, left-handed, low-down, low-rent
4. *tough:* hard-boiled, heavy-duty, mean
5. *risqué:* adult, blue, hot, juicy, rauncy, spicy, strong

307. Dishonesty

n. 1. dodge, emag (backsl. = game), funny business, graft, lurk (Aus.), racket; spec. payola (bribery to gain publicity)

v. 2. *to be dishonest:* fall down on, go back on, lay down on (see also Crime: 460 ff)

adj. 3. *dishonest:* bent, – as a nine bob note, fishy, funny, iffy, off, sneaky

4. *untrustworthy:* bent, cronky (Aus.), lurky, wrong

phr. 5. *of distrust:* I wouldn't trust him/her as far as I could throw him/her

308. Unfairness

n. 1. carve-up, dirty deal, dirty pool, dirty work (at the crossroads), funny business, not cricket, raw deal, the dirty, the shaft

v. 2. *to treat unfairly:* do one dirt, do the dirty (on), hit below the belt, play (one) dirty, pull off some funny business, – off

adj. 3. *unfair:* below the belt, crummy, low-down, low-rent

adv. 4. *treated unfairly:* shafted, screwed

309. Dissoluteness; Dissipation; Self-Indulgence

n. 1. the life of Riley, the Life (US black underworld), the fast lane, – track

v. 2. *to live 'fast':* fly high, go for broke, go it, – the pace, hit the high spots, kick up one's heels, play the giddy goat, rip it up, run in the fast lane, – the fast track, step high (wide and handsome), tear it up, whoop it up

3. *to indulge oneself:* bust loose, kick over the traces, let oneself go, let loose, loosen up, take the lid off

adj. 4. *dissolute:* fast, sporty

DECEPTION

310. Deception; Deceit

n. 1. bill of goods, bull, bullshit, bunk, bunkum, con, crap, eyewash, hanky-panky, jiggery-pokery, jive, kidology, moonshine, put up job, shuck, snowfall, snow job, window dressing

2. *trick:* all done by mirrors, bunco, dirty pool, dodge, fast one, gaff, gag, okey-dokey (US black), old moody, (one's) little game, racket, ramp, ripoff, sucker trap; spec. crib (examination aid); long con (long-term con trick), short con (short-term con trick) (see also Confidence Trick: 491)

3. *hoax, swindle:* cod, con, dry shave, fast shuffle, fiddle, gyp, hook, job, mace, number, put-on, shakedown, sell, skin, touch

v. 4. *to deceive:* bamboozle, blag, blow past, chi-ike, chump, con, criss-cross (US black), deal them from the bottom of the deck, do brown, – down, – in the eye, drop one in it, flimflam, flummox, get the drop on, give (one) a fast shuffle, give (one) the business, hand a lemon, have on toast, have one on, lead up the garden path, play for a sucker, play the con, – the nut role, pull an act, – a fast one, put down a routine, put it across (on), – the shuck on, – one over (on), rat fuck, RF, ring it on, rip off, rope in, run one way and look another (US black), sam, scale (Aus.), sell a bill of goods, sham on (US black), show out, shuck, snow, string along, suck, take for a ride, – for a sucker, two-time, work

5. *to fool:* cod, goose, jive, josh, kid, pull one's leg, – the wool over one's eyes, send on a humbug trip (US black), throw a curve (to), – dust in one's eyes

6. *to defraud:* ace, – out of, beat for, beat (one) out of, burn, chisel, chizz, diddle, do, – a job on,

– brown, – over, flim-flam, fuck out of, game, get the fat off (Aus.), gazump, gessump, gyp, give a fucking, – a screwing, hook for, lay for, take for, jip (out of), half-ounce (rhy.sl. = bounce = short-change), have, have one over, – one on, Jew (derog.), knock, mace, milk, nail, pluck, promote, ring the changes, rip off, roll, rook, scale (Aus.), screw, sell (one) a pup, send to the cleaners, shake down, shanghai, shave, skin, stick it up, sting, take to the cleaners, trim, tuck up, weed; spec. gas and run (fill up without paying); walk the check (leave without paying)

7. *to hoax:* BS, bull (along), bullshit, cod, feed a line, – load of baloney, have on a string, hand a line (of bull, baloney, etc.), hokum, jolly (along), josh, keep (one) on a string, kid (along), lay it on thick, pile it on (thick), play (along), shoot the bull, – a line, string along, toss a line

8. *to be tricked:* be bamboozled, – done up brown, – given a fast shuffle, had, etc. (see v. 4, 6), fall for, get a haircut, – it in the neck, – suckered, go for, jump at, play out of the pocket (US black), swallow (hook, line and sinker), tumble for

adj. 9. *deceitful:* full of shit, leery, near the mark, snaky

10. *cheating:* macing, stuffing (US black)

11. *cheated:* done, x-ed out (US black)

phr. 12. *warning:* don't take any wooden nickels

311. Falsification; Sham

n. 1. bunkum, dud, phony, phonus balonus, ringer, Sexton Blake (rhy.sl. = fake), snide; spec. Oliver (rhy.sl. = Oliver Twist = fist = false entry in a ledger); slum (fake jewellery)

2. *pretence:* act, blind, front, put-on, smoke screen

v. 3. *to falsify:* cook (the books), pad (a bill), ring, sell a pup

4. *to pretend:* come it, come the old soldier, drum up, fake it, go through the motions, make like, play dumb, pull an act, swank; spec. pass (for a Jew to act as a Christian, a gay to act as a heterosexual, etc.)

adj. 5. *false:* brummagem, bent, bum, cheesy, cooked (up), doctored (up), dud, hokey, jive, not all that it seems, phony, snide

adv. 6. *faked:* ain't holding no air (US black)

312. Falsehood; Lie

n. 1. ackamaracka, balls, BS, bull, bullshit, crap, fanny, fib, fish story, get up, good one, jiggery-pokery, jive, likely story, moody, one (US black: one big lie), pitch, porky (rhy.sl. = pork pie), sell, snow, snow job, straight shit, tall story, – tale, whopper

v. 2. *to lie:* blow smoke up one's arse, BS, bull, bullshit, clock a daffy (S.Afr.), crap, draw a long bow, feed one a line, – one stuff (US black), fib, fudge, fly a kite, give a little leg, jive, lumber, pile it on (thick), play stuff (US black), prop up, shit through one's teeth, three-sheet

adj. 3. *exaggerated:* gross, howling, thumping, thundering, whacking, whopping

phr. 4. *am I lying?:* can you see green in my eyes? (S.Afr.), would I shit you (you're my favourite turd)?

313. Treachery

n. 1. dirty work (at the crossroads), funny business, the shaft

v. 2. *to be treacherous:* dingo (Aus.), give one some funny business, – the shaft, play (one) dirty, stab in the back

3. *double-cross:* cross, cross up, two-time
adj. 4. *treacherous:* two-faced, two-timing

314. Betrayal
n. 1. squeal, tipoff
v. 2. *to betray:* do the dirty (on), fink (on), front one off (US black), play Judas, put the finger on, rat on, sell down the river, sell out, spill the beans on, turn in (see also Crime: 481, Crime: 501)
3. *to turn against:* go back on, go sour on, lay down on, poop out on

315. Entrapment
n. 1. fit up, fix, frame up, put up job, set-up
v. 2. *to entrap:* drop (right) in, fit up, frame up, put in the frame, set up; spec. plant (to 'discover' false evidence); (see also Crime: 497)

CULPABILITY
316. Accusation; Blame
n. 1. beef, knock, rap
v. 2. *to accuse:* call the turn on, drop on, finger, hang something on, knock, pip (something) on, put the finger on, – the shoe on the right foot (US black), shift the weight, throw down on (see also Crime: 481)
3. *to blame unfairly:* bark up the wrong tree, put the shoe on the left foot (US black), smear
4. *to take the blame for:* be left holding the baby, – holding the bag, carry the can (for), take the rap (for)

317. Vindication
n. 1. let-off, let-out
2. *excuse:* blind, (load of) flannel, song-and-dance, stall
v. 3. *to acquit:* give an out, slide; spec. spring (to free a prisoner); (see also Crime: 504)

4. *to make an excuse:* alibi out of, clean up (US black), give a song and dance, stall along
5. *to apologise:* eat crow, – dirt, – one's words

318. Punishment
n. 1. rap
2. *chastisement:* dose, dressing-down, going over, shellacking, trimming, what-for
3. *beating:* anointing, basting, clouting, fanning (one's arse), hiding, larruping, lathering, leathering, licking, polishing, seeing-to, shellacking, strap oil, swishing, tanning (one's arse/hide), toco, welting, whacking; spec. kneecapping (IRA punishment)
v. 4. *to punish:* attend to, bear down on, bust loose on, come down on, crack down on, do, – for, go after, – for, fix, get on one's arse, – one's case, – one's tail, give a dose, – a dressing-down, etc. (see n. 2), give (merry) hell, – it to, – the business, – the works, – one Larry Dooley (Aus.), hang one to the wall, have one's guts for garters, let one have it, – it in the neck, – have what-for, go at, – to town on, jump on (with both feet), knock it out of, land on, lay on, light into, make it hot for, pour (it) on, nail to the wall, put through the grinder, – the mill, – through it, – through the hoop, – under the cosh, raise Cain with, – merry hell with, settle one's hash, skin alive, spifflicate, turn inside out, walk into (see Crime: 502, Crime: 503)
5. *to beat:* anoint, bash, baste, beat the daylights out of, – the devil out of, – the hide off, beat up, dust one's coat, fan, give a basting, – a clouting, etc. (see n. 3), hammer, knock the stuffing(s) out of, larrup, lather, lay into, leather, lick the hell out of, – the tar out of, – the pants off, – to a frazzle, nail to the wall,

pan, shellac, sock, swack, swish, tan (one's arse/hide), tickle one's tail, wallop, whale the shit out of, – the tar out of, whop

6. *to be punished:* cop it, draw the crow (Aus.), eat shit, get it in the neck, take it on the chin, – one's lumps, – the fall, – the gas, – the knock, catch (merry) hell, catch it, get it (good and hot), get toco; spec. have it coming and going (be punished twice) (see Crime: 502, Crime: 503)

7. *to accept one's punishment:* face the music, get what's coming to one, – one's come-uppance, pay the piper, stand up and take it, take it (like a man), – one's medicine, – the rap

8. *to deserve punishment:* be riding for a fall, be for it, – in for it, – on the spot, have it coming, let oneself in for it

9. *to escape punishment:* beat the rap, duck the rap (see Crime: 504)

REPARATION
319. Confession
n. 1. come-across, cough (up), squawk, squeak

·v. 2. *to confess:* come across (with the goods), come clean, – one's cocoa, – one's fat (Aus.), – one's lot, cough (up), fess up, get (it) off one's chest, – (it) out of one's system, – (it) off one's mind, level (with), open up, out with (it), put up one's hand, sing, spill (it), spill one's guts, – the beans, – it out, squawk, squeak, talk, unload (see also Crime: 481, Crime: 501)

3. *force to confess:* break (down), crack, – wide open, make one sing, put the arm on, third degree

320. Reform
n. 1. clean-up; spec. Black justice (black self-determination)

v. 2. *to reform:* clean up, clean up one's act, go legit, – square, – straight

---

RELIGION
321. Religion
n. 1. spec. fish-eater, Taig (derog: Roman Catholic); God slot (compulsory religious hour on UK TV)

adv. 2. *religious:* holier-than-thou, nearer-my-God-than-thee, pi

322. Religious Activities
v. 1. *spec. take a collection:* pass the hat

323. Religious Person
n. 1. bible-banger, bible-basher, bible-puncher, Holy Joe

2. *spec. Salvation Army:* Sally Ann, Salvo (Aus.)

3. *preacher, priest:* Holy Joe, sky pilot

4. *charlatan:* mitt man

324. Religious Buildings and Organisations
n. 1. *church:* Godbox

2. *YMCA:* Y

3. *Salvation Army:* Sally Ann, Salvo (Aus.)

325. Supernatural Beings
n. 1. *euphemisms for God:* dad, gad, gawd, golly, gor, gorra, gorry, gosh, gor, gum, Lawd, lawdy, lawks, laws, lor, Lordy

2. *euphemisms for Christ:* Christmas, Christopher (Columbus), crikey, criminy, cripes, gee, geez, jayzus, jeez, Jesus H. Christ

3. *the Devil:* deuce, dickens, divil, Old Bendy, – Billy, – Blazes, – Boots, – Boy, – Cain, – Clootie, – Dad, – Driver, – Gentleman, – Gooseberry, – Harry, – Horny, – Lad, – Ned, – Nick, – One,

– Poger, – Poker, – Roger, – Ruffin, – Scratch, – Serpent, – Toast, Sam Hill

4. *ghost:* bogeyman, boogieman, spook

326. Afterlife
n. 1. *heaven:* happy hunting grounds, harp farm

2. *hell:* blazes, blue blazes, Hades

327. Sorcery; Magic
n. 1. hocus-pocus
v. 2. *to put a spell on:* hex, hoodoo, put the hex on

Human Relations

FRIENDLINESS
328. Friendship
n. 1. *welcome:* glad hand
v. 2. *to make friends:* buddy up, chum up, get next to, get one's feet under the table, hit it off, pal up (with)
3. *to get on with:* click (with), knock along with
4. *to be popular with:* be in good with, – on the right side of, – in with, etc. (see adv. 9), rate, stand good with, sit right with
5. *to be overfriendly:* glad hand; spec. press flesh (for a politician to shake hands)
6. *to associate with:* hang around with, hook up with, mob up with, run with, tie in with, – up with
adv. 7. *friendly:* buddy-buddy, chummy, down with, hope-to-die (US black), in one's corner, one on one, pally, palsy-walsy, running with, thick with, tight with
8. *intimate:* on speakers; spec. just quietly (Aus. between you and me)
9. *popular with:* aces with, in good with, in solid (with), in with, into, next to, on the right side of
excl. 10. *terms of friendship:* ace, amigo, baby, babes, babycakes, bless your little cotton socks, buggerlugs, diddums, ducks, love, lovey, sunshine

329. Kindliness; Consideration
n. 1. TLC (tender loving care)
v. 2. *to be kind:* have one's heart in the right place
3. *to be lenient:* ease up on, let down easy, let up on, pull one's punches

adj. 4. *kind:* big hearted, soft
excl. 5. don't worry it may never happen, upsidaisy, worse things happen at sea, you can't win them all

330. Reconciliation
v. 1. *to reconcile:* square up
2. *to be reconciled:* bury the hatchet, get clear with

HOSTILITY
331. Estrangement
n. 1. break-up, bust-up, splitsville
v. 2. *to become estranged:* break it off, – up, – with, bust up, call it a day, – it quits, chuck, ditch, dump, give one the brush(-off), part brass rags, split (with), throw over, wash one's hands of (see also Reject: 224, Jilt: 353)

332. Enmity; Disfavour
n. 1. frost, hard word; spec. shit list (black list); spec. Jim Crow laws (racist laws in US)
v. 2. *to dislike:* be down on, – off, go off, – sour on, have a down on, have a hard-on for, – a hate on, – it in for, – no love lost for, not go nap on (Aus.)
3. *to earn disfavour:* get in bad with, – on the outs with; spec. one's name is mud (to be unpopular)
adv. 4. *on bad terms:* in bad (with), in Dutch (with), – the doghouse, – wrong (with), off of, on the outs, on the outer (Aus.), out with, washed up with, went down like a pork chop at a Jewish wedding

333. Jealousy
v. 1. *to be jealous:* eat one's heart out
phr. 2. *of jealousy:* all right for some, I should be so lucky, nice work if you can get it

334. Malice
n. 1. cussedness, shenanigans
2. *grudge:* axe to grind, bitch, bone to pick, down, peeve
v. 3. *to cause trouble for:* louse (one) up, mess over, put the mockers on, rubbish, trash; spec. put the black on (blackmail); set up (place in a vulnerable situation)
4. *to provoke trouble:* gee up, head-hunt (US black)
5. *to hold a grudge:* be down on, have an axe to grind, – a bone to pick, – a down on, – a peeve with, – it in for
adj. 6. *malicious:* mean, mean-hair, ornery, shitty

335. Retaliation; Revenge
n. 1. comeback, paybacks (US black)
v. 2. *to take revenge:* come back at, even the score, fix, settle one's hash, settle up, square (it), stuff
3. *to seek revenge:* be out for blood

336. Intimidation
n. 1. big stick, frighteners, screws
v. 2. *to intimidate:* buffalo, bulldoze, bullyrag, come down on, come down fonky (US black), – heavy, hang tough, hard-talk, heavy, lean on, put the arm on, – the bull on, – the cosh on, – the frighteners on, – the screws on, – the squeeze on, – the wind up, stand over (Aus.), weird out; spec. kneecap (IRA punishment) (see also Cowardice: 300)
excl. 3. *threats:* or else!, I don't mean maybe!, I'll knock your block off!

4. *counter to threats:* oh yeah!, sez who!, you and whose army!

337. Rough Treatment
n. 1. muscle, rough-house, rough stuff, strong arm stuff (see also Kill: 118); spec. heading, nutting; knuckle sandwich
2. *a blow:* backhander, bang, haymaker, lick, old one-two, one (ie 'fetch him one'); spec. Christmas hold (on the testicles), king (Aus. kinghit = knockout punch)
v. 3. *to manhandle:* be rough on, bounce, cut up rough, – up rusty, hand out punishment, – a bit of stick, get tough with, rough up, tough up
4. *to hit:* banjo, barrel (Aus.), bash, bean, belt, boff, boot (around), burst, bust (one) up, clip, clobber, clock, clunk, conk, crown, dance on one's lips, deck, dish it out, do a job on, do over, drive on (US black), duff over, duff up, duke, dust (one), flatten, get in one's eye (US black), give a fourpenny one, give one the leather, go down on, go the knuckle (Aus.), go upside one's head (US black), grunge, hang one on, jam one up (US black), job (Aus.), kick (one's) arse, kick the stuffing out of, knee, knock one's block off, knock the bejazus out of, – the stuffing out of, lump, nut, paste, pepper one up (US black), plaster, pop (in the eye), put a hurting on (US black), put one on, – one's arse in sling, – the boot in, – the leather in, ring one's bell, roak (US black), run over, run sets on (US black), run up the side of one's head (US black), scone (Aus.), scrag, slosh, slug, sock, spank, stick one on, stomp, take a pop (at), tan one's hide, throw a punch, throw hands (US black), tump over, whack, whale the piss out of, – the shit out of, – the tar out of, whap, whup, wooden (Aus.), work over

5. *to knock out:* cold-cock, cold-deck, drop, kayo, knock cold, KO, lay out, put (one) away, put one's lights out
6. spec. chive, let the daylights into, stick (stab); skullneck (decapitate); stripe (slash)
7. *to shoot:* bang off, blast, blow away, blow one's head off, chop, drill, give it to, – (one) lead poisoning, let have it, nail, perforate, plug, put the blast on, shoot the daylights out of, take a crack at
8. *to wound, hurt:* hurt, nip; spec. mark up (bruise)
9. *to kick:* give the leather, leather **adv.** 10. *hit on the head:* boned

338. Attack; Assault
n. 1. *a fight:* aggro, barney, bovver, confusion (WI), ding-dong, donnybrook, dust-up, fair, fist junction (US black), kick-up (WI), knock-down drag-out, knuckle, mash-up (WI), pasting, punch-up, rashing (US black), ruffle (US black), rumble, scrap, spillin' (US black), stoush (Aus.), thumb (US black), up-and-downer; spec. shin battle (a fake battle); spec. queer bashing, Paki-bashing, nigger-bashing (attacks on gays, Pakistanis, blacks)
2. *rape:* drumstick case (US black)
v. 3. *to fight:* bop, duke it out, get down from the Y (US black), give the works (to), go from the Y, go from the fists, go from the shoulders, gunzel (US black), kick (some) ass, lay into, lock arseholes, mess up, mess with, mix it, rain on, rough-house, shuffle, snap arseholes, sort out, straighten
4. *to attack:* beat up (on), blaze on (US black), do, do up, get tore in, get stuck into, go down, go round with, jack up, make a pass at, muscle in, rip into, sail into, sandbag, sic onto, snag, tear into,

tear one a new arsehole, vamp on (US black)
5. *to beat, defeat:* beat the can off, – the pants off, – the shit out of, boff, bop, break in half, brown-slice (WI), cream, crease, do over, do to a turn, do up (brown), donkey-lick (Aus.), dough-pop, eat up, flatten, floor, give it to (one) good, give lumps, give the chop, give the works to, hang one out to dry, have one's guts for garters, jam one up (US black), jump all over, knacker, knock bowlegged, – for a loop, – hell west and crooked, – into the middle of next week, – one's socks off, – one's teeth down his throat, – silly, leave for dead, lick, make mincemeat of, mogador (rhy.sl. = floor), mullah, paste, push one's face through the back of one's neck, put (one) away, shove one's fist down his throat, smear all over the map, take to the cleaners, wax one's tail, wax, whale the shit out of, – the tar out of, whip one's arse, wipe out, work over good; spec. mummy (US black: beat to death)
6. *to rape:* gorilla, jam one up (US black)
7. *to ambush:* jap, jump, snag **adv.** 8. *beaten up:* done over, done up (like a kipper)
9. *aggressive:* scrappy

CO-OPERATION
339. Co-operation
n. 1. cahoots, get-together, hook-up, tie-in, tie-up
v. 2. *join in:* case out, hook up with, lock into, muck in, play ball (with), tie up with, tie into; spec. re-up (US milit: to re-enlist)
3. *to involve:* get one in (on an act), ring in, rope in
4. *to do one's share:* do one's bit, keep one's end up, pull one's weight, weigh in
5. *to make a deal:* cut up the cake

adv. 6. *united:* crewed up, in cahoots, hooked up, mob-handed, solid, team-handed, tied in, – up
phr. 7. *let's co-operate:* you scratch my back and I'll scratch yours

340. Agreement
n. 1. click, hook-up, tie-up
v. 2. *to agree:* be on, get behind, go a bundle on, go for, go (along) with, swing with, tumble for
3. *to sign a contract:* ink, pact
phr. 4. *agreement:* put it there!, shake!
5. *agreed:* and how, aren't we all, bags I, check, check and double check, count me in, don't mind if I do, I'm on, I'll go for that, I'll say, I'm with you, me and you both, 'nuff said, put it there, shake, same here, that's (for) me, you're on

341. Assistance
n. 1. boost, leg-up; spec. log-rolling (mutual aid)
v. 2. *to help:* boost, chip in, give a leg-up, pinch-hit, reach (US black)
3. *to support, back up:* boost, front for, go overboard for, get behind, get one's back (US black), go to the mat for, stooge for
4. *to defend oneself:* throw a punch
5. *to give a chance to:* give a break, – half a chance, – a squeeze
6. *to let someone get on with:* let the dog see the rabbit
7. *to do a favour:* do a solid (US black), lemon (rhy.sl. = lemon flavour = favour)

OPPOSITION; CONFLICT
342. Opposition
n. 1. spec. needle match
2. *litigation:* Sue City
v. 3. *to oppose:* thumb the nose at, throw one's hat in the ring
adj. 4. *rebellious:* bolshy, uppity

343. Disagreement
v. 1. *fail to agree:* get out of line

adv. 2. *in disagreement:* no deal, – dice, – go, – sale, – soap, – way, nothing doing

344. Contention
n. 1. *argument, quarrel:* argy-bargy, barney, blow-up, blue (Aus.), bull and cow (rhy.sl. = row), ruck, ruckus, run-in, shoot-out, spat, to-do; spec. demo (demonstration); Mexican stand-off (no-win situation); sporting encounter: blinder
v. 2. *to pursue, compete:* breathe down one's neck, duck-shove (Aus.), go for pinkslips, have a hit on, jockey, lock assholes, tangle assholes
3. *to argue:* have it out, pick a bone with, weigh in
4. *feel aggressive:* feel froggy (US black)
5. *to challenge:* buy a (wolf) ticket (US black), call (one) out, choose off (US black), step out on the green (US black)
adv. 6. *in contention:* head up, mano-a-mano, one-on-one
7. *aggressive:* bad-ass, chippy, hard-boiled
phr. 8. *challenges:* leap and you will receive (US black), want to make something of it?, who (are) you screwing?

COURTESY
345. Courtesy; Politeness
n. 1. spec. cool (street gang peace)
excl. 2. *social remarks:* age before beauty, be my guest, bully for you!
3. *thank you:* ta, ta muchly, thanks a bunch, – a million
4. *you're welcome:* forget it, keep the change, no sweat, skip it, that's cool
5. *no thank you:* I'll freeze, that's cool

346. Greeting
n. 1. howdy, howdydo; spec. dap,

soul shake (ritual black palm-slapping)
v. 2. *to greet with mutual palm-slapping:* give some skin, – spli, give the drummer some, high-five, slap, – five, – the plank (US black)
excl. 3. *hello:* bhani ghani (US black), cop a squat, getting any?, Hello, John (got a new motor?), hi-de-hi! (response: hi-de-ho), how's it hanging?, how're they hanging?, how's tricks?, lay some on me! (US black), long time no see, look what the cat's brought in, – the wind's blown in, park your carcase, roll your own (US black), skin me! (US black), what can I do you for?, what gives?, what's cooking?, – going on?, – happening?, – new?, – shaking?, – the deal?, what sup?, wotcher; spec. Miss Thing (homosexual use)
4. *goodbye!:* Abyssinia!, (see you later) alligator, catch some rays, – you later, cheerie-bye, cheerio, chin-chin, don't call us, we'll call you, don't do anything I wouldn't do, – spend it all at once, – take any wooden nickels, hooroo (Aus.), oh reservoir, pip-pip, seeya, seeyabye, see you in church, – in court, – the funny pages, so long, stay loose, ta-ta, TTFN (ta-ta for now), teuf-teuf, toodle-bye, toodle-oo, toodle-pip

---

DISCOURTESY
347. Impudence; Audacity
n. 1. *cheek:* brass, chutzpah (Yid.), crust, face, neck, lip, moxie, once a week (rhy.sl. = cheek), piss and vinegar, sass, stalk
2. *cheekiness:* guff, jaw, lip, mouth, sauce, sass
v. 3. *to be impudent:* cock a snoot (at), have a brass neck; spec. gross out (to shock); spec. take tea with (to outwit)

adj. 4. *impudent:* bold, bold as brass, faastie (WI), fresh, leery, lippy, more front than Brighton beach, mouthy, pushy, rumbunctious, rumbustious, smart-arse, smart-alecky, snotty, wise-ass
excl. 5. *don't be cheeky!:* can you beat that!, what a nerve!, less of it!, of all the . . . , don't be smart!

348. Slight; Snub
n. 1. brush (off), cold shoulder, frost, frozen mitt, go-around, kick in the pants, run-around, smack in the eye (see also Ejection: 62)
v. 2. *to slight, snub:* freeze on, give one the belt, – the brush (off), – the cold shoulder, – the freeze (out), – the frost, – the go-around, – the runaround, have a shot at (Aus.), high-hat, see off, send away with a flea in one's ear, shoot down, shine on (US black), upstage; spec. cold-cunt (lesbian use: ignore)
phr. 3. *of ignorance:* don't know one from a bar of soap (Aus.)
excl. 4. *of contempt:* in your eye!

LOVE
349. Love
n. 1. *infatuation:* crush, pash
v. 2. *to be in love:* be stuck on, fall for (like a ton of bricks), go for, have a thing for, – eyes for, – one's nose open (US black), – a ring through one's nose, – the hots (for), rush, take a shine to, wear the ring (US black)
3. *to fascinate:* get under one's skin
adv. 4. *in love with, obsessed:* after, bitten, crazy for, cuckoo over, dead set (on), gooey about, – over, goofy about, gone on, head over heels, in a bad way, in deep, lovey-dovey, mad about, moony (over), nuts about, smitten, snowed over, soft on, sweet on, on a tight leash, wild about

350. Courtship
n. 1. dating, macking,
nanny-goating (rhy.sl. = courting);
spec. basket picnic (gay use: looking
over prospective pickups)
2. spec. heavy date (very important
date)
v. 3. *to pick up:* chat up, give the
business, hoopdie-swoop (US
black), mack, pluck (US black)
4. *to appraise sexually:* give the glad
eye, make a dead set for, – a play
for, prop up, pull a quick park (US
black), put the hard word on, scope
(on); spec. cruise (gay use)
5. *to go out:* spec. double
(double-date), sit (a woman) (US
black)
6. *to steal someone else's date:* cut
out, snake
7. *to interfere with courtship:* (play)
gooseberry

351. Caressing
n. 1. (bit of) slap and tickle, bush
patrol, finger pie, groping,
lovey-dovey, parking, PDA (public
display of affection), pecking and
necking (US black), stink(y)-finger;
spec. first base (initial sexual
contact); ga-ga, jam (gay
use)
2. *a kiss:* French kiss, kissyface, hit
(rhy.sl. = hit and miss), soul kiss
(US black), smacker, tongue sushi
v. 3. *to caress:* canoodle, climb all
over, cock pluck (US black), cop a
feel, dry-fuck, feel up, finger-fuck,
get to first base,
4. *to kiss:* chew face, mug, poof,
suck face, swap spit
adv. 5. *physically affectionate:* H^2
(hot and heavy)
phr. 6. *rejection of caresses:* not
tonight Josephine

352. Flirtation; Philandering
n. 1. *philandering:* catting (US
black); spec. little black book
(bachelor's address book)

2. *a flirt:* cock-teaser, cunt-teaser,
prick-teaser
3. *flirtatious glance:* bedroom eyes,
come-hither look, glad eye, goo-goo
eyes
4. *flirtatious talk:* chat, line,
lyricising (WI)
v. 5. *to philander:* cat around,
cruise, fan one's ass, – one's pussy
(US black), flag (gay use), fool
around, give up rhythm (US black),
hit and run, jack around, jazz
around, perv about, play around,
play the field, put it about, shoot
the thrill (US black), tomcat; spec.
basketeer (gay use: to size up
possible conquests); play checkers
(gay use: to move around a cinema
looking for sex)
6. *to flirt:* play hard to get
7. *to approach for sex:* bumchat, hit
on, jeff (US black), mack on (US
black), make a pass, pick up,
sweet-talk, shoot a line, talk
business (US black); spec. front one
off (US black: to seduce for gain,
not lust)
8. *to frustrate:* cocktease, pricktease
9. *gay use:* have kidney trouble
(solicit in public lavatories)
10. spec. red-light, shell-road (to
throw a girl out of a car if she
refuses to have sex)

353. Jilting
n. 1. air, brush, chuck, dump,
freeze, frost, kiss-off, let-down,
push
v. 2. *to interfere in a relationship:*
bird dog, cock block, gigolo, play
chicken, rank one's style (US black)
3. *to cheat:* burn, chippie, chippy
on, two-time
4. *to have an affair:* carry on, tip out
(US black)
5. *to end an affair:* chuck, dump,
give the air, – the brush, etc. (see n.
1), kiss off, run out on, throw over,
tip (US black), unload (see also
Reject: 224)

6. *to miss a lover:* carry a torch, torch for
adv. 7. spec. on the rebound

354. Engagement
n. 1. spec. bottom drawer
v. 2. *to be engaged, go out with:* date (Aus.), get it together, go steady, have something going
3. *to propose:* pop the question
adv. 4. *engaged:* dropped, taped up (US black)

355. Marriage; Living Together
1. ball-and-chain
2. *living together:* LTR (living together relationship), shack job, shack-up
3. *uncertain relationship:* see-saw (US black)
4. *marrying someone younger:* baby-snatching
v. 5. *to marry, be married:* be spliced, – hitched, have papers (US black), make the legal move, tie the knot
6. *to live together:* bungalow, knock on together, shack (up)
adv. 7. *married:* cash and carried, cut and carried (rhy.sl.), hitched, spliced
8. *unhappily married:* hen-pecked, pussy-whipped

356. Divorce; Parting
n. 1. bust-up, splitsville
v. 2. *to divorce, part:* blow one out, bust up, call it a day, – quits, split
3. *to repel:* turn off

SEX
357. Sexuality
n. 1. *desired object:* cookies
2. *desire, passion:* hard-on, load (US black), hot nuts, – pants, zazzle (US black); spec. blue balls (frustration)
3. *to desire:* be hot for, go for, gun for, have hot pants for, – hot nuts

for, honk for, lech (after), feel one's oats
4. *to excite:* get one going, – get one's nose open (US black), (this will) put lead in your pencil, prime one's pump, turn on
5. *to be sexually active:* have some rabbit, put it about
6. *to expose the genitals:* flash
7. *to be bisexual:* swing both ways
adj. 8. *sexy:* foxy, hot, raunchy, rude, warm
9. *bisexual:* AC/DC, ambidextrous, bi, half-and-half
10. *pornographic:* adult, blue, hard, strong
adv. 11. *excited:* begging for it, dripping for it, fruity, horny, hot (for), hot to trot, randy, sexed up
phr. 12. as the actress said to the bishop; nudge nudge wink wink know what I mean say no more

358. Sexuality: Homosexual
n. 1. spec. debut (first gay experience); mother-love (gay male's relationship with a heterosexual woman); talking (lesbian use: a relationship when one partner is in jail); bambi effect (for a young gay male to turn to heterosexuality); second closet (an admission of homosexuality); squelch (sex without affection)
v. 2. *to hide one's homosexuality:* pass, stay in the closet, wear a mourning veil; spec. lose one's gender (to abandon homo- for heterosexuality); wear a cut-glass veil (fail to hide one's homosexuality)
3. *to reveal one's homosexuality:* come out, discover one's gender, drop one's beads, – one's hairpins, lay it out, learn a new way, wear one's badge; spec. be brought out (to be initiated into the gay life); turn the tables (for a homosexual to blackmail a heterosexual)

4. *to act effeminately:* camp, foop, poof about, ruin, swish, wreck
5. *to become homosexual:* turn the corner
adj. 6. *effeminate:* la-di-dah
7. *homosexual:* bent, camp as a row of tents, chichi, having a dash, lavender
8. spec. longwinded (taking a longtime to reach orgasm)
9. spec. on the fence (ambivalent about homosexuality)
10. spec. enthroned (soliciting in a public lavatory), dethroned (ejected from a public lavatory)

359. Intercourse
n. 1. ball, bang, bit of how's-yer-father, – of the other, bunk-up, bush patrol, dash in the bloomers, dead shot (US black), Donald Duck (rhy.sl. = fuck), fickey-fick, fratting, fucking, fucky-fucky, fugging, ground rations, horizontal jogging, – rumble, horry (Aus.), hot fling (US black), indoor sledging, interior decorating, Jack in the box (US black), jig-a-jig, lay, legover, nasty, naughties, naughty, nobbing, nookie, oats, parallel parking, roll in the hay, root, rub-a-dub, seeing-to, thrill and chill (US black), turking, Ugandan discussions, wellington (Aus. rhy.sl. wellington boot = root), you know what; spec. knee-trembler (intercourse while standing up); straight shot (intercourse without contraception)
2. *spontaneous intercourse:* bip bam thank-you ma, bump, fast-fuck, quicke, wham bam thank-you mam
3. *lunchtime intercourse:* afternoon delight, funch, nooner
4. *place of intercourse:* killing floor, whip shack (US black)
5. *coitus interuptus:* getting off at Redfern (Aus.), – out at Gateshead, leaving before the gospel

6. *to have intercourse:* ball, bang, beanbag, biff, bust some booty (US black), cha-cha, charver, chingazo (Sp.), cut a side (US black), cut a slice off the joint, dance on the mattress, dip it, dip one's wick, – the fly (US black), dive into the dark (US black), do, do a kindness, do the do (US black), – the nasty, – the natural thing, – the pussy (US black), drill, drop one's load, empty one's trash (US black), exercise the ferret, feature with (Aus.), fill one up (US black), frig, fuck, fug, fugh, futz, gee, get a shot of leg (US black) , – into one's pants, – into, – on top of, – one's ashes hauled, – one's cookies, – one's end away, – one's greens, – one's jollies, – one's leg over, – one's oats, – one's rocks off, – some big leg, – some cock, – some pussy, – some tail, – some, give her a length, give her one, – one a tumble, – some body, – the dog a bone, go all the way, go with, grind, have a cut off the joint, have a dash in the bloomers, have a shag, – a slice off the joint, – a tumble, – it away (with), – it in, – one's greens, – one's oats, hide and salam, hide the salam, honeyfuck, honeyfuggle, hop on a babe, hump, jack up, jazz, jump, jump up and down, knock it off, knock it out (US black), – off a piece, lay, lay some pipe, make it (with), mash the fat (US black), meddle, mess around, mount, off, pile (US black), plank, play mothers and fathers, – mummies and daddies, – night baseball, plonk, plough the back forty, plough poke, pole, pork, prod, punch, ride, roger, root, rout, rump, schtup (Yid.), score between the posts (Aus.), scrape (Aus.), screw, see the King, shaft, shag, skeet (US black), skin the cat, slip her a length, slip it to, snag, spear the bearded clam (Aus.), stick it to,

stoop, stroke (US black), stuff, take a turn on Shooter's Hill (US black), throw, tom, tonk, tumble, twang; spec. roof it (to have sex on the roof); spec. talk fuck (to talk obscenely during intercourse); come across (surrender to seduction)

7. *to copulate enthusiastically:* bang like the shithouse door in a gale, go in out like a fiddler's elbow, go up her like a rat up a drain, rip her guts down (US black), screw the arse off, shag like a rattlesnake

8. *to have an orgasm:* come, come one's cocoa, – one's fat, cream, pop one's cork; spec. have a double shot (ejaculate twice)

9. *to give an orgasm:* ring one's bell, – one's chimes

10. *to have many sexual partners:* climb trees to get away from it (Aus.), get more arse than a toilet seat, have more pricks than a second-hand dart-board, have to swim underwater to get away from it (Aus.), hump 'em and dump 'em, so busy I've had to put a man on to help (Aus.), swing

11. *to deflower a virgin:* cherrypop, cop a cherry, crack a cherry, cut the cake, pop a cherry, split the cup (US black)

12. *to seduce:* Georgia, Georgy (US black), get across, – off with, – next to (US black), – one's leg over, go case with, have, – it away with, have one over, make, nail, prong, race off (Aus.), reel in the biscuit; spec. strike out (fail to seduce); are you saving it for the worms (an attempt to persuade an unwilling girl)

13. *to lose one's erection:* mess with nature (US black)

adj. 14. *promiscuous:* fast

15. *seduced:* had

16. *having intercourse without contraception:* bareback

adv. 17. *having intercourse:* at it, firkin, frigging, fucking, in the saddle, on the job, – the nest, – top of; spec. been there (referring to a previous sexual partner); spec. dog-knotted (for partners to be locked together during intercourse through muscle spasm)

18. *satiated:* plucked (US black)

phr. 19. it takes two to tango

20. *sexual distaste:* don't fancy yours, I wouldn't fuck her with your prick, – with a borrowed prick, I wouldn't touch it with yours, – with a ten-foot barge-pole

360. Varieties

n. 1. *oral sex:* head, lunch, sixty-nine, soixante-neuf; spec. rubbernecking (auto-fellatio)

2. *fellatio:* blow-job, deep throat, face-fucking, gob-job, head, lunch, sixty-eight ('you suck me and I'll owe you one'); spec. punishment (gay use: taking on an extra-large penis); glory hole (a hole in a public lavatory – the penis is pushed through for fellation)

3. *cunnilingus:* box lunch, dining at the Y, dipping in the bush, head, mouth music, punch in the mouth, sack lunch, skull (US black); spec. red wings (Hell's Angel use: cunnilingus with a menstruating woman)

4. *anilingus:* felch, reaming, ream job, rimming, rim, rim-job; spec. black wings, brown wings (Hell's Angels use)

5. *sodomy:* arse fucking, back jump (US black), brown-eye, browning, going up the arse, – the chute, – the tan track etc. (see Parts of Body: 121), Greek culture, hoop, ring, trip to the moon (gay use)

6. *group sex, orgy:* all in one, bunch punch, daisy-chain, gang-bang, gang-shag, group grope, team cream (gay use), threesome, three-way deal, triangle; spec. sloppy seconds (a girl moving from one partner to the next)

7. *fringe sex:* B&D, English culture (bondage and discipline) bagpiping (intercourse under the armpit), freak fuck, leg work (intercourse between the thighs), S&M (sado-masochism), Swedish culture (rubberwear); tightbuck (gay use: foetal position used for S&M or bondage)

8. *spec.* collegiate fucking, Princeton rub (gay use: body-to-body rubbing); flat-fucking (lesbian use: body rubbing)

9. *masturbation:* J. Arthur (rhy.sl. = wank), five-finger Mary, four sisters on Thumb Street, hand job, hand shandy, J/O scene, jerking the gherkin, Jodrell Bank (rhy.sl.), Lady Five Fingers, mother fist and her five daughters, Mrs Palm and her five daughters, Onan's Olympics, one-legged race, – off the wrist, one stick drum improvisation, pocket pool, slaking the bacon, wank, whizzing the jizzum; *spec.* circle jerk (group masturbation); playing chopsticks (gay use: mutual masturbation)

10. *coprophilia:* scat

v. 11. *to have oral sex:* eat, fress (Yid. = eat), give up one's face, go around the world, – down (on), – down south, gobble, take it any way (gay use)

12. *to fellate:* bite one's crank, blow, blow one's cookies, – one's glass, – the skin flute, cop one's bird, – one's joint, deep throat, eat one's meat, feed one's face, french, gam, give cone, – head, gnaw the 'nana, go down on, gobble, – the goo, kiss, – the worm, lay the lip, plate (rhy.sl. = plate of ham = gam), play hoop-snake with (gay use), smoke, suck off, swing (gay use), tongue lash; *spec.* ride a blind piece (gay use: to fellate an uncircumcised penis); spit out of the window (gay use: to spit out semen); spray the tonsils (ejaculate in the mouth); bag (US black: swallow semen)

13. *to practise cunnilungus:* blow some tunes (US black), brush one's teeth (US black), clean up the kitchen (gay use), dine at the Y, dip in the bush, dive, – in the canyon, drink at the fuzzy cup, eat, – hair pie, – out, face the nation (US black), go way down South in Dixie, gorilla in the washing machine (US black), go under the house (US black), grin in the canyon, have a moustache, scalp (US black), sip at the fuzzy cup (US black), sneeze in the cabbage, – in the canyon, tongue (gay use), yodel, – in the canyon (of love) – up the valley; *spec.* sit on one's face (cunnilingus with the female superior)

14. *to practise anilingus:* eat jam, eat pound cake, go way down South in Dixie, rim (out)

15. *to sodomise:* ask for the ring, ass-fuck, brown, bunghole, burgle, butt-fuck, buy the ring, cornhole, dive into the sky, go up the old dirt road, get some brown, – some brown sugar, – some duke, go Hollywood, hose (gay use), lay the leg, leather (gay use), pack peanut butter, plug, punk, shoot one's star, throw a buttonhole on (US black); *spec.* use the English (wriggle the buttocks during penetration)

16. *to permit sodomy:* duck, flopover, pick up the soap for, pratt for, take it up the arse, – up the butt, – up the (poop-) chute, etc. (see also Parts of Body: 121), take on some backs (US black)

17. *to have group sex, an orgy:* gang bang, gang shag, line up on, make a sandwich, turn out; *spec.* run a double train (for two men to penetrate a woman simultaneously); pull a train (to suffer gang-rape)

18. *to molest:* diddle, touch up

19. *to masturbate (male):* bang the bishop, beat one's little brother,

– one's meat, beat off, – one's dummy, – one's hog, – one's meat, belt one's hog, bring oneself off, burp the worm, butter one's corn, choke the chicken, – the chook (Aus.), clean one's rifle, consult Dr Jerkoff, crank one's shank, dinky one's slinky, do oneself off, do a dry waltz with oneself, feel in one's pocket for one's big hairy rocket, file one's fun-rod, fist fuck, fist one's mister, flex one's sex, flick one's Bic (US black), flip oneself off (Aus.), flog one's mutton, – the dolphin, – the dog, – the log, get one's nuts off, grease one's pipe, hack one's mack, hand-gallop, haul one's own ashes, hump one's hose, jack off, jerk off, Levy (rhy.sl. = Levy and Frank = wank), milk the chicken, pack one's palm, paint one's ceiling, play a flute solo on one's meat whistle, play pocket billiards, – the male organ, – with oneself, please one's pisser, point one's social finger, polish one's sword, pound one's pork, – one's pud, – one's flounder, prompt one's porpoise, prime one's pump, prune the fifth limb, pull one's joint, – one's pud, – one's pudding, – one's taffy, – one's wire, – the pope, rub off, – up, run one's hand up the flagpole, sew (US black), shake hands with the guy who stood up when I got married, shine one's pole, shoot the tadpoles, slam one's hammer, slam one's spam, slap one's wapper, spank the monkey, – the salami, – with the wife's best friend, stir one's stew, strike the pink match, stroke one's beef, – one's poker, – the dog, talk with Rosy Palm and her five little sisters, thump one's pumper, tickle one's pickle, toss off, twang one's wire, tweak one's twinkie, unclog the pipes, varnish one's pole, walk the dog, wank, watch the eyelid movies, wax one's dolphin, whip off, whip one's dripper, – one's wire, whack off, whank, whip it, wonk one's conker, yang one's wang, yank the yam, – one's crank; spec. catch a buzz (to masturbate with a vibrator)
20. *to masturbate (female):* beat the beaver, buttonhole, clap one's clit, cook cucumbers, grease the gash, hide the hot dog, hit the slit, hose one's hole, make waves, pet the poodle, slam the clam, stump-jump
21. spec. fist, fist-fuck (gay use: to insert the fist into the anus)
22. spec. pick up the vibrations (gay use: watch a gay sex-show); take one's meat out of the basket (gay use: to reveal the genitals to another man)
adv. 23. *aberrant:* geared

SOCIAL LIFE

361. Sociability

n. 1. *'good life':* life of Reilly, sporting life
2. *invitation:* stiffy
v. 3. *to lead a social life:* get around, put oneself about; spec. sit eggs (US black: overstay one's welcome)
4. *to visit:* blow by, fall by, knock up, pop in, slide by, stop by
adj. 5. *sociable:* chummy, pally, palsy(-walsy)

362. Social Engagement

n. 1. *meeting:* date, meet, one to meet
2. *a meeting place:* hang-out; spec. cottage (gay use); meat market (student use)
3. *to meet:* bump into
4. *to break a date:* duck out, give one a miss, stand up
5. *to have a date broken:* be shafted, stood up
6. *to stay at home:* bing it (US black)

363. Social Entertainment; Party

n. 1. bash, bean-feast, beano, beer bust, beer-up (Aus.), blast, bunfight, bust, do, gang-shag (US black), get-together, heller, knees-up, racket, rave, ruckus, rug beat (US black), shake, shindig, shindy, thrash, turn (Aus.), wing-ding; spec. hen party (all women); stag party (eve-of-wedding men-only party); be-in (hippie gathering)

v. 2. *to go out:* creep, hit the high spots, night-club; spec. party-hop (to move from party to party); get home with the milk (return after a night's revels)

3. *to have a good time:* cut it up, juke, party, whoop it up

4. *to entertain:* do the honours, throw a party, – a bash, – a beano, etc. (see n. 1)

364. Dancing
n. 1. bopping, boogying, cutting the rug, juking; spec. breaking, hip-hop, hoofing

2. *a dance, ball:* bollock, clutch

v. 3. *to dance:* boogaloo, boogie, cut the rug, juke, shake a leg, shake it, strut one's stuff

---

POSSESSION: ACQUISITION
365. Acquisition; Gains
n. 1. goodies, killing, pickings, rake-off, take

v. 2. *to obtain:* bag, collar, come in for, cop, freeze onto, get one's hooks on, glom, gobble up, land, load up on, mop up, nab, nip, pull down, rope in, rustle up, scare up, snag, sneeze, whistle up; spec. trouser (to pocket)

3. *to take everything:* go the whole hog, sweep the board

4. *to obtain by fraud:* chisel out of, ease out of, promote for, wangle out of, work for (see also Influence: 219)

adv. 5. *gaining:* on a roll

phr. 6. *I want!:* bags I!, dibs on!

366. Possession; Property
n. 1. traps; spec. dead man's shoes

(property of a dead person); OPs (other people's property)

2. *luggage:* bindle, keister

v. 3. *to have plenty:* be cochealed, – lousy with, pack, reek with, roll in, stink of, swim in

adj. 4. *supplied:* cochealed, stinking

adv. 5. *well-supplied:* crummy with, filthy with, loaded, long on, lousy with, rolling in, stinking with, swimming in

6. *lacking:* clean out of, fresh out of

phr. 7. *how much do you have?:* how are you fixed?; spec. are you holding? (do you have drugs)

367. Joint Possession; Sharing
n. 1. piece, rake-off, shake, slice, split; spec. Dutch treat (both parties share payment); even Steven (fair shares); short end, – straw (the lesser share)

v. 2. *to share:* chip in, cut up, divvy (up), go Dutch, – fifty-fifty, – halves, – splits, muck in with, split; spec. deck up (drug use)

3. *to give a share:* cut in, deal in, give a cut, – a piece, etc. (see n. 1), ring in, split with

4. *get one's share:* come in for, cut a piece, – a slice, etc. (see n. 1), get a cut, – a piece, – a slice, etc. (see n. 1); spec. get in the ground floor (get a share at the outset); hog, muscle into (take an extra share)

5. *to share out:* dish out

adv. 6. *sharing:* even Steven, fifty-fifty, going halves, – Dutch

7. *excluded from a share:* out of the game, – the picture, – the running

368. Borrowing and Begging
n. 1. *a request for something:* bite, hit-up, mooch, shakedown, tap, touch

v. 2. *to beg:* bite one's ear, bludge (Aus.), bot (Aus.), brace up, bum off, coat and badge (rhy.sl. = cadge), fang (Aus.), get into one's ribs, grub, make a touch,

mump, ponce off, put the bee on,
– the bite on, – the lug on, – the
touch on, shake down, soak, stick
one for, tap, throw the hooks into,
touch; spec. work a crowd (beg
from an audience)

3. *to extort:* bleed (white), put the
bite on

adv. 4. *begging:* on the bot (Aus.),
– the coat and badge (rhy.sl. =
cadge)

phr. 5. *lend me some money:* let me
hold some change

369. Loss

n. 1. wipe-out; spec. losing streak
(continual losses)

v. 2. *to lose:* drop a packet, – a
bundle, – one's roll, – one's wad,
get the short end (of), kiss goodbye,
kiss off, lose one's shirt

POSSESSION: BESTOWAL

370. Giving

n. 1. *gift:* freebie, handout, pressie,
prezzie

v. 2. *to give:* chip in, come across
(with), come up with, cough (up),
deal out, dish out, dob in (Aus.),
eevige (backsl.), fork out, – over,
hand out, kick in, shell out, sub
(up); spec. give one the pink slip (to
cede something of value); mash it
on one (US black: to give someone
their dues)

3. *to contribute:* chip in, kick the tin
(Aus.), weigh in with

4. *to tip:* cross one's palm, grease;
spec. stiff (fail to tip)

5. *to treat:* blow one to, go for, pick
up the tab, shout; spec. my shout
(my round of drinks)

6. *to be generous:* spread oneself

adj. 7. *generous:* handsome

371. Reward

n. 1. payoff; spec. pie in the sky
(fantasy reward)

2. *deserts:* come-uppance

3. spec. leather medal, wooden
spoon (metaphorical prize for the
poorest loser)

v. 4. *to give one's deserts:* cook
one's goose, give one's come-
uppance

5. *to be rewarded:* bring home the
bacon, pick the plums, take the
cake; spec. get it coming and going
(get double rewards)

372. Bribery

n. 1. dash (Nigeria), fix, grease job,
kickbacks, payoffs

2. *a bribe:* backhander, bung, drink,
hush money, kickback, payoff,
straightener, take

v. 3. *to bribe:* bung, get to,
grease, – one's palm, juice, oil,
palm, patch (Canada), piece off, put
the fix in, schmeer (Yid. = grease),
sling (Aus.), square on off,
stiffen, straighten, take care
of

4. *to accept bribery:* be on the take,
dip one's beak, get one's hands
dirty, take

POSSESSION: ECONOMY

373. Extravagance

n. 1. splurging

v. 2. *to be extravagant:* blow one's
wad, flash one's dough – one's wad,
have a hole in one's pocket, live
high off the hog, ride high wide and
handsome, splash it about, splosh it
on, splurge, throw one's money
away

373. Thrift

n. 1 *something in reserve:* ace in
the hole, card up one's sleeve

v. 2. *to live on the cheap:* take the
bus

3. *to hide away:* keep on ice, put in
cold storage, rat-hole

adj. 4. *mean:* cheap, chinky, Jewy
(derog.), mingy, tight

POSSESSION: ESTATE
375. Wealth
n. 1. barrel of money, pot of dough
2. *funds:* bundle, pile, roll, wad
v. 3. *to be rich:* have money to burn, live high on the hog, ride the gravy train, roll in money
adj. 4. *wealthy:* cashed up, filthy rich, flush, in the money, loaded, made of money, rolling, stinking, stuffy, up in the dough, – in the money, well in, – away, well-fixed, – -heeled, – -lined
adv. 5. *comfortable:* high on the hog, in clover, in good shape, living off the tit, on a good wicket, on Easy Street, on the sunny side (of the street), on velvet, set, sitting pretty

376. Poverty
n. 1. Queer Street
2. *insufficient funds:* ain't long enough, not a bean, – a brass razoo (Aus.)
v. 3. *to be poor:* be down to one's bottom dollar, – in Queer Street, – in a hole, feel the pinch, have the wolf at the door, not have a pot to piss in, – have a prayer, – a red

cent, rough it, scrape the bottom of the barrel, skate on one's uppers, touch bottom
4. *to lose money:* drop; spec. alley-whipped (unpaid for work performed)
adv. 5. *poor:* at the bottom of the barrel, – the end of one's tether, beat, boracic (rhy.sl. boracic lint = skint), bought and sold and done for, broke (to the wide), busted, clean broke, cleaned out, cold in hand (US black), dished, doesn't have a pot to pee in, done for, – up, down on one's luck, flat as a pancake, – broke, hard-up, heart of oak (rhy.sl. = broke), hung for bread, hurting, in a hole, – a tight corner, nigger-rich, on one's beam ends, – one's uppers, – the Rory (rhy.sl. Rory O'Moore = floor = poor), out (of pocket), poor as a church mouse, – as a shithouse rat, pushed (for), raggedy-ass, skint, stony (broke), strapped (for cash), touching bottom, up against it, washed up, wiped out; spec. beggar my neighbour (rhy.sl. visiting the Labour = Unemployment Office)
6. *indebted:* in hock

People

PERSONS: GENERAL
377. People
n. 1. *person:* article, artist, bastard, bim, bimbo, bird, bleeder, blighter, bloke, bozo, cat, civvie, critter, customer, dude, egg, face, fish, fuck (as in 'dumb fuck', etc.), guy, head, jamoke, Joe Blow, joker, Mr Average, momser (Yid.), nosper (backsl.), number, (ordinary) Joe, people, proposition, punter, scout, sort, stiff, ticket, whatshis(her)face, whatshis(her)name; spec. breeders (gay use: non-homosexuals); textiles (nudist use: non-nudists)
2. *self:* yours truly
3. *suffix:* -nik

378. Group; Crowd
n. 1. crew, idrin (WI: brethren), mob, outfit, pack, posse, push (Aus.), team; spec. slag (unpleasant people)
2. *everyone:* all and then some, all hands, – the world and his wife, – the world and his brother, every mother's son, every man Jack, every Tom Dick and Harry, whole kit and caboodle, – shbang, – shooting match, – works
3. *cults, clubs, etc.:* bodgies (Aus.), bopping club, – gang, Brussel sprouts (rhy.sl. = Boy Scouts), greasers, mods, rockers, punks, sharpies (Aus.), skinheads, Sloanes, Valley Girls, widgies (Aus.)

379. Men
n. 1. bloke, bozo, bugger, chap(pie), cock, cove, cuss, customer, dude, geezer, hombre, ice cream freezer (rhy.sl. = geezer), John, joker, meat, moosh, nam (backsl.), old bean, – boy, – chap, – cock, – horse, – top, omee, regular Joe, sport, wallah

380. Women
n. 1. apron, babe, band (US black), biddy, bim, bimbo, bird, bit of fluff, bitch, booty (US black), broad, butter (US black), chick, cock, cono (Sp.), cookie, coot, crack, crotch, cuddle and kiss (rhy.sl. = miss), cunt, dame, dish, doll, dolly (bird), filly, fish, fluff, fox, frail, gash, hairy, haybag, hen, jane, judy, kitty-cat, minge bag, moll, moo, mustang, mystery, nammo (backsl.), nemmo (backsl.), one good woman, oyster, piece, piece of ass, – of tail, polone, potato (Aus. rhy.sl. = potato peeler = sheila), pussy, quail, rag baby (US black), real woman (US black), sheila (Aus.), sister, skirt, slit, snatch, sort, squirrel, tart, totty, trout, tuna, twist, womon, wool; spec. -widow (a woman whose husband is occupied elsewhere)

PERSONS: BY AGE
381. Young Persons
n. 1. spec. youthquake
2. *baby:* ankle-biter, chickabiddy, crumb-crusher, – -snatcher, diddums, lambkin, little man, rug rat
3. *child:* dustbin lid (rhy.sl. = kid), gawdelpus, God forbids (rhy.sl. = kids), goober, kiddiwink, kiddo, nipper, pogue, shaver, short, sprog, sprout, snotnose; spec. moppet

(young girl); bub (young boy); drop (US black: orphan)
4. *young man:* bimbo, geepie, pup(py); spec. Queerbait (pretty young man); toy-boy (young boy pursued by older women)
5. *young woman:* bimbo, bint, bobby-soxer, bopper, bubble-gummer, bud, schoolie, teenybopper, yummy; spec. gaolbait, San Quentin quail (sexy underage girl); schlubette (stupid girl); little madam (self-opinionated)
6. *immature youngster:* candy-butt, cootie, poopbutt (US black), puppy dog, rootiepoot (US black), young blood
7. *virgin:* cherry, puppy, raw sole (US black)

382. Old Persons
n. 1. antique, buster, crumbly, dusty, fossil, geri, grunters, oldie, old coot, – timer, wrinkly
2. *old man:* buffer, codger, deelo nam (backsl.), gramps, joskin, mossyback, old buzzard, – cocker, – geezer, – sweat, pop(s), pot and pan (rhy.sl.); spec. DOM (dirty old man), sugar-daddy (provider for a younger girl), (see also Man: 379)
3. *old woman:* battleaxe, boiler, bunty, delonammon (backsl.), drago, leather, old bag, – biddy, – boiler; (see also Woman: 380)

PERSONS: INHABITANTS
383. Nationality
n. 1. *American:* septic (rhy.sl. = septic tank = yank), uncle, Uncle Sam, yank, yankee-doodle; spec. WASP (white anglo-saxon protestant)
2. *Australian:* Aussie, digger; spec. Alf, Fred, ocker (unsophisticated Australian); Roy (sophisticated Australian)
3. *Canadian:* Canuck

4. *Chinese:* Chink, Chinky, tiddley-wink (rhy.sl.)
5. *Dutchman:* butterbox
6. *Englishman:* John Bull, jumble, kipper (Aus.), limey, pom(my) (Aus.), pongo (NZ); spec. expat (expatriate English)
7. *Frenchman:* frog
8. *German:* boche, Fritz, Heinie, hun, jerry, kraut, Otto, squarehead
9. *Greek:* bubble (rhy.sl. = bubble and squeak)
10. *Hawaiian:* kanaka
11. *Indian (US):* spec. breed (half-breed)
12. *Irish:* bogtrotter, green nigger, harp, Mick, narrowback, Paddy, Patsy, tad; spec. lace-curtain Irish (genteel Irish)
13. *Italian:* dago, eyetie, ghinny, ginney, ginzo, guinea, guinzo, mountain wop, spag, spaghetti bender, wop; spec. moustache Pete (early Italian immigrants to US); paisan (fellow-Italian)
14. *Japanese:* nip
15. *Mexican:* bato, beaner, bean eater, chico, cholo, chuc, dago, greaseball, greaser, pachuco, spic(k), taco bender, – head; spec. wetback (illegal immigrant to US)
16. *New Zealand:* Kiwi
17. *Pakistani:* Paki, Pakki
18. *Philippino:* flip
19. *Russian:* Ivan, Russki; spec. commie, commo (Aus.), pinko, red
20. *Scot:* Jock
21. *South African:* rock spider (Afrikaaner)
22. *Welshman:* Taffy
23. *West Indian:* Bimi
24. *Yugoslav:* Yug
25. *foreigners:* ding (Aus.), reffo (Aus.), snow (Aus. Latins)
26. spec. PIGS (Poles, Italians, Greeks, Slavs: US 'ethnics')

384. Race and Religion
n. 1. *blacks (by whites):* boog, boogie, chocolate, chungo bunny,

coon, dark meat, darkie, dinge, egg and spoon (rhy.sl. = coon), eightball, groid, harvest moon (rhy.sl.), jig, jigaboo, Jim Crow, jungle bunny, Lucozade (rhy.sl. = spade), nigger, nignog, oogie, Rastus, razo (rhy.sl. = razor blade = spade), sambo, schvug (Yid.), schwartze (Yid.), shadow, shine, silvery spoon (rhy.sl.), smoke, smut-butt, soap dodger, spade, spearchucker, spook, stove lid, swartzer (Yid.), wog, zigaboo; spec. touch of the tar brush (black ancestry); pickaninny (black child); Afs, munt (S.Afr. use); boong (Aus. aborigine)

2. *blacks (by blacks):* all-originals, black 360°, bleed, blood, boot, brothers, homeboy, homegirl, member, original, skillet, speck, suede; spec. butterhead (US black: embarassing person); bungo (WI: fool); royal (WI: non-West Indian black)

3. *spec. dark complexioned black (by blacks):* black bird, – dust, inky-dinky, midnight, smokestack, zombie

4. *spec. light complexioned black (by blacks):* bright, buckwheat, casper, grey, lemon, pinkie; spec. high yaller, – yellow, yellow ass, – girl (mulatto)

5. *spec. rebellious black (by blacks):* bad boy, – nigger, bad-ass nigger, cut-throat, field nigger, hardhead; spec. John Henry (tough, hard worker despite odds); firsts (blacks who are first to invade white purlieus)

6. *spec. subservient or bourgeois black (by blacks):* Aunt Jemima, – Jane, Dr (Mr) Thomas, fade, faded boogie, handkerchief head, house nigger, HN (house nigger), oreo, seddity, shuffle, (Uncle) Tom, yard negro

7. *gypsy:* diddicoi, gyppo

8. *Jews (derog.):* abe, Abie

Kabibble, abie, bagel bender, eskimo, fast-talking Charlie (US black), five-to-two (rhy.sl.), four by two (rhy.sl.), front-wheel skid (rhy.sl. = yid), Goldberg (US black), goose, half-past two (rhy.sl.), hebe, hooknose, ikey mo, kangaroo (rhy.sl.), kike, lox jock, moch, mockie, quarter-to-two (rhy.sl.), Red Sea pedestrian (Aus.), saucepan lid (rhy.sl. = yid), sheeny, shonk, shonnicker, slick-'em-plenty (US black), three balls (US black), Yid, yiddle; spec. JAP (Jewish-American princess)

9. spec. Litvak, Polack (immigrant Jews from Lithuania, Poland)

10. *spec. non-Jews (by Jews):* goy, goyim, yoks; flour mixer (rhy.sl. = shikse), shikse (gentile girl)

11. *orientals (derog.):* chopstick, dink, gook, little people, ricer, slant, slit, slope, yellow peril

12. *whites (by blacks):* beast, blanco, chalk, Charlie, devil, fay, fey, gray, hay eater, honk(ie), hunkie, kelt, lily, man with fuzzy balls, Mr Charlie, – Cracker, – Peanut, ofay, paleface, peck, peckerwood, pink, rabbit, whitey, yacoo; spec. gringo (Mexican use); gub, Mr Gub (aborigine use); roundeye (oriental use); pepper and salt (US black: a mix of blacks and whites); superhonkie (ultra-authoritarian, possibly racist white)

13. *white females (by blacks):* bale of straw, Lady Snow, Little Eva, Miss Amy, – Ann, – Lillian, pinktoes, silk, snow, white meat; spec. gringa (Mexican use)

14. *subservient US Indians (by Indians):* apple (red on the outside, white inside), Uncle Tomahawk

385. Inhabitants

n. 1. spec. banana bender (Aus: Queenslander), brummy (inhabitant of Birmingham, UK), crow eaters (Aus: South Australians);

cornpone, cracker (US: poor Southern white), ethno (Aus: any immigrant, usually Italian, Greek, Yugoslav), fly-over people (US: 'middle America'), raddie (UK: Italian living in London), scouse (Liverpudlian), Wooloomooloo yank (Aus. one who attempts to ape US style); yellow-belly (inhabitant of Lincolnshire)

386. Townspeople
n. 1. slicker, townee; *spec.* town (student use; local residents, rather than 'gown' – students)
2. *neighbour:* Texan rude nam (backsl. = next door man)
3. *resident:* old identity (Aus.)
4. *spec.* blockbuster (first white or black family to live on a black or white block)

PERSONS: TYPES
387. Person of Importance
n. 1. big cheese, – chief, – deal, – enchilada, – fish, – gun, – noise, – pot, – stuff, – wheel, – wig, biggie, BMOC (big man on campus), Boss Charlie (US black), celeb, gaffer, guvnor, hammer man (US black), head cook and bottle-washer, headliner, heavyweight, (high) mucky-muck, high-up, high monkey-monk, his nibs, honcho, hook, hot-shot, kingfish, main man, men in suits, mensch (Yid.), Mr Big, pitch and toss (rhy.sl. = the boss), pooh-bah, sachem, shtarka (Yid.), shtarker, the cheese, – gorilla, – man, top cat, – dog, wheel; *spec.* higher-higher (US milit. use: high command); blue-eyed boy, fair-haired boy, white-haired boy (favourite)
2. *conceited person:* doll

388. Insignificant or Petty Person
n. 1. bebopper (US black), bit of fluff, crumb, dud, feeb, frip, half-pint, jobsworth, lightweight, Melvin, no big deal, – great shakes, nobody to write home over, one-eyed scribe (US black), pint-size, pipsqueak, piss-ant, slob, small change, stooge, tick, tinhorn, twerp, zero; *spec.* grunt (USMC use); shower (group of insignificant people)

389. Polished and Sophisticated Person
n. 1. cool cat, hipster, jumping cat (US black), Mr Cool, smart guy, smoothie

390. Unsophisticated Person
n. 1. booboisie, Great Unwashed, Johnny-come-lately, square, working stiff; *spec.* squaredom (world of 'squares')
2. *peasant:* apple-knocker, boonie, carrot cruncher, clod, farmer, hayseed, hick, honyok, hoosier, neck, red, redneck, rube, shitkicker, swede, woollyback
3. *lout:* ape, baboon, bohunk, boob, clunk, dumbo, dummy, geek, goop, honky, hunk(y), jibone, lob, lug, lump, lunkhead, ox, palooka, plug, swab, yahoo
4. *socially inept:* diddy-bop (US black), ditty-bop, flamer

391. Gullible Person; Dupe
n. 1. boob, chump, fall guy, gobshite, lollipop, loogan, mark, meal ticket, mug, pigeon, puppethead, pushover, sap, soft-cop, soft touch, square, steamer (rhy.sl. = steam tug = mug), sucker, Trick Willy (US black), turkey on a string (US black)
phr. 2. there's one born every minute

392. Ill-bred Person
n. 1. grunge, lowlife, sleaze, sleazo, yob(bo)
2. *snobbish abbrevs.:* NB (no

background), NQOCD (not quite our class dear), SQPQ (suspiciously quiet, probably queer)

393. Awkward, Careless Person
n. 1. baggage smasher, butterfingers, mollydooker (Aus.), shithook, spas(tic), stumblebum
2. *uncoordinated:* non (US black)

394. Superior, Admirable Person
n. 1. *admirable:* bottler (Aus.), brick, cool head, curly wolf, good news, killout (US black), natural (born) man/woman (US black), notch (WI), regular guy, straight shooter, through and through (US black); spec. soul child (US black: high in black consciousness)
2. *superior:* big shot, high mucky-muck, Mr Big, toff; spec. OMCD (gay use: out of my class darling)

395. Terms of Disparagement
n. 1. animal, ape, arsehole, ball-buster, basket, beige, butterhead (US black), chippy-chaser, cocksucker, crud, cunt, cunt-lapper, dickhead, dog, dork, dos a reno (backsl. = sod), douchebag, dratsab, (backsl. = bastard), dub, dumb cluck, – fuck, four-letter man, fuckwit, granny-jazzer, horse's arse, J. Arthur (rhy.sl. = wanker), kiss of death, knucklehead, long thin streak of piss, lug, lummocks, mammy-jammer, – -rammer, – -hugger, – -tapper, m.f., mollyfock, momma-hopper, momser (Yid.), mooch, mother, mother-fouler, – -flunker, – -raper, – -fucker, – -grabber, – -hugger, – -jiver, – -jumper, mug, naus, nellie, nerd, out-and-out (US black), peck, pheasant plucker, piss-cutter, poppa-lopper, ponce, poopbutt (US black), pootbutt (US black), prick, pug(gy), putz (Yid.),

rat arse, – bastard, – prick, ratbag, sap, schmo (Yid.), scumsucker, shit, shit on a stick (US black), shit-for-brains, slag, sleeping Jesus, smartiepants, so-and-so, SOB, sod, sonofabitch, sonofagun, stinker, sucker, sumbitch, triple clutcher, turkey, twat, twot; spec. REMF (US milit: rear-echelon mother-fuckers), SOHF (UK 'society': sense of humour failure); (see also: Insignificant Person: 388, Low-bred Person: 392, Contemptible Person: 396, Vexatious Person: 397, Selfish Person: 399, Weakling: 403, Effeminate Person: 404, etc.)
2. *thug:* ass-kicker, goombah, goon, jibone

396. Contemptible Person
n. 1. bad egg, – hat, – lot, – penny, bastard, beat off, Berkeley Hunt (rhy.sl. = cunt), bitch, bitch's bastard, blood claat (WI), bugger, bum, cocksucker, creep, cunt, dipstick, dipshit, droob (Aus.), fart, flake, fuck, fucker, jel, lower than the spots on a snake's ass, – than whale-shit, merchant banker (rhy.sl. = wanker), Mr Do-You-Wrong, motherfucker, mucker, pain in the arse, piece of crap, – of shit, poison, prick, rat, shithead, shitheel, skull-and-crossbones (US black), so low he can look up a snake's asshole and think its the North Star, sod, tick, TL (Yid: tochus-lekker = arse-licker), toe-rag, turd, wanker (see also Insignificant Person: 388, Ill-bred Person: 392, Terms of Disparagement: 395, Vexatious Person: 397, Selfish Person: 399, Weakling: 403, etc.)

397. Annoying Person
n. 1. blister, crasher, gangster, gawdelpus, god-help-us, pain in the arse, – in the neck, PITA, pill, poison; spec. mudcrusher (US

black: bully); jobsworth (petty official)

398. Meddler or Inquisitive Person
n. 1. back-seat driver, buttinski, finick, fleabag (US black), kibitzer, stickybeak (Aus.), stirrer (see also Talker: 422)
2. *obsessive:* neatnik

399. Selfish or Greedy Person
n. 1. *mean:* cheap Charlie, cheapie, cheapskate, clam, crawfish, doggy (US black), Jew (derog.) meanie, meany, penny-pincher, piker, skinflint, Scotchman (derog.), tick, tight as Kelsey's nuts, – as O'Reilly's balls, tightwad
2. *egocentric:* jackanape (US black), jake flake (US black)
3. *greedy:* gannet, glut (glutton), gross-out artist, guts, hog, pig; spec. foodie (gourmet)
4. *obstinate:* cuss, donkey, hardhead, hard nut to crack, mule, 'ornery cuss, pighead, tough customer, – proposition

400. Unselfish, Helpful Person
n. 1. good thing, pussycat, softie, soft touch, stand-up guy
2. *helper:* helping hand, meal ticket, rooter; spec. angel (theatrical backer)
3. *representative:* dep, double, stand-in, sub
4. *go-between:* fixer, front
5. *advisor:* back-seat driver, kibitzer, tipster, woppitzer

401. Vain Person
n. 1. *braggart:* all wind and piss, – mouth and trousers, bigmouth, big note artist (Aus.), bilge artist, blatherskite, blowhard, bullshit artist, ear-basher, fatmouth, man with a paper ass (US black), smart arse, – guy, swellhead, windbag, wise arse, – guy, wisenheimer (see also Talker: 422)

2. *show-off:* bit of a lad, diddy-bop (US black), hot-dogger, Jack the lad, lair (Aus.), teddy bear (Aus. rhy.sl. = lair)
3. *self opinionated:* acts like shit would melt in his/her mouth, hard-on (derog.), thinks his/her ass is icecream and everyone wants a bite, thinks he/she shits lollipops, – he/she is so nice his/her shit don't stink
4. *snob:* Lady Muck, Lord Muck, sadit (US black), stuffed shirt, upways (US black)
5. *flashily dressed:* butterfly (US black)

402. Brave and Reckless Persons
n. 1. chancer, fire-eater, redhot, shtarka (Yid.)
2. *street fighter:* diddley-bop

403. Weakling; Coward
n. 1. baa-lamb, bottler, candy-ass, Caspar Milquetoast, chicken, chickenshit, copout, creampuff, creeping Jesus, CS, div, drip, 4-F, fraidy-cat, funk, funker, girl's blouse, jellyfish, lightweight, limp-dick, Mary Ann, microbe, milksop, milquetoast, mollycoddle, mother's boy, namby-pamby, panty-waist, puss gentleman (US black), pussy, rabbit, scaredy-cat, sheep, snow (Aus.), softy, sook (Aus.), sop, tired people (US black), wanker, waterboy, weak sister, wimp, wimp-guts, yellowbelly
2. *whining person:* creeping Jesus

404. Homosexuals
n. 1. *male homosexuals (derog.):* arse bandit, bananas, battyman (WI), bent, birdie, bitch, boy-ass, brown artist, – family, – hatter, browning family, sisters, bufu, bugger, bum-boy, bunker, burglar, butch, buttercup, buttfucker, chutney ferret, cocksucker, dead-eye dick, dicky-licker, dirt

tamper, Dorothy's friends, dung-puncher, eye doctor, fag, faggot, fagola, fairy, fancy-pants, femme, flit, fooper, four-letter man, fruit, funny man (US black), gay, gender-bender, ginger (rhy.sl. = ginger-beer = queer), grand duchess, haricot (Aus. rhy.sl. = haricot bean = queen) he-she, homo, iron (rhy.sl. = iron hoof = poof), jam duff, jocker, ki-ki, lily, mouser, muzzler, nance, nancy-boy, nellie, nelly, nola, off-colour, omee-polone, one of those, pansy, pillow biter, pixie, poof, poofta, poofter, poove, (powder) puff, quack (US black), queen, queer, shandy (rhy.sl. = chandelier = queer), she-man, shirt-lifter (Aus.), sissy, skippy (US black), so, sweet (US black), swish, tan tracker, that way, three-letter man, tonk, tooti-frooti (US black), turd-burglar, – packer, Turk, waffle, white liver, wind jammer, wolf, yoo-hoo boy; spec. fats and fems (overweight or effeminate gays, barred from many clubs)

2. *female homosexuals (derog.):* Amy-John, charlie, dike, dyke, finger artist (US black), jasper (US black), lady lover, les, lesbo, leso (Aus.), lezzie, lezzo, malflor (Sp.), nelly, pinky, Sappho, thespian; spec. bluff (bisexual lesbian); spec. beard (a man acting, for appearances, as lesbian's husband)

3. *'masculine' lesbian:* bull, bull dagger, bull-dyke, bumper, collar and tie, daddy, dagger, diesel, diesel-dyke, drag-dyke horsewoman, jockey, mantee, pap, top sergeant, truck driver

4. *'feminine' lesbian:* fem, femme, fluff, mama, pinky, puss, ruffle, twist; spec. sil (silly about = a partner in a love affair)

5. *male homosexual types:* auntie, chicken hawk, – queen, dirty dowager, dowager, grand duchess, john, mother, mother ga-ga, Mother Superior, your mother (older men); belle, bronco, butterbox, chicken, cornflakes, daughter, debutante, ga-ga, lamb, pogue, poggler, tender box, tail, twinkie (novice or youngster); husband, pitcher ('masculine' homosexual); bitch, wife ('feminine' homosexual); peek freak, peer queer, watch queen (voyeur); church mouse (one who solicits in churches); angel, cousin, gazooney, gonsil, possesh (older man's young lover), show stopper (particularly attractive boy); body lover (homosexual frotteur), rim queen (one who practises anilingus), top man, bottom man (dominant and passive partners in a sado-masochistic couple), privy queen, tearoom queen (one who solicits in lavatories), body queen (one who prefers body-builders), ill piece (unattractive man); brilliant (ostentatious queen), drag-queen (one who dresses as a woman), kiki (an active or passive homosexual), oncer (promiscuous male, never repeating a partner); uniforms (members of the armed or uniformed services); sea food (sailors); rough trade (genuine or fantasising 'proletarian' sexual partners); size queen (one who prefers large penises); golden shower queen (one who enjoys urolagnia); toe queen (foot fetishist), felch queen (scopophiliac); angel with a dirty face, closet case, – queen (one who dare not reveal his homosexuality); breeders (married homosexuals who father children); kid simple, pee-pee lover (one who prefers very young boys); jam fag (one who is devoted only to sex); sister-act (homosexual couple, or a homosexual man copulating with a heterosexual woman); RFD (Rural Free

Delivery) queen (homosexual living in the country); payoff queen (one who prefers to pay for sex); jam, straight (a non-homosexual male); pretender to the throne (one who poses as homosexual for his own purposes)

405. Gloomy or Irritable Persons
n. 1. *gloomy:* crab, crag, fuddy-duddy, gloom, meanie, misery, misery-guts, party pooper, sad sack, sourpuss, wet blanket
2. *irritable:* carpet-biter, grassfighter (Aus.), grouch, hothead, sorehead

406. Humourist; Amusing Person
n. 1. bundle of laughs, card, caution, cutup, kidder, laugh riot, Mr Laffs, stitch; Carl Comedian (one whose jokes are not appreciated)

407. Stable, Conservative Person
n. 1. dodo, do-right man, eightball, grey, Mom-Dad-Buddy-and-Sis, mossyback, shell-back, square, square John, stick-in-the mud, straight; spec. heterosexual (gay use); spec. dusty bread (US black: conventional girl)
2. *unemotional:* iceberg

408. Unstable, Irresolute Person
n. 1. bug, jellyfish, man-a-hanging (US black), pussyfooter, shilly-shallyier, yoyo

409. Eccentric, Unconventional Person
n. 1. bat, card, cough-drop, crazo, dag (Aus.), dorf, flip-out, fruitcake, galoot, GB, geek, goof, goofball, half-saved, headcase, honker, nut, nutcase, odd stick, oddball, outfit, psycho, rum 'un, – customer, rummy, squirrel, wacko, weirdo, zod
2. spec. hippie, hipidity, mind-tripper

3. spec. little green man (extraterrestrial)

410. Enterprising, Energetic Person
n. 1. ball of fire, comer, eager beaver, fool (for), go-getter, heller, hotshot, Johnny at the rathole, Johnny on the spot, live one, – wire, mover, pisser, player, wheeler-dealer, zip; spec. -oholic (general suffix); buck private (US milit. use: a private who is 'bucking' for promotion)
2. *older (1):* battleaxe, warhorse
3. *hard worker:* grind, stayer, sticker

411. Lively or Passionate Young Woman
n. 1. goer, hot dish, – honey, – number, – one, – stuff, hotsy, piece, – of fluff, pushover, sassy box (US black)

412. Lazy or Unenterprising Person
n. 1 corner cowboy, dag (Aus.), deadbeat, dead duck, – 'un, drag-ass, feather-merchant, fuck-off, goldbrick, jerk-off lard-ass, layabout, lazybones, passenger, piker, poop-butt (US black), skiver, sleeper, slowcoach, sooner (Aus.), weary Willie
2. *dreamer:* wanna be (US black)

413. Successful Person
n. 1. big-timer, comer, hitter, hot-dog(ger), hotshot, it, jumping cat (US black), knockout, Mr Shit, natural, top dog; spec. butter-and-egg man (small-town success)

414. Failure
n. 1. also-ran, back number, blind Freddy (Aus.), bum, deadbeat, dero (Aus.), dud, dudley, duffer, flake, fuck-up, gimp, goner, jerk, nebbish (Yid.), no-hoper, pooch, ring-ding, schlemiel (Yid.),

schlepper (Yid), shmeggegge
(Yid.), trash, washout, yesterday's
papers, Z-bird (see also Terms of
Disparagement: 495, Contemptible
Person: 396, Weakling: 403)

415. Wealthy Person
n. 1. fat cat, green thumb (US
black), lobster (US black), Mr Big,
pound-note geezer, silvertail (Aus.),
silk stocking (US black), tall poppy
(Aus.), zillionaire; spec. nouveau,
nouvy (newly rich)
2. spec. cock (one on whom one can
sponge)

416. Poor Person
n. 1. broker, dosser (see also
Parasite, etc.: 417)

417. Parasite; Dependant; Beggar; Borrower
n. 1. *parasite:* bludger (Aus.),
crasher, freeloader, friend in need
(US black), goldbrick, leech; spec.
doley (Aus. one who draws the
dole)
2. *beggar:* dero (Aus.), glimmer,
mooch, mook, panhandler,
schnorrer (Yid.)
3. *tramp:* bag lady, bindle stiff,
bum, dino, dosser, hurricane lamp
(rhy.sl.), pikey, scat; spec. street
people
4. *lodger:* artful dodger (rhy.sl.)

418. Praiser; Flatterer
n. 1. apple-polisher, ass-kisser,
– licker, bootlicker, brown-noser,
bull artist, bum-sucker,
mealy-mouth, politician, shmooser
(Yid.), suck-up, tom, Uncle Tom
(US black), yes-man; spec. flack
(promo man); log-roller (one who
praises their friends)

419. Critic; Opposer
n. 1. Dutch uncle, knocker, Monday
Morning quarterback, yenta; spec.
crix (show business: critics)

2. *reformer:* bluenose, comstock,
killjoy, longnose, smuthound,
snoop(er), wowser (see also
Meddler: 399)
3. *arguer:* rucker
4. *nag:* ball-buster, – -tearer

420. Talker
n. 1. bag of wind, blowhard, gasbag,
gasser, loudmouth, spruiker (Aus.),
storefront preacher, tub thumper,
tummler (Yid.), windbag; spec.
barrack-room lawyer (self-taught
expert); (see also Vain Person: 401)
2. *gossip:* blabbermouth,
gatemouth, mixer, motormouth,
sack mouth (US black), shit-stirrer,
tattle-tale, whistle-blower; spec.
dish queen (gay use)
3. *user of obscenity:* garbage mouth,
sewer mouth
4. *barker, pitchman:* gee man
(Aus.), spruiker (Aus.)
5. *teller of tales, exaggerator:* bull
artist, bullshit artist, bullshitter,
slickster (US black), smoothie,
wind-up merchant
6. *one who reminds:* elbow shaker
(US black)

421. Listener
n. 1. spec. dummy (deaf mute)

422. Observer; Spectator
n. 1. spec. pinktea (gay use)

423. Eater; Drinker
n. 1. barfly, chow-hound, dustbin,
guts, gutso, sponge
2. *drunk:* one-pot screamer (Aus.)
3. *solo drinker:* Jimmy Woodser
(Aus.)

424. Traveller
n. 1. *'outlaw' motorcyclists:* biker,
easy rider, one percenter, ton-up
boy

PERSONS: PHYSIQUE
425. Attractive
n. 1. *attractive woman, girl:* angel, babe, banana (US black), beat, bit of all right, – crackling, – stuff, brickhouse (US black), butter baby (US black), candy, charmer, cheesecake, chick, classy chassis, cookie, creamie, crumpet, cupcake cutes, cutesie-pie, dish, doll, doll city, dollface, dolly, donah, dreamboat, eyeful, fleshpot (US black), frail, ginch, glamour puss, good-looking, grouse gear (Aus.), hamma, hammer (US black), honey, hot number, jam, (little) cracker, little pretty, looker, lovely, Mercedes (US black), mink (US black), nifty, – piece, page three girl, pancake, patootie, peach, pie, poodle (US black), Porsche, (US black), poundcake, real babe, scorcher, sexpot, sleek lady (US black), stallion (US black), star, sweet potato pie (US black), sweetie, talent, ten, thoroughbred black (US black), tomato, toots, tootsie, – roll (US black), yummy; spec. Barbie Doll (pretty and ultra-conventional); melted butter (US black: light-skinned girl); all tits and teeth (blatantly sexual)
2. *attractive male:* beefcake, buf, glamour-puss, hunk, little pretty, sexpot, smoothie

426. Unattractive
n. 1. face like a douchebag, – like a toilet seat, fright, grub, horror, picklepuss, pretty mess, sight, sourpuss
2. *unattractive woman:* BB head (US black), bad news, bag, bat, bear (US black), buzzard, chicken (US black), chromo, cow, crow, cull bird, dog, dogface, doggie, double-bagger, douchebag, drack (Aus.), grubber, hairbag, hedgehog, heifer, hog, mule, nailhead (US black), pitch, ragmop (US black),

Ruth Buzzy (US black), scab, scuzz, skank, sleaze, snot, sweat hog, tackhead (US black), thunder chicken (US black), welfare mother (US black); spec. PTA (US black: pussy, tits and armpits – all smelly)
3. *unattractive male:* dick

427. According to Size
n. 1. *heavyweight:* bohunk, bozo, bruiser, brute, hunk(o), lug, lump, moose, ox, palooka, wham (US black)
2. *fat person:* barrel, blimp, chubette, dumpling, fat-arse, fatso, fatty, guts, gutso, hully (US black), lard-arse, pig, pudge, tick, tub of lard; spec. Miss Piggy (gay use: a fat homosexual)
3. *fat woman:* Bahama mama (US black), butterball, Judy with the big booty (US black), pig(ger), pigmouth, shuttlebutt, teddy bear (US black)
4. *small person:* crumb, feather merchant, half-pint, – portion, microbe, midget, peewee, pint-size, pipsqueak, sawn-off, shrimp, squirt; spec. lofty (as nickname)
5. *tall person:* beanpole, daddylonglegs, high-pockets, lofty; spec. shorty, tiny (as nickname)
6. *thin person:* bag of bones, broomstick, long (thin) streak of piss, string bean
7. spec. gallon head, pumpkin head (person with a large head)

428. According to Hair, Facial Look, etc.
n. 1. *redhead:* bluey, coppernob
2. *bald person:* skinhead, suedehead
3. *bearded person:* beaver, fuzzface, muff
4. *according to eyes:* boss-eye
5. *similar people:* dead fetch, – ringer, – spit, spitting image
6. *left-handed person:* lefty, southpaw
7. spec. Afro (US black: one

wearing such a hairstyle);
crinkle-top (US black: woman with
an Afro); duck's butt (US black:
woman with messy hair)
8. spec. long-hair (a hippie)
9. with glasses: four-eyes

429. Sick and Injured Persons
n. 1. exhausted person: burn-out,
crasher, crispy
2. cripple: basket case, gimp,
raspberry (rhy.sl. = raspberry
ripple)
3. invalid: cot-case (Aus.), gomer,
gork, vegetable
4. alcoholics: alky, dipso, wino
5. corpse: goner, stiff

PERSONS: MENTAL STATE
430. Intelligent; Experienced
n. 1. bear-leader, brain, egghead,
gallon head (US black), high-brow,
know-it-all, longhair, marv, maven
(Yid.), pointy-head, razor, smart
cookie, smartypants, wise guy,
wisenheimer; spec. old dog (US
black: expert in a given field);
culture-vulture, pseud (fake
intellectual)
2. able person: ace, clever dog,
crack hand, dab, good head, hot
stuff, natural, nobody's fool, no
slouch, (boss) player (US black),
sensation, the cheese, the tops,
up-and-comer, whiz, wizard
3. experienced person: old hand, old
timer, vet
4 predictor: crystal-gazer, dopester,
doper, steerer, tipster
5. scholar: spec. sponge (one who
learns easily)

431. Unintellectual; Stupid
n. 1. addlepate, airhead, ass,
asshole, BF (bloody fool), berk,
Berkeley hunt, Berkshire hunt,
birdbrain, blockhead, bonehead,
boob, boofhead, bozo, brenda,
bubblehead, bugs, busher,

cement-head, chowder-head,
chucklehead, clod, clodpoll, clown,
cluck, clunk, coot, crackpot,
crapbrain, deadhead, dickhead,
dildo, dill (Aus.), dingaling,
dingbat, diphead, dipshit, dodo,
dope, dork, dorkbrain, drongo
(Aus.), Dublin University graduate,
dum-dum, dumb-ass, dumb-bell,
dumbellina, dumb fuck, dumbhead,
dumbo, dummy, dumbski,
dunderhead, fathead, flipwreck
(Aus.), FNG (fucking new guy),
fruitcake, fuckhead, fuckwit, galah
(Aus.), get, gig (Aus.), gink, git,
goober, goof, gook, goop, greener,
greenhorn, hammerhead (US
black), head-banger, herbert,
horse's arse, – hangdown, ig man
(US black), ignant (US black),
Irving, klutz, kook, lame,
lamebrain, log, loogan, loon(y),
lug, lunchbox, lunk, lunkhead,
meathead, mental job, mo-mo,
momo, mug, mule, musclehead,
mutt, nana, ning-nong (Aus.), nit,
nitwit, nong (Aus.), no-no, noodle,
numbnuts, numbskull, nutcake,
nutter, pinhead, poon (Aus.), poop,
poophead, prat, prawnhead (Aus.),
pud, puddinghead, quashie (WI),
ring-ding, rookie, room to rent,
rube, schlemiel (Yid.), schlub
(Yid.), schmeggege (Yid.), schmuck
(Yid.), schnook (Yid.), screwball,
section eight, semolia (US black),
shitkicker, sickie, silly, silly-billy,
simp, spaz, squarebrain (US black),
stumer, stupe, stupe-head, stupid
fuck, thickie, thicko, three-dollar
bill, tool, toolhead, twit, veg,
wet foot, wethead (US black),
whacko, whizpop, wienie, wise,
zipalid; spec. schoolbook chump
(US black: one who is intellectual
but not intelligent); spec.
square-eyes (one who watches too
much TV)
phr. 2. one who looks like he
wouldn't piss if his pants were on

fire; (to a dullard) one of these days you'll wake up dead

PERSONS: MORAL STATUS

432. Good; Respectable

n. 1. baa-lamb, good time, real McCoy, regular guy, right guy, square John, – shooter, straight arrow, stand-up guy, white man
2. *'good girl':* quandong (Aus.)

433. Disreputable

n. 1 alley cat, – rat, bad egg, – hat, – penny, baddie, bar steward, bugger, cloth-ears, face-ache, freak, fucker, hard, – case, heel, hood, lare (Aus.), lowlife, naus, oik, raas, raasclat, shitbird, shithead, shitheel, shit-for-brains, shtarka (Yid.), SOB, son of a bitch, sweep, wedgeass, wrong 'un, yob(bo)
2. *foulmouthed:* salty dog, trashmouth
3. *thug:* bruiser, bucko, goon, gorilla, hard case, hard egg, hatchet man, heavy, hood, husky, lowlife, muscle, plug-ugly, punch-out artists, SAN (stop-at-nothing) man, torpedo, tough guy, – nut, ugly customer; spec. goon squad (group of hired thugs)
4. *bodyguard:* heavy, minder, muscle
5. *rebel:* cowboy (US black)
6. *fugitive:* lamster, over the hill, runout man, skip(per); spec. draftnik (draft evader)
7. *freak:* geek
8. *assassin:* hitman

434. Dishonest

n. 1. chiseller, cowboy, gyp, hydraulic (Aus.), rip-off artist, rooker, shark, shicer, shyster, spiv, tealeaf (rhy.sl. = thief)

435. Deceitful; Untrustworthy

n. 1. actor, bad actor, Carl Rosa (rhy.sl. = poser), cross man, dreykop (Yid.) false face (US black), fly-by-night, four-flusher, grifter, high and goodbye (US black), merry-go-round (US black), PhD (piles it higher and deeper), real greek, sharpie, sly slick and wicked (US black), slyboots, snake, Spanish athlete (he 'throws the bull'), Turk McGurk, two-timer, welcher, wide boy, wrong guy, wrong 'un
2. *liar:* holy friar (rhy.sl.), one-eyed scribe (US black), Tom Pepper
3. *informer:* blab, blabbermouth, peach, snitch, squawker, squealer, stoolie (see also Crime: 481)
phr. 4. his guts are moving the wrong way, does a lot of shitting but his pants aren't down, doesn't know whether to suck or blow, – to shit or go blind, you need an ear scoop to filter his horseshit; don't pick up soap in his shower, he'd steal a rotten doughnut out of a bucket of snot, he'd fuck a snake if somebody would hold its head; you can't trust him further than you can throw a bull by the prick, – than you can see up an alligator's ass (in a dust-storm) (at midnight)

436. Sexual Choice

n. 1. *fellator:* barbecue (US black), face-artist, fluter, French active, – passive, Frenchman, icing expert, mouth worker; spec. glutton for punishment (one who continues to fellate after orgasm)
2. *one who performs cunnilingus:* cannibal, cuntlapper, fish queen, gash-eater, high diver, meat-eater, muff diver
3. spec. sandwich man (one male plus two females)
4. spec. butt-plunger (man who enjoys inserting a dildo into his own anus)
5. *child molester:* monster, nonce, perv, secko (Aus.)
6. *exhibitionist:* flasher

7. *trans-sexual, transvestite:* TS, TV
8. *bisexual:* double-life man, switch hitter
9. *masturbator:* jack-off, jerk-off, rod walloper, wanker
10. spec. cradle-snatcher (one who prefers much younger partners)
11. *celibate:* priest
12. *voyeur:* looker, peeper
13. spec. mystery mad (one who prefers stray young girls)

437. Promiscuous

n. 1. swinger
2. *promiscuous male:* alligator (US black), cock-hound, cocksman, come-freak, cum-freak, rooster (US black), saloon-bar cowboy, stud, swordsman
3. *promiscuous female:* baggage, bike, bimbo, broad, bum, carpenter's dream, charity girl, chippie, cooze, dead cert, dirty leg, easy lay, – ride, floosie, floozie, free for all, gash, gin-and-fuck-it, goer, knock, lay, leg, Little Miss Roundheels, lust dog, motorcycle (US black), mount, nymph(o), paraffin lamp (rhy.sl. = tramp), piece, piece of ass, – tail, pig, punch, pushover, quickie, quiff, right sort, screamer and a creamer, scrubber, shack job, shack-up, shagbag, slag, sleepy-time girl, steamer, stinker, tart, town bicycle, – pump, – punch, whore; spec. groupie, band rat; snow bunny (girls who specialise in rock groups, skiers); buttered bun (girl having sex with several men in succession); splash (the victim of gang-rape)
4. *promiscuous male homosexual:* fantail, glutton
5. *promiscuous lesbian:* clithopper
phr. 6. no better than he/she should be, one who's had more arse than a toilet seat, – more pricks than a second-hand dart-board

PERSONS: SOCIAL POSITIONS

438. Friends

n. 1. abc, ace, – boom boom, – boon coon, – coon poon, asshole buddy, blood (US black), bro (US black), brother, buddy, butty, china (rhy.sl. = china plate = mate), chum(my), cobber (Aus.), cutty, Dutch (rhy.sl. = Dutch plate = mate), family, good ole boy, home squeeze (US black), homeboy, homegirl (US black), landsman, main man, mate, mellow (US black), Mister Ed, mucker, off the block, pal, pard, PLU (people like us), road dog, running partner (US black), splib, splib-de-wib (US black), (main) squeeze, oppo, yardie (WI); spec. smiling faces (US black: false friends); sight for sore eyes (a friend in need)
2. *allies:* spec. cognoscenti, sisters (gay use); friendlies (military); crew (a gang); blue-eyed soul brother, paleface nigger (US black: white who is accepted by blacks); coon-lover, nigger-lover (derog.: a white who rejects racism)
3. *fan:* rooter

439. Hanger-on

n. 1. ligger
2. *fan:* celebrity fucker, grouper, groupie, star fucker
3. *spec. gay use:* fruit fly, fag hag, half-iron, scag hag
4. spec. walker (rich woman's male social companion)
5. *toady:* apple polisher, arse-kisser, – -licker, brown-noser, – -tongue, creep, suck-arse, yes-man

440. Stranger; Enemy

n. 1. *novice:* Johnny-come-lately, new fish, tenderfoot
2. *alien:* beastie, ding (Aus.), Queen's Park Ranger (rhy.sl. = stranger)

441. Lovers
n. 1. crush, dreamboat, flame, heart-throb, honeybunch, pash, sweetie, sweetie-pie
2. *male lover, boyfriend:* daddy one (US black), Lord Right, Mr Right, old man, sweet daddy
3. *female lover, girlfriend, mistress:* chick, dolly, frail, honey, jam tart (rhy.sl. = sweetheart), Lady Right, Miss Right, main bitch (US black), mat (US black), monotony, mum, old lady, ordinary (US black), Renee, Richard (the Third) (rhy.sl. = bird), steady, sweet patootie, sweetpea, toots, tootsie; spec. Mayfair Merc(enary) (using sex to succeed socially)
4. *adulterous lover:* back-door man, bit on the side, fancy man
5. *couple:* item, shack job
6. *'great lover':* fast worker, heaver (US black), makeout artist, stallion, stickman, stud, wolf; spec. 4-F club ('find 'em feel 'em, fuck 'em and forget 'em)
7. *former lover:* ex
8. *new lover:* fresh hide (US black)
9. *inter-racial lovers:* coal burner, gin-jockey (Aus.); spec. dinge queen (gay use); gin shepherd (man who attempts to keep races apart)
10. *physical preference:* arse man, chubby-chaser, leg man, tit man
11. *casual partner:* it, one-night stand, pick-up, trick
12. *flirt, teaser:* cunt-teaser (male), cock-teaser, prick-teaser (female)

442. Sentimentalist
n. 1. sopcan; spec. moon-ass, puppy (infatuated person)

443. Flirt; Philanderer
n. 1. *flirtatious woman:* cock-teaser, dick-teaser, gold-digger, man-eater, prick-teaser, vamp
2. *male philanderer:* chippy chaser, Jody (US black), hard-leg (US black), lady-killer, letch, masher,

plumber, sharp-shooter, skirt-chaser, slugger, sport, steed, swordsman, tomcat, wolf
3. spec. MTF (must touch flesh), NSIT (not suitable in taxis) (UK 'society' use)

444. Relatives
n. 1. *family:* Mom-Dad-Buddy-and-Sis
2. *father:* my old guvnor, old boy, – fellow, – man, pop(s), sorry and sad (rhy.sl. = dad)
3. *mother:* ma, mam, mum(s), mumsie, old lady
4. *husband:* hubbie; spec. weekend man (US black: one who sees his family only at weekends)
5. *wife:* ball and chain, better half, carving knife (rhy.sl.), Dutch, Duchess of Fife (rhy.sl.), her indoors, old Dutch (rhy.sl.), – lady, trouble and strife (rhy.sl.)
6. *sister:* skin and blister (rhy.sl.)
7. *illegitimate child:* bachelor's baby
8. *grandparents:* gramps, nan(a)
9. *widow:* sod widow (as opposed to 'grass widow', whose husband is only absent)

445. Single Person
n. 1. loner, lone wolf, stag
2. *unattached girl:* bit of spare
3. spec. fishing fleet (girls who look abroad for husbands)

446. Sociable
n. 1. cookie-pusher, drugstore cowboy, lounge lizard, raver, stage-door johnny, wildcat (US black)
2. *uninvited guest:* crasher

447. Hedonist; Pleasure-seeker
n. 1. cutup, funster, good-time Charlie, hell-raiser, Mr Laffs; spec. nightstick (US black: one who enjoys night-life)
2. *tourist:* boing-boing, rubberneck

448. High Society; Elite
n. 1. blue-blood, carriage trade, high-hat, nob, swell, toff
2. *spec.* glitterati (fashionable academe); preppie (student at a US prep – UK public – school); Wellies (upperclass members of Exeter University, UK); hooray, Hooray Henry (boorish upperclass UK youth)
phr. 3. *an excess of leaders:* all chiefs and no indians

449. Masses; Rabble; Proles
n. 1. Joe Public, John Q. Public, the Great Unwashed

450. Fashionable; Chic
n. 1. clotheshorse, fancy pants, Mr Firstnighter, shoe, slicker, supersoul (US black), swing daddy (US black); *spec.* zubber (one dressed in top hat, tails, etc.)
2. *spec.* made (US black: one who has their hair straightened)
3. *spec.* glitterati (fashionable academe), preppie (member of US prep – UK public – schools), Sloane Ranger (British upperclass female), yuppie (young upwardly mobile professional)

451. Unfashionable
n. 1. boojie, boogie, cull, fish 'n' chip mob, gape (US black), geek, goose, greaser, grockle, ham and egger, jello squad, MCM (middle class monster), Nashville (US black), nerd, nerk, puck, rag head (US black), Santa Claus (US black), slummy, wally, zonko; *spec.* nubian (US campus: black students)
2. *badly dressed:* caution sign (US black)

452. Unsociable
n. 1. homeboy, homegirl, stay-at-home
2. *social failure:* clunk, creep, drag, drip, dumbell, dumbo, dummy, feeb, iceberg, lemon, pain in the arse, – in the behind, – in the neck, pill, schmo, schnook, stick-in-the-mud, stiff, washout, wet blanket; *spec.* tired woman (US black: unsophisticated)

WORKERS
453. Worker
n. 1. jockey, wage-slave, working stiff
2. *assistant:* dogsbody, gofer, gopher, off-sider (Aus.), tickler; *spec.* candy-striper (US hospitals: voluntary workers); *spec.* head cook and bottle washer (general factotum)
3. *hard worker (at school, college):* cereb, conch, egg, gome, grub, hack, pencil geek, schoolbook chump (US black), spider, squid, swot, throat, tool, wonk
4. *hard worker:* eager beaver, grafter, workoholic
5. *strike-breaker:* blackleg, fink, goon, – squad, scab
6. *privileged worker:* IDB (abbrev. in Daddy's business)

454. Unskilled Worker
n. 1. *beginner, novice:* butterboy, greener, greenhorn, new fish, rookie, wet foot; *spec.* boot, yardbird (US military: recruit); prospect (recruit to an 'outlaw' bike club); fresher (freshman at university, college)
2. *spec.* pearl diver (washer-up)
3. *labourer:* ape, humper, roughneck, roustabout; *spec.* shovel stiff (one who digs); McAlpine fusilier (worker for a construction firm); lump (freelance unskilled workers, esp. in construction industry)

455. Domestic; Servant
n. 1. biddy, daily, flunky, keep-up (US black), shikse (Yid.)

456. Specialist

n. 1. *military:* boonie rat, dogface, doggie, doughboy, eleven-bravo, GI, grunt, swaddy, tommy (soldier); gyrene, leatherneck (US Marine), swab jockey (sailor), point (head of patrol), drag (last man), slackman (2nd man in patrol), Band-aid (corpsman); black gang (naval engine room crew); padre (chaplain); flyboy (pilot); deck ape (deck hand); grape (deck hand on carriers); early out (serviceman due for retirement); gunny (US: gunnery sergeant); bird dog (air spotter); lifer (career soldier), looie (lieutenant)

2. *medical:* croaker, medico, quack (doctor), butcher, sawbones (a poor surgeon), gynae (gynaecologist), headshrinker, looney doctor, nut doctor, shrink, trick cyclist (psycho-analyst); cock doctor (venerealogist)

3. *media:* sob sister, agony aunt (advice columnists), hack, journo, pencil pusher, scribe (writer), stringer (local correspondent); newsie (paper-seller)

4. *law:* ambulance chaser, brief, legal eagle, loudmouth, mouthpiece (lawyer), silk (Queen's Counsel); Barnaby Rudge, smear and smudge (rhy.sl. = judge); garden gate (rhy.sl. = magistrate); dick, gumshoe, shamus (private detective); repo man, skip tracer (debt collector)

5. *entertainment:* bouncer, chucker-out, wollyhumper (steward); hoofer (dancer); red (Butlins redcoat); carney (carnival worker); DJ, jock (disc jockey); muso (musician); combo (group of musicians); roadie (rock music road manager); lenser, megger (film director); gabriel (trumpeter); canary (singer)

6. *bureaucracy:* flak catcher (complaints officer), paper pusher, pencil pusher, red-taper (lowest form of civil servant); spec. sniffer (DHSS investigator)

7. *social:* walker (rich woman's companion)

8. *craftsman:* chippie (carpenter); sparks (electrician); mush faker (umbrella repairer); brickie (bricklayer); retchub (backsl. = butcher)

9. *political:* politico, flesh-presser, palm-presser; spec. lefty, parlour pink, pinko, Trot (left-wingers); lame duck (US politican who has lost office but still serves out time); libber (feminist activist)

10. *education:* chalkie (Aus.), schoolie (teacher); lollipop man/lady (road safety supervisor)

11. *travel:* hostie, stew (air hostess); clippie (bus conductress)

12. *scientists:* back-room boys, boffins

13. *taxis:* hack(er), hackie, mushie, musher (drivers); brown coat, white coat (inspectors at London Cab Office)

14. *cleaner:* garbo (Aus.), honey-dipper, sanno (Aus.); Mary Ellen (dockyard, boat cleaners)

15. *docker:* wharfie (Aus.), yardbird

16. *business, commerce:* drummer (salesman); uncle (pawnbroker); hired gun (expert); Collins Street farmer, Pitt Street farmer (Aus.: absentee rural landlords)

17. *chemist:* druggie

18. *sportsman:* jock; slugger (boxer), tanker (boxer who deliberately loses); jock (jockey)

19. *petrol station:* pump jockey

20. *farming:* cowpoke (cowboy)

21. *oil rigs:* roughneck, roustabout (labourer)

22. *services:* milko (Aus. = milkman); saw (US black: rooming house owner)

23. *spy:* spook

24. *general specialist:* artist, merchant, pro

25. *cook:* babbling brook (rhy.sl.)

457. Superintendent; Manager
n. 1. boss, bossman, Edmundo
(rhy.sl. = Edmundo Ros = boss),
gaffer, guv, guvnor, master-dog (US
black), pitch and toss (rhy.sl. =
boss), skip(per), top dog

2. *military:* brass hats, white
hats (officers); full bird (full
colonel); topkick (first sergeant);
Shake and Bake (graduate of US
NCO school); mustang (officer
promoted from the ranks); first skirt
(senior officer in WAC); -pipper
(lieutenant)

Specialist Jargons

CRIME: PERSONS
458. Persons
n. 1. *criminal:* babbler (Aus.), babbling brook (rhy.sl. = crook), bandit, body, buck, face, hardhead (Aus.), merchant, perp; spec. good people (former criminals); mooner (US: 'moonstruck' – a pathological lawbreaker); operator, the Man (major criminal); rounder (Can. sophisticated criminal); Ten (FBI's Ten Most Wanted Criminals list) (see also Persons, Disreputable: 435, Dishonest: 436, Deceitful: 437)
2. *gang:* crew, firm, mob, push (Aus.), team; spec. the Mob, the wise guys (US Mafiosi); made man (US: member of Mafia); coolie (street gang use: an unaffiliated youth); deb (street gang member's girlfriend)
3. *small-time criminal:* cruncher (Aus.), heel, international milk thief, meter thief, parking meter bandit, pie-eater (Aus.), tearaway; spec. soldier, button man (US: lower echelon Mafioso)
4. *young or novice criminal:* JD (juvenile delinquent), schoolboy, virgin; spec. MINS (US jail use: Minors in Need of Supervision); CHINS (Children In Need of Supervision); gunsel, gonsil (criminal's young – poss. homosexual – accomplice)
5. *violent criminal:* dropper, hatchet man, hit man, stick-up artist, trigger man
6. *sex criminal:* spec. player (pimp); junior jumper (US: underage rapist); diddler, monster, short eyes, shut eyes (child molester)
7. *thief:* blagger, jump-up merchant, – man, second-storey man; spec. in-and-out man (spontaneous thief)
8. *swindler, con-man:* alias man (WI), ginnal (WI), illywhacker (Aus.), ringer, samfie (WI); spec. bait (attractive girl used to lure victims); hedge (the crowd that gathers around a street con-man); ringer (one who steals, improves, then sells cars)
9. *arsonist:* firebug; spec. blanket man (arsonist's assistant)
10. *receiver:* buyer, fence; spec. placer (middleman between thief and receiver)
11. *planner:* set-up man
12. *go-between:* bag man, bird dog
13. *look-out:* earwig
14. *pickpocket:* dip, hoister, knockabout man (Aus.), legshake artist (Aus.), whiz, wire
15. *shoplifter:* booster, hoister, (US black), blockerm, stickman
16. *gambler:* KG (known gambler); spec. digits dealer (numbers racketeer); operator (controller of gambling game); subway dealer (US: card sharp)
17. spec. *seducer* (US black: one who provides means of making illicit cash)
18. *court personnel:* spec. beak (judge, magistrate); interrupter (interpreter); penitentiary agent (inadequate defence lawyer)
19. *legitimate person:* pop corn
adj. 20. spec. -handed (number: three-handed, four-handed, team-handed, etc.)

CRIME: PHYSICAL
459. Health
n. 1. spec. crush-out (the obliteration of a corpse by crushing it in a junkyard metal crusher)
adv. 2. *dead:* DOA (dead on arrival), slabbed and slid, tits up

---

CRIME: PLACES
460. Locality
n. 1. *police station:* bill shop, cop shop, factory, pig heaven, – sty
2. *police divisions:* ground, manor, patch, toby
3. *storage enclosure:* flop, slaughter; spec. Aladdin's cave (UK: a thief's home or the hideaway for his loot)

461. Establishments; Resorts
n. 1. spec. clip joint, gyp joint (swindling night-clubs)

CRIME: PROPERTY; BOOTY
462. Money
n. 1 (see Commerce: 516); spec. California roll (US), flash (UK), (large roll of low-denomination notes, wrapped in a high-value note to give illusion of wealth)
2. spec. case dough (limited funds); drops (money hidden away); earner (high-paying criminal enterprises; bribe); fall money (funds set aside for legal fees); indoor money (daily expenses)
v. 3. *to profit from crimes:* earn, score

463. Valuables
n. 1. red (gold), tom (rhy.sl. = tomfoolery = jewellery); spec. groin, groyne (UK: any ring)
2. *fake jewellery:* fool's gold, patacca; spec. mug's ticker (dud watch)
3. *safe:* can, crib, damper, peter

464. Booty; Illicit Goods
n. 1. goods, good stuff, hot stuff, swag; spec. drop (delivery of booty, money, etc.); five-finger discount (proceeds of shoplifting); LF gear (UK: proceeds of 'long firm' fraud); overs (booty yet to be disposed of); carve-up, cut, taste (a share)
v. 2. spec. mash it on (one) (US black: pass on contraband)
3. *to share out:* cut up touches

CRIME: IMPLEMENTS
465. Implements; Devices
n. 1. spec. autograph (blank paper used to obtain victim's signature); billy, Mr Wood, rosewood, shit-stick (billy-club, truncheon); stonicky, swailer (cosh); car key (screwdriver used to break into cars), can opener (safe-breaking tool); combo (combination lock); bracelets, cuffs, darbies (handcuffs); come-along (manacle); flash case (US black: case holding drugs, contraband); happy bag (case carrying a shotgun); HBI (house-breaking implements); jemmy, jimmy, tool (crowbar); jigglers (skeleton keys); keister, peter (bag of tools); jumper (jump-lead); loid, Lloyd (celluloid lock-pick); monkey (padlock)

466. Weapons; Explosives
n. 1. *gun:* equaliser, Roscoe; spec. crowd pleaser (US policeman's weapon); sawed off, sawn-off (sawn-off shotgun); Chicago piano, – typewriter (machine-gun)
2. *knife:* shank; spec. shin (US jail use)
3. *explosives:* dinah (nitroglycerine); jelly (gelignite)
v. 4. *to be armed:* carry, hold
adv. 5. *armed:* CCW (US: carrying a concealed weapon), carrying, holding, rodded
6. *unarmed:* clean

CRIME: FOOD; LIQUOR, ETC.

467. Food
n. 1. spec. CNR strawberries (Canadian prison-issue prunes)

469. Tobacco
n. 1. burn, snout; spec. tailormade (factory-produced cigarette)

CRIME: COMMUNICATION

469. Communication; Correspondence
n. 1. spec. batphone (UK: police radio); dep (UK: deposition); squawk (UK: petition to authorities); stiff (UK: illicit jail communication)

470. Speech
n. 1. spec. toast (US jail: long epic poem)
v. 2. spec. cut up touches (reminisce over crimes, etc.)
adv. 3. *agreed verbally:* on a promise
phr. 4. spec. on the earie! (be quiet! someone is listening); Edna! (UK: rhy.sl. = Edna May = on your way!)

471. Signals; Symbols
n. 1. spec. show out (UK: signal between policeman and an informer who meet in public)

472. Information
n. 1. bubble (rhy.sl. = bubble and squeak = speak), dope, scream, squeal, the score, tickle, tip; spec. hooking (attempting to smear the police through false information); crude (US: informer's rather than public's tip-off)
2. *informer:* backmark (US black), canary, car park (rhy.sl. = nark), cheese-eater, dog (Aus.), dog's nose, finger, fizgig (Aus.), guinea pig, grass (rhy.sl. = grasshopper = shopper), mule mouth, nark, noah's ark (rhy.sl. = nark), nose, pig

brother (US black), rat, singer, slim, snitch, snout, stool-pigeon, stoolie, Tom Slick (US black), tout (IRA use); spec. narc (narcotics informer); supergrass (major informer)
v. 3. *to inform:* blow one's nose, cop out (on), copper, cough, give the man the play (US black), grass, holler cropper, put the bubble in, QE (turn Queen's Evidence), scream, spill, – the beans; blow through (phone in information); put it around (circulate rumours); turn one around (to persuade a criminal to turn informer)
adj. 4. *untrustworthy:* copper-hearted

473. Betrayal; Accusation
n. 1. spec. fix, frame-up (concoction of evidence)
2. *informer:* budgie, snitcher, squealer; spec. faded boogie, pig brother (US black: black informer to white authorities)
v. 3. *to betray:* blab, blow the gaff, – the whistle on, drop a dime on, – a quarter on, – a dollar (US black: cash sums vary as to degree of betrayal, all refer to using the telephone), finger, grass, give a body, go bent, lolly, pin on, put a body up, – a name up, – away, – in the acid, – one in (Aus.), – the nigger on, – the whisper on, rat on, rat one out, shop, snitch, squeal, tip in, tom out (US black), top off (Aus.); spec. narc one over (betray to the drug squad)
4. *to concoct evidence:* frame, frame up, fit up, fix (up)
adv. 5. *betrayed:* bubbled, grassed up, etc. (see also Information: 472), lollied (rhy.sl. = lollypopped = shopped)

CRIME: OBSERVATION

474. Guarding
n. 1. *guard, lookout:* dogger out (US), six-man (Can.)

adv. 2. *on guard:* on the earie

CRIME: TRAVEL
475. Transportation Methods
n. 1. *driver:* wheelman; spec. skid artist, stoppo driver (UK: getaway driver)

2. *police car:* black and white, blue and white, blue dangers, hurry-up, salt and pepper; spec. nondescript, Q-boat (UK: unmarked police cars); noddy (UK: police motorcycle)

3. *'Black Maria':* cattle car, go-long, hurry-up wagon, meat wagon, paddy wagon

CRIME: TRAMPING
476. Vagrancy
n. 1. *vagrant:* wag; spec. vag (vagrancy charge)

477. Begging
adv. 1. on the bow, on the earhole

CRIME: CRIME AND PUNISHMENT
478. Crime
n. 1. caper, job; spec. across the pavement (UK: any street crime); back-alley deal (US black); rackets (underworld); the Life (US black: the underworld); MO (modus operandi: a given criminal's 'trademarks'); ways (US: ethos and style of the Mafia); aka (false name)
v. 2. *to commit crime:* do a job, get one's feet muddy, make one, perform, pull a caper, – a job; spec. put one together (plan a crime); chip (US: carry out petty crimes); have an in (have useful contacts); make one's rep (to establish one's criminal status); row in (to enrol in a criminal plan)
3. *to give up crime:* go straight
adj. 4. *criminal:* naughty

adv. 5. *involved in crime:* at it

479. Theft
n. 1. heist, hist, screwer; spec. B&E (breaking and entering); high-wall job, second-storey job (theft involving climbing); sneak job (house-breaking); sticksing (WI: pickpocketing); boosting, hoisting (US: shoplifting); snow-dropping (stealing from washing lines); creaming, the weed (stealing from one's employer's tills); Black Power dance (looting); cartnapping (stealing supermarket trolleys); matchbox (anywhere easily robbed)
2. *thief:* gazlon (Yid.), gonef, gonnif, macer, tealeaf (rhy.sl.); spec. nighthawk (specialist in night work)
3. *specialists:* bumper, cannon, fork, hooker, nudger, stall, pick (pickpockets); moll buzzer (pickpocket who prefers female victims); jack roller, lush worker, roller (one who robs drunks); breaker, crib-man, screwsman, second-storey man (house-breaker); pete-man, peterman (safe-breaker); booster, lugger, skin worker (shoplifter); creep(er) (sneak thief); git-'em-up-guy (hold-up man); reader, slow walker (US: one who follows postmen to rob them); dunnigan worker (one who robs in public lavatories); shitter (one who excretes where he has stolen)
v. 4. *to rob:* blag, clout, fleece, half-inch (rhy.sl. = pinch), kipe, knock off, – over, liberate, pinch, skank (WI), skulk, swipe; spec. dance (from upper floors); do a crib, jack in the box (to house-break); boost, hoist (to shoplift); drag, gleep a cage (US), make a car (US) (to steal from cars); work the hole, – the well (to pickpocket on public transport); drop sticks (WI), fan (to pickpocket); kiss the dog (to

pickpocket face-to-face); case (the joint) (to appraise a location prior to a robbery)

adj. 5. *larcenous:* sticky-fingered

adv. 6. spec. at the wash (stealing from public lavatories); creeping and tilling (US black: robbing from shop tills); on the bottle, on the whiz, at the push-up (working as a pickpocket); swagging (US prison: stealing prison property)

phr. 7. spec. it fell off the back of a lorry, they give them away with a pound of tea

480. Swindling

n. 1. bunco, con, flim-flam, FP (false pretences), high game, grift; spec. big con (large-scale confidence tricks); short con, – stuff (small-scale confidence tricks); slow con (slowly matured trick); fonfen (Yid. the 'line' used by a con-man); hit-and-get (moving quickly from town to town); pitch (site of a three-card monte game); bucket gaff, – job (fraudulent company); market (bait that lures the victim); donah ('the lady' in a three-card monte game)

2. *confidence tricks:* double-dooring (hotel fraud); drop game (using planted wallets); drumming (posing as a 'salesman'); the Hype, the Bill, twenties (confusing shopkeepers over change); LF, long firm (credit fraud); murphy (game) (beating and robbing of a prostitute's client); smack (coin-tossing fraud); tat (tricks using dice); tweedling (selling allegedly 'stolen' goods)

3. *confidence trickster:* bunco artist, con artist, grifter, megsman; spec. amster (Aus. rhy.sl. = Amsterdam = ram); bunco-steerer, buttoner, inside man, ram (Aus.) (con-man's confederate); broadsman (card-sharp); thrower, slide (members of a three-card monte team)

4. *victim:* flop, live one, mark, mug, percher, pigeon, punter

5. *to swindle:* con, take (for a ride)

6. spec. chop the clock (turn back a mileometer); do the party (lure victims in a three-card monte game); fly a kite (pass dud cheques); reload (permit the sucker to win); cook the mark (calm down the fleeced victim)

adv. 7. spec. at the switch (swindling shops); on the knocker (posing as a salesman); on the plastic (using stolen credit cards); at the mark-up (taking an excessive share of loot or profits)

481. Illicit Business

n. 1. dodge, lay, put up job, racket, scam; spec. shakedown (blackmail, extortion); corner, lawing (confidence tricks based on selling supposedly 'stolen' goods); brooming (UK cabbies: refusing all but profitable fares); mule (amateur smuggler)

2. *false appearance:* front

3. *illicit businesses:* spec. granny (business used as a front); laundromat (a business used to 'launder' money)

v. 4. spec. launder, wash (to 'decriminalise' illicitly acquired funds); scalp (to work as a ticket tout)

adj. 5. *illicit:* moody

phr. 6. *justifying possession of stolen goods:* it fell off the back of a lorry; they give them away with a pound of tea

482. Corruption

n. 1. *corruption:* graft

2. *bribe:* bung, drink, grease

3. spec. grass-eater (US: policeman who is satisfied with the bribes he is offered), meat-eater (one who demands higher payments)

v. 4. *to take bribes:* cop, cop a drop, drink

adj. 5. *corrupt:* a bit swift, bent, dodgy, wide
adv. 6. *accepting bribes:* mumping, on a pension, – contract, – the take, – the wrist; spec. on the tin (US: free meals, gifts offered policemen)
phr. 7. spec. can I speak to you? (UK: asking a policeman: can you be bribed?)

483. Counterfeiting and Forgery

n. 1. *counterfeit money:* funny money, slush (UK)
2. *counterfeiter:* cobbler, penman, scratcher; spec. lay-down merchant, slinger (one who passes forged banknotes); kiter, paper hanger (one who passes dud cheques)

484. Kidnapping

n. 1. snatch
v. 2. snatch, sneeze

485. Violence; Coercion

n. 1 (see Rough Treatment: 337, Assault: 338); GBH (grievous bodily harm), push-in job (mugging on the victim's doorstep), RWV (robbery with violence); spec. cement kimono, – overcoat (the hiding of a corpse by burying it in cement); father and mother stuff (street gang use: attacking 'civilians')
2. spec. juice man (collector for a loan-shark); minder (bodyguard); sledge (one who carries a sledgehammer)
v. 3. *to hurt:* do a mischief (to), give it to, muscle, strongarm
4. *to rob with violence:* knock over, mug, stick up
adv. 5. *violent:* on the muscle
6. *marked for death:* on the spot

486. Evidence; Suspicion

n. 1. dope, goods, stuff (on); spec. dirty dishes (planted evidence); dabs (fingerprints); frame (general situation regarding suspicions); wild prints (prints as yet unidentified)
2. *surveillance:* ob(b)o, plant, stake-out; spec. blinker (police helicopter)
3. *identification:* ID, make; spec. mug shot (identifying photo of criminal)
4. *a suspect:* chummy
v. 5. *to suspect:* measure one's dick (for), row in
6. *to identify:* ID, make (for); mug (to take identifying photos)
7. *to plant or fake evidence:* fit up, flake, frame, plant, stitch up
8. *to hide evidence:* wax up
9. *to exonerate:* drop one out, row out
10. *to divert suspicion:* take the dairy off
adv. 11. *under surveillance:* pegged
12. *'framed up':* jobbed
13. *under suspicion:* hot, in the frame

487. Evasion

n. 1. fade, lam, powder, runout powder
2. *hiding place:* slaughter, stash
3. *escapee:* runner, take-off artist, trotter
4. spec. outfit (prison escape kit); outers (any means of escape)
v. 5. *to escape:* cop a heel, – a moke, cop and heel, do a runner, go over the hill, have it away (on one's toes), make one, make one out, take off; spec. jump bail (break one's bail conditions and flee)
6. spec. spring (to help one escape)
phr. 7. spec. one away! (UK prison officers cry of alarm)

488. Search; Pursuit

n. 1. *raid:* swoop
2. *search warrant:* brief, ticket, W
3. *to stop and search:* fan, frisk, jack up, pat (one) down, pull, rumble, turn over; spec. spin, – a drum (to search premises)

4. spec. go out poncing (UK: to search for working pimps); house (UK: to trace a suspect to a given place)

phr. 5. the heat's on!

489. Apprehension; Arrest

n. 1. bail up (Aus.), bounce (US), bust, capture, clear-up, collar, hook, jam, pinch, pull, tug; spec. accommodation collar, flake (US: arrest simply to fill a quota); lay down (UK: remand in custody); humbug, hummer, swift 'un (false arrest)

v. 2. *to arrest:* bail up (Aus.), book, borrow, bounce, bust, capture, claim, collar, drop the hook on, feel a collar, grab, have (it) off, hook, jam, life, nab, nick, pinch, pull, put the sleeve on, run in, scoop, spear, swag, swamp, toss in the bucket, toss in the can, tug; spec. railroad (to arrest unfairly); scratch for work (UK: to need an arrest)

3. *to be arrested:* get a capture, – a tug, – one's collar felt, fall, take a fall

adv. 4. *arrested:* bagged, captured, collared, hooked, etc. (see n. 1.), done up (like a kipper), nicked, popped, tucked up; spec. on the pavement (arrested in the street)

5. *caught red-handed:* bang to rights

6. *due to be arrested:* due

phr. 7. spec. it looks like rain (an arrest is imminent)

490. Examination of Prisoners

n. 1. line-up; spec. beef (court case)

2. *hard interrogation:* heat, third degree; spec. Mutt and Jeff ('good' and 'bad' role-playing by interrogators)

3. *statement:* verbal; spec. dock asthma ('surprised' reactions of the accused on hearing their confessions in court)

4. *charge:* rap; spec. bad rap (serious or unfair charge)

v. 5. *to interrogate:* strap (interrogate harshly); spec. verbal (for police to fake a confession)

6. *to confess:* come clean, – one's cocoa, – one's fat, – one's lot, – one's guts, cough, dob in (Aus.), sing, – like a canary, sneeze (it out), spill one's guts, stand up; spec. hold the bag, take the rap, wear it (confess to another's crime)

7. *to plead innocent:* plead

8. *to withstand interrogation:* beat the rap, stand up

adv. 9. spec. very swift (of corrupt police methods)

phr. 10. *charge him!:* stick him on!

491. Sentence

n. 1. bit, bird (rhy.sl. = bird lime = time), lagging, porridge, time

2. spec. chuck (US: 'not guilty' verdict); toothbrush day (the day of sentencing: one should take a toothbrush to court)

3. spec. baby life (US: 6 yrs, 4 mths); big bit, – time, lagging, long bit, nice bit (long sentences, 3 years+); carpet (UK: 3 mths); double carpet (6 mths); fin up (US: 5 yrs to life); haircut (UK short sentence); half a stretch (UK: 6 mths); handful (US: 5 yrs); leggner (UK: 12 mths); maximum, minimum (US: longest/shortest times that must be served in an indeterminate sentence); nickel (US: 5 years); dime (US: 10 years), pontoon (UK: 21 mths); pound (US: 5 yrs); rofe (backsl. = 4 yrs); short time (short sentence, end of sentence); SS (UK: suspended sentence); stretch (UK: 12 mths); two (UK: 2 yrs); beggar's lagging, tramp's lagging (UK: 90 days); weekend (UK: very short sentence); woodener (UK: 30 days); zip-five (US: maximum 5 yrs)

v. 4. *to imprison:* send away, – down, – up, weigh off; spec. dish

out gravy (sentence harshly); cop a plea, cop out (plea bargain)
5. *to be imprisoned:* go away, – down, pull time
6. *to be found 'not guilty':* beat the rap
adv. 7. *on trial:* standing on the top step, up the steps, – stairs

492. Capital Punishment
n. 1. *electric chair:* chair, hot chair, – seat, – squat
v. 2. *to electrocute:* bake, fry
3. *hang:* stretch (one's neck)

493. Commutation and Release
n. 1. *bail:* Royal Mail (rhy.sl.)
2. *parole:* jam roll (rhy.sl.); back door parole (UK: dying in jail)
3. *rejection of parole:* blank, flop, knockback
4. *parolee:* early riser; spec. PV (parole violator)
5. spec. bleat (petition for repeal); lifeboat (pardon)
6. *release:* blue papers (UK), walking papers (US) (official statement of release date); get-up (release date); gate fever (pre-release nerves)
v. 7. spec. carry a case (to be freed on bail); on the count (US black: walking the streets); recoup (US black: to start post-prison life afresh); feed the bears (pay a parking fine)

494. Prison Life
n. 1. big house, boob, brig, bucket (Can.), calaboose, chokey, clink, college, coop, cross-bar hotel, glasshouse, hoosegow, Joe Gurr (rhy.sl. = stir), joint, jug, lagging station, pen, pokey, quod, slammer, sneezer, stir, tank, Texas steel; spec. drunk tank (lockup for drunks); the Island (Parkhurst, IOW); juvie (US: juvenile prison); the Moor (Dartmoor), outhouse (US: hostel) outside (the free world); Q (San Quentin); the Scrubs (Wormwood Scrubs); upstate (prisons in New York State); the Ville (Pentonville)
2. *places in prison:* range (US/Can. open areas outside cells); block, chokey, cooler, damper, Florida (US), hole, Siberia (US) (solitary confinement); crazy alley, paddy, pads (padded cells); limbo room (Can.: corporal punishment room)
3. *cell:* cheder (Yid.), flowery (rhy.sl. = flowery dell), slot (Aus.), peter, slams; spec. Rory (rhy.sl. = Rory O'Moore = cell door)
4. *prisoners:* con, gaolbird, (old) lag, yardbird (US black), spec. (new) fish (new inmate); flipflop (US: recidivist); short (nearing release); aces high, real man, right guy (US: popular prisoner); centreman, jointman (Can. sycophant to guards); stoolie (informer); red band (UK: trusty); atlas, OBC (one brutal convict) (strong convicts) baron, carvie (UK: tobacco trader); sweet kid (young homosexual); prison wolf (older homosexual); bug pass (Can. insane prisoner); politician (one who secures privileges); gaolhouse lawyer (one who studies law); wallflower (UK: one who plans an escape); lifer (serving life); three-time loser (US: serving mandatory life after a third conviction); recluse (a long-term prisoner with no outside contacts); lugger (Can. smuggler of contraband); knight of the golden grummet (US: prison homosexual); star (UK: first offender); daddy (UK Borstal use; powerful prisoner)
5. *prison officers:* flue (rhy.sl. = screw), hack, herder, screw, twirl; spec. bully beef, screwdriver, white shirt (senior officer); bitch's bastard, caser (severe officer); bent screw, safe screw (corrupt officer); light of love (rhy.sl. = guv = governor);

dep (deputy governor); particulars (US: external authorities); tube (UK: officer who eavesdrops on prisoners), zombie (UK: sour, surly officer); Gabriel (chapel organist); convictitis (paranoid fear of prisoners)

6. *imprisonment:* porridge, time; hard bit, – time (difficult sentence); first bird (first sentence); good time (remission); dead time (US: imprisonment that does not diminish the sentence); cons, jacket, mileage, PC (previous convictions); previous, rap sheet, sheet, yellow sheet (criminal record)

7. spec. bingo (Can.: riot); blanket party (US: initiation rite); break (an escape); cell task (UK: pin-up); cobitis (UK: dislike of jail food); duffer (UK: pudding, US: bread); fall money (US: legal fees); friend form (US: visiting order); grab (UK: pay); hominy gazette (Aus.: rumours); joey (UK: contraband); jo-jos (Can.: overcoat); jug-up (Can.: mealtime); bug juice, liquid cosh (Can./UK: major tranquilisers used for restraint); outfit (escape kit); pussy in a can (US: sardines); rim slide (US: fart); reader (UK: any reading matter); rower (UK: argument); scratcher (UK: match); whodunnit (UK: meat pie); wicked lady (cat o'nine-tails); kit (contraband communication; any prison paperwork); bug (Can.: homemade water-heater); KB (UK: knockback – rejection); full sheet (UK: prisoner's complaint against an officer)

v. 8. *spec. (prisoners):* blow one's copper (US: lose remission); choose up (US: select a homosexual partner); do a bit (serve time); get the Book, get the glory (become religious); give (one) the office (to initiate a newcomer); flash the range (US/Can.: scan the prison landing with a mirror); go up (the river) (to be imprisoned); have some rabbit (US: yearn to escape); lay in (US: reject exercise periods); play too close (US black: invade privacy); ride the deck, swap cans (US: have anal intercourse); cop a heel (US: attack from behind)

9. *spec. (prison officers):* bang up, dub up, chubb, miln up (UK: lock the cell door); ducket (Can.: place fellow-officer on report); get the book (US: to be reprimanded); put the block on (UK: tighten up prison regulations); ghost (move prisoners at night); case (UK: place a prisoner on report)

adj. 10. spec. chosen (US: selected as a homosexual partner); nicked (UK: put on report); scammered (homosexual)

adv. 11. *imprisoned:* away, inside, in the nick, in chokery, – stir, etc. (see n. 1.), jugged, on jankers, on the corn (Aus.), under glass, up the river; spec. carpy (UK: locked up for the night); two-ed up, three-ed up (UK: two or three men sharing a cell); stir bugs, – crazy (insane); baroning (trading in consumables)

12. *in solitary confinement:* behind one's door, buried (US), iced, OP (Can.: off privilege); spec. in the peek (under observation); on Rule 43 (UK: in voluntary solitary confinement)

13. *escaped:* away, on the lam, over the hill

phr. 14. *aimed at a complainer:* if you can't do the time, don't do the crime

495. Police

n. 1. Alice Blue Gown (gay use), Babylon (WI), bear, Big John (US black), Bill, blue meanies, bluebottles, blues, bobby, bogey, bogie, bull, button, chapper (Yid.), cop(per), cozzer, deputy do-right (US black), divine right (US black), esclop (backsl. = cop), flatfoot,

flattie, fuzz, gendarmes, gestaps (US black), gum heel, harness bull, hawkshaw (WI), heat, hood (Aus.), irvine (US black), John Law, John Hop (Aus. rhy.sl. = cop), Johnny-be-good (US black), Kojak, law, little boy blue (US black), Lucy Law (gay use), mallet (US black), nab (US black), nail 'em and jail 'em (US black), Old Bill, ossifer, paddy, Peter-Jay (US black), pig, reppock (backsl. = copper), rozzer, Sam and Dave (US black), scuffer, Sherlock Holmes (US black), the Man, three-bullet Joey (US black), Tilly (gay use), uncle nabs (US black), union wage (US black), walloper (Aus.), weakheart (WI), whips (US black); spec. rusty gun (veteran); active, hungry (enthusiast); saint (uncorruptible); horseman (RCMP 'mountie'); five-day wonder (UK: graduate of police college); aid (Temporary Detective Constable); dickless Tracy (woman officer); choirboys, wollies (novices); skip (sergeant); guv, guvnor (UK: any senior rank, usually as form of address) boffin (forensic expert); bobbsey twins (gay use: squad car officers); mother superior (gay use: sergeant)
2. *detectives:* ace, brains, busy, clothes, D (Aus.), eye, filth, G-man, gumshoe, jack, mod squad, Scotland Yard (US black), shoo-fly; spec. T-man (US Treasury agent); peeper (private detective)
3. *traffic police:* bald-tyre bandits, bear in the air (US: using a helicopter), brown bomber (Aus.), Freeway Freddie (US black), green hornet (Can.), grey ghost (Aus.), Kojak with a Kodak, pirates, Smokey
4. *group of police:* button mob, heavy mob, team; spec. heavy mob, Sweeney (rhy.sl. = Sweeney Todd = squad), the squad (flying squad); pussy posse, queer detail, Vera Vice

(vice squad); narco (narcotics squad); bunco squad (fraud squad); Met (UK: Metropolitan Police); Home and Colonial (UK: regional crime squad); rubber heels, umbrella brigade (UK: Special Branch); rubber heels, shoo-fly (internal disciplinary officers); COs (UK: Commissioner's Office – taxi-cab authorities)
5. *police work:* the job; spec. batting average (US: arrest record); rubbish (UK: tedious duties); shout (an emergency call); SOP (standard operating procedure); advice (UK: a reprimand)
6. *police badge:* buzzer, potsy, tin
7. *Scotland Yard:* hollow tooth, Kremlin, the Yard
8. *police station:* Bridewell, factory, nick, old bill, (see also Crime: 460)
9. spec. dido (UK: internal complaint); Kilburn (rhy.sl. = Kilburn Priory = police diary)
v. 10. spec. walk the bricks (patrol); go out with (share professional attitudes); cover the sheet (fill an arrest quota); give a coating (to reprimand); cast (UK: to be discharged); put in one's papers (UK: to resign); crash (UK: drop enquiries); plot up (UK: study a given villain); blow out (UK: for a case to collapse); shape up (for a case to develop well)
adv. 11. spec. copping on the wrist, on the take (accepting bribes); over the side (UK: shirking duty for private interests); cooping (US: sleeping on duty); on dab (UK: on a disciplinary charge)
phr. 12. derog. ACAB (all coppers are bastards)
13. spec. APB (all points bulletin: general alert); ten-four (message received and understood)
phr. 14. spec. have you got a coat (UK: have you found a feasible suspect?)

CRIME: MISCELLANEOUS
496. Miscellaneous Terms, etc.
n. 1. spec. black (blackmail);
bleeding dirt, the mouse
(blackmailing homosexuals); Jewish
lightning (deliberate arson for
insurance fraud); bustle-punching
(acting as a frotteur); moprey
(exposing one's genitals to a blind
woman); copper jitters (irrational
fear of police); Follies (UK:
Quarter Sessions)
v. 2. spec. do it for oneself (UK
cabbie use: take a fare without using
the meter); torch (commit arson)

PROSTITUTION
497. Prostitution
n. 1. pussy game, the Game
2. *prostitute:* ass peddler, bangtail
(US black), bird (US black), brass,
business girl, call-girl, charlie
(Aus.), chromo (Aus.), cruiser,
Edie, flash-tail, flatbacker, grunter
(Aus.), ho (US black), hook(er),
hoowah, KP (Aus.: common
prostitute), kurve (Yid.), lady,
moonlighter, nafka (Yid.), noffka
(Yid.), open game (US black),
pavement princess, pro,
professional woman, prossie, prosso
(Aus.), puta (Sp.), short-time girl,
stepper (US black), stick (US
black), tom, working girl; spec.
square broad (non-prostitute);
industrial debutante (specialist in
conventions)
3. *part-time prostitute:* B-girl, charity
moll (Aus.), chippy, half-brass,
weekend ho (US black), – warrior,
summertime ho (US black)
4. *senior prostitute:* old timer, vet
5. *worn-out prostitute:* fleabag, over
the hill ho (US black)
6. *incompetent prostitute:* flaky ho
(US black), hold-out, mudkicker,
nag, slouch; spec. outlaw (one who
works without a pimp)
7. *experienced prostitute:* bottom

woman, main bitch, rose among the
thorns, star of the line,
thoroughbred
8. *under-age prostitute:* baby-pro
9. *male prostitute:* ass peddler,
– pro, bird taker, broad, boy, buff
boy, bunny, business boy, call boy,
career boy, cocksman, cocktail, coin
collector, come-on boy, commercial
queer, crack salesman, dick
peddler, fag boy, flesh peddler,
floater, foot soldier, gigolo, goofer,
he-whore, Hollywood hustler, party
boy, prick peddler, puto (Sp. =
whore), rent, rent-boy, sport,
sporting goods, two-way man,
trabajadao (Sp. = worked over),
trade, working girl
10. *thieving prostitute:* ginger,
rip-off artist
11. *prostitutes working for a pimp:*
flock, nest, stable; spec. choosing
money (cash given by a prostitute to
her new pimp); pimp crazy (a
prostitute who prefers sadistic
pimps)
12. spec. hand gig (gay use:
prostitute who masturbates (with)
client); vegetarian (prostitute who
will not fellate); three-way girl
(offers all bodily orifices for sex);
trapeze artist (specialist in
cunnilingus)
13. *working targets:* catch, trap;
spec. git-down time (start of
working day)
14. spec. trick baby (prostitute's
client-fathered child)
v. 15. *to work as a prostitute:* hawk
one's fork (Aus.), – one's mutton,
– one's pearly, hook, peddle pussy,
sit on one's stuff (US black), step
(US black), turn tricks; spec. break
one's luck (meet the day's first
client)
16. *work as a male prostitute:* hawk
one's brown, peddle one's arse
adv. 17. *working as a prostitute:* on
the bash, – the bat, – the battle
(Aus.), – the bottle, – the Game,

steppin', trollin'; spec. on the case (earning steadily from one client)
phr. 18. *used by prostitute to client:* wanna do a thing?, – go out?

498. Pimps and Pimping

n. 1. mackery, the Life; spec. the Book (verbally transmitted 'book of pimping rules')
2. *pimp:* Alphonse (rhy.sl. = ponce), Charlie Ronce (rhy.sl.), fence (Aus.), hoon (Aus.), Joe Bonce, Joe Ronce (rhy.sl.), macaroni (US black), mack man (US black), ponce, sweetman; spec. bit of mess (UK: a male lover, neither client nor pimp)
3. *small-time pimp:* chili chump, – pimp, coffee and pimp, popcorn pimp, simple pimp
4. spec. boss player (superior pimp); faggotter (pimp for male prostitutes); gorilla pimp (violent pimp); promoted pimp (experienced, senior pimp); sugar pimp (kind pimp); macaroni with cheese (pimp who has other interests); Madam (male/female brothel proprietor)
5. spec. bonds (clothes given to his prostitutes); copping clothes ('best suit' used when enticing a new prostitute); kimible (noticeable 'pimp walk'); pimp's arrest (revocation of statutory bail bond for a given prostitute when she wants to leave); pimp dust (cocaine); pimp fronts (pimp-style clothes); pimp ride (expensive car); pimp shades, – tints (dark glasses)
v. 6. *to entice prostitutes:* cast the net, cop, – for, hit on, take an application
7. *to run prostitutes:* drive one's hos, put one on the block, – one on the corner, turn (one) out; cop and blow (exploit a prostitute); lock (ensure a prostitute's fidelity); ponce off (live off immoral

earnings); work from a book (run call – not street – girls)
8. *to discuss pimping:* run down game, talk game
9. spec. file (to give instruction to a prostitute); rig a jig (prepare a sexual con-trick); put snow in one's game (ensnare a white person for financial gain); creep (to defraud a client); work a ginger (Aus.: to rob a client); drop a lug (US black: to confront or argue with)
adj. 10. *pertaining to pimping:* mack

499. Clients and Services

n. 1. fare, gonk, john, trick, TOS (trick off the street); spec. freak trick, special (devotee of any sexual speciality, see n. 2); phoney (mean client); champagne trick (generous client); live one (good client)
2. spec. beat (masochist); beer bottle beat (one who likes to be hit with a bottle); cream-puff freak (cake-thrower); dress-up (uses the girl's clothes/make-up); facial (the girl sits on his face); gorilla (sadist); jim, tin soldier, twank (voyeurs, 'assistants', etc.); leapfrog (one who watches two girls play leapfrog); needle freak (sadist, with needles); no freak (likes to simulate rape); phone freak (calls the girl to talk sex); sniffer (sniffs underwear); talker (only talks to the girl); underwear (underwear fetishist); word freak (listens to obscenities); toys (appliances used for bondage, S&M, etc.)
3. *sex show:* circus, dig (US black), gazoopie, gazupie; spec. T&A, tits and ass (burlesque, strip-show)
4. *services:* around the world (licking, sucking of entire body); B&D (bondage and discipline); English culture, – guidance (flagellation and bondage); fifty-fifty (gay use: alternating fellatio and sodomy); fladge (flagellation); French culture (fellatio); golden

showers (urolagnia); Greek culture (anal intercourse); party (any form of sex act); R/S (rough stuff, including sado-masochism, urolagnia, rubberwear, etc.); Roman culture (orgies); short time (basic intercourse); Swedish culture (rubber); telephone J/O (masturbation while listening to the telephone); tongue bath (see around the world); water sports (urolagnia); middle finger (prostitute's trick that speeds up orgasms); freebie, free shot (sex for free)
5. spec. ten-two (US payment for sex: $10 for girl, $2 for room)
v. 6. *to lick and suck the client's body:* go around the world, – all over town (with), round-house
7. spec. kerb-crawl (to solicit street girls from a car)
8. spec. georgy (to hire a whore and then refuse to pay)
9. spec. freak off (offer sex for free)
10. spec. sell a boy (gay use: to hire a prostitute as a 'gift' for a third party)

500. Locations

n. 1. *brothel:* barrelhouse, benny house, call house, case, cathouse, chicken ranch, hook shop, house, knocking shop, leaning house (US black); spec. punch house (US black: place where pimps and whores meet); rap parlour (euphemism for 'massage parlour'); peg house, show house (homosexual brothel)
2. *pimp uses:* office (wherever a pimp conducts business); fast track (centre of whoring in a city, US East Coast cities in general); slow track (US West Coast cities)
3. *the street:* ho stroll (US black), pitch, stroll, track
adv. 4. *on the street:* on the bricks

COMMERCIAL SEX
501. Pornography
n. 1. smut
2. *books:* eight-pager, fuck book, one-hand job, stroke book, Tijuana bible; spec. fag hots (gay-orientated material)
3. *films:* blue film, horn movie, skin-flick, stag movie
4. spec. close-ups: beaver shot (female genitals); flap shot, liver shot, meat shot, pink, wide-open beaver (inner labia, open vagina, etc.)
adj. 5. *pornographic:* adult, blue

DRUGS
502. Selling
n. 1. *seller:* candyman, connection, dealer, man, pusher, watermelon man (US black); spec. seedy (US black: seller of pills)
2. spec. buy (purchase of drugs); meet (appointment to buy drugs); green house (location, popular for buying drugs); jam house (location where cocaine is available); hop joint, shooting gallery (location where narcotics can be bought and used)
3. spec. Dr Feelgood, hungry croaker, writing doctor (doctors who write illicit prescriptions for drugs)
4. *measures of drugs:* amp (ampoule); bag (measure of narcotics); bindle, deck, paper (small fold of paper holding narcotics), birdseye (small amount of narcotics); blow, toot (one line of cocaine); brick (appx. 1 kilo of marijuana); can (1 oz of marijuana); cap (capsule); deck, dime bag ($10 worth of a drug); fifty-cent bag ($50 worth of marijuana); football (appx. 0.5 grain of a narcotic); half-lo (15 bags of heroin); jar (500/1000 pills); key (one kilo); LB (one pound weight); lid (22 gms appx. of

marijuana); line (one snort of a narcotic); match, matchbox (half-oz of marijuana); mic (one microgram, used to measure LSD); oz (1 ounce weight); paper, piece (appx. 1 oz of heroin); pinch (small amount of marijuana); spoon (2 gms heroin); taste (small amount of any drug); teaspoon (1 gm heroin); ten-cent bag ($10 worth of marijuana); weight (1 oz of heroin, 1 lb of marijuana); baggie (small plastic bag to hold marijuana)

5. *adulterated drugs:* blank ('narcotics'); catnip ('marijuana'); six and four (heavily diluted heroin)

6. spec. one-shot credit (a buyer is allowed only one default in payment)

7. spec. dog tag (a legitimate prescription for narcotics)

8. *to sell drugs:* deal, hustle, serve; spec. lay on (to offer free or sample drugs)

9. *to buy drugs:* connect, cop (for), score; spec. front (advance cash for a purchase)

10. spec. write script (for a doctor to write prescription for narcotics)

11. *to measure out drugs for sale:* bag, bag up, cap (into capsules)

12. *to sell adulterated, fake or short weight drugs:* burn, rip off

13. *to adulterate drugs:* cut, hit, step on

adv. 14. *in possession of drugs:* anywhere, carrying, holding

phr. 15. *do you want drugs?:* do you need a boy?

16. *have you any drugs?:* are you anywhere?, – carrying?, – holding?

503. Use and Addiction
n. 1. *pill-taker:* a-head, downer, freak, pillhead, pill-popper, speed freak

2. *narcotic user:* AD, hophead, globetrotter, hype, junkie, junk hawk, mainliner, schmecker, smack freak, – head, stuffer, unkjay, user

(heroin); cokey, coke freak, – head, snow bird (cocaine); needle freak, pin-jabber (one who prefers to inject); snooter (one who prefers to sniff drugs); hog (one who uses an excess of narcotics); swellhead (US black: one who has collapsed from drug use)

3. *soft drug user:* doper, druggie, freak, head, pothead, weedhead (cannabis); acidhead, acid rapper, tripper (LSD); space cadet, zonker (an excessive user); bud sesh (smoking drugs together); teahouse (place for communal smoking); bowl, chalice, chillum, cutchie (WI) (device for smoking)

4. spec. stash (drug hiding place; thus the given drug itself)

5. *addiction to narcotics:* habit, jones, monkey (on one's back); burning down habit, oil-burner habit (very heavy addiction); coffeeand habit (mild addiction); white line fever (cocaine addiction); honeymoon (early use of heroin)

6. *withdrawal from drugs:* belly habit, bogue, cold turkey, kicking (the habit), sweats, sick; spec. detox (detoxification: post-withdrawal period); chucks, chuck horrors (excessive eating that follows withdrawal)

v. 7. *to be addicted:* be strung out, have a habit, – a jones, – a monkey on one's back, hurting (for)

8. *to stop using narcotics:* go cold turkey, kick, kick the habit

9. spec. make for a stash (to steal drugs from a fellow user)

10. spec. bogart (take an excess of marijuana)

adv. 11. *using drugs:* on the needle; spec. pinned (tiny pupils, a sign of heroin use)

adj. 12. *no longer addicted:* clean, straight

504. Pills
n. 1. *general pills, capsules, etc.:*

ace, beans, blunt, candy, cap, dolls, hors d'oeuvres (US black), Jacks (and Jills) (rhy.sl. = pills), ju-ju, M&Ms, prescriptions, rainbows, roundhead, vitamins, yum-yums

2. *stimulants:* a (amphetamine); b (benzedrine); bam (bambita = amphetamine); bennies, benny, benz (benzedrine); black beauties, – bomber, – widow, blues, bomb(er), Christmas tree (deximal); crank, crystal (powdered Methdrine); dex(y) (dexedrine); leaper, meth (methdrine); olly (rhy.sl. = Oliver Reed = speed); pep-em-ups (US black), ph, pink lady, purple heart, rouser (US black), speed, uppers, ups, white cross, whites, whiz, widow

3. *depressants, tranquillisers:* barbs, blue angel (amytal barbiturate); borders, Christmas tree (Tuinal); downer, F-40s (Seconal); F-60s (Histadyl); F-66s (Tuinal); goofball, gumdrop (US black), jacket (nembutal); jiblet (US black), Lilly (Seconal); nebbie, nembie (Nembutal); reds, sleeper, slow-'em-ups (US black), sopor, tranks, Vallie (Valium); yellowjackets, yellows

4. *methaqualone:* ludes (Quaalude); mandies (Mandrax)

5. spec. silk and satin, up-and-downer (pill combining amphetamine and barbiturate); Mickey Finn (knock-out drug, poss. chloral hydrate); Monday pills (US milit: malaria pills)

6. *to take pills:* drop

DRUGS: TYPE
505. Hard

n. 1. *narcotics:* hard stuff, stuff; good stuff (better than average drugs)

2. *heroin:* beast, big H, boy, Chinese no. 3, dog food (US black), duji, gold dust, H, henry, hop, horse, junk, scag, schmeck, shit, skag, skezag, (pig Latin), stuff; spec. quill (heroin hidden in a matchbook cover)

3. *cocaine:* blort, blow, bowser, C, candy, cecil, charlie, coconuts, coke, flake, fly, freezer, girl, golden girl, gonzo, jam (US black), lady, leaf, nose, nose candy, pimp dust (US black), rock, snow, sophisticated lady (US black), toot, white shit

4. *opium:* black, brown stuff, button, canned stuff, card, green ashes, high hat, hop, mud, O, red smoker, san lo, tar, yen pok

5. *morphine:* cube, Dr White, dolly, God's own medicine, GOM, M, Miss Emma, mojo, sweet Jesus, white nurse, – stuff

6. spec. PG (paragoric); paracki (paraldehyde)

7. *drug cocktails:* 'Frisco speedball (heroin, cocaine & LSD), speedball (heroin and cocaine)

8. *drug injection:* bang (in the arm), fix, hit, Jimmy Hix (rhy.sl. = fix), jolt, shot; spec. wake-up (first injection of the day); main, mainline (the vein into which one injects); joy bang, – pop (occasional use) ab (an abcess caused by injecting); marks, tracks (scars of regular injections); hot shot (injection of poison deliberately used to murder a drug addict)

9. *hard drug paraphernalia:* gun, hypo, spike (hypodermic syringe); fit, gizmo, outfit, works (needle plus other equipment for making an injection); collar (wrapper that ensures needle and dropper fit tightly); cooker (a container in which a mixture of heroin and water can be heated); cotton (cloth through which heroin is sucked into the syringe); tie-up (a means of tying off the vein prior to injection); rope (a vein)

v. 10. *to inject drugs:* bang up, crank

(up), do a thing, – in, – up, fix, geeze, jack up, hit the mainline, mainline, pop, shoot up, take off, use; spec. chippy (to use narcotics occasionally); tie off (to isolate the vein); skinpop (inject under the skin rather than into a vein); fire up, shoot gravy, jack off (pump the mixture of blood and heroin into the arm); spill (to miss the vein); get one's wings (to start injecting drugs); brew, cook (heat a mixture of heroin and water prior to injecting oneself)

11. *to sniff or inhale drugs:* blow, get one's nose cold, horn, jam (US black), sniff, snort, toot; spec. base, freebase (to inhale cocaine mixed with ether); chase the dragon, kick the gong around (inhale heated heroin); toot (a device for inhaling cocaine)

12. *to addict to drugs:* hook

adj. 13. *narcotic:* heavy

adv. 14. spec. caught in a snowstorm (under the influence of cocaine); on the sleeve (injecting narcotics)

506. Soft

n. 1. *hashish:* charas, dope, hash, kaker (Yid.), kif, shit; spec. tincture (tincture of cannabis); THC (tetrahydrocannabinnol); temple balls, Lebanese gold, – red, Afghani, Af, black Pak, Turkish pollen (geographical 'trade' names)

2. *marijuana:* ace, baby, bale, bar, black gungeon, – moat, – Russian, bomber, boo, brand X (US black), brick, bu, bush, charge, collie, dagga, dew, djamba, dope, duby, esrar, gage, ganga, gangja, gangster (US black), gauge gear, grass, greapha, greefo, griefo, gunja, gunny, hay, hemp, herb, joy, juanita, locoweed, maharishee, mariweegee, Mary Warner, Mary, Maryanne, Maryjane, moocah, mootah, mooter, mother nature's

own tobacco, mother nature, mu, muggle, muggles, pot, reefer, root, smoke, tea, turnip greens (US black), twist, 'wana, weed, wheat, zombie (Aus.); spec. sinsemilla, Mexican green, Durban poison, Congo bush, Acapulco gold, Acapulco red (geographical 'trade' names); homegrown (home cultivated); bad shit (better-than-average drugs)

3. *marijuana or hashish cigarette:* bag of bones, bomber, bones, doobie, dubee, duby, j, joint, ju-ju, no-brand cigarette, no-name cigarette, off-brand cigarette, skoofer, skoofus, skroofus, spliff, stencil, stick, stogie, toke, toothpick (US black), tuskie (US black); burnie, roach (remains of a cigarette); crutch, roach clip (gadget to hold the hot 'roach'); papers, skins (cigarette papers); makings (content of a 'joint'); hit, toke (puff of a cigarette)

4. *hallucinogens:* acid, LSD; spec. clear light, mellow yellow, Owsley, strawberry fields, sunshine, window pane ('trade names'); angel dust, hog, steam (phencyclidine); businessman's trip (DMT); mesc (mescalin)

5. *amyl nitrate:* aroma, poppers

6. *to smoke drugs:* blast, do a number, take a hit, toke (down); spec. bogart, double-clutch (take more than one's share); shotgun (blow smoke into another's mouth); cuff (to hide a burning cigarette)

507. Experience and Effects

n. 1. *hard drug use:* rush (immediate effects of a narcotic injection); spec. OD (overdose)

2. *soft drug use:* charge, high, stone, turn-on; spec. hashover (cannabis hangover); trip (LSD experience)

3. *bad experience:* bring-down, bummer, bum trip, freak-out, horrors

v. 4. *to take a drug:* do, do up, get behind

5. *to 'get high':* blow one's mind, do one's head, fly, get Chinese, – high, – low, make one right (US black), ride the wagon (US black), – tough (US black), toot one's horn; spec. freak out (have an unpleasant drug experience; come down (to feel the effects of the drug end); go on the nod, nod, nod out (to fall asleep when using heroin)

6. *to look after a drug user:* babysit

adj. 7. *'drugged':* spacey, trippy, weird

adv. 8. *experiencing drugs:* annihilated, bent out of shape, blocked, bombed, charged up, destroyed, fried, fucked up, goofed, have the slows (US black), high, hopped up, loaded, messed up, on it, ossified, out of it, – of one's brain, – of one's gourd, – of one's mind, – of one's nut, – of one's skull, pilled up, psychedelic to the bone (US black), ripped, skulled, spaced (out), toasted, twisted, wasted; on the nod, smacked out (intoxicated with heroin)

phr. 9. DFFL (dope forever, forever loaded); someone blew out his/her pilot light

---

COMMERCE
508. Commerce

n. 1. *large sum of money:* big bucks, bundle, fat knot (US black), megabucks, packet, pile, sting, wedge

2. *small sum of money:* chickenfeed, grubstake, pin money, razoo (Aus.), walk-about money

3. *cheque:* goose's neck (rhy.sl.), total wreck (rhy.sl.); spec. bum map, frog, kite, leaper, rubber cheque, stumer (bad cheque)

4. *rent:* burton (rhy.sl. = Burton-on-Trent), Duke of Kent (rhy.sl.)

5. *corruption:* lurkola (Aus.), payola (payoffs for media exposure); gayola (payoffs that permit the running of gay clubs)

6. spec. California bankroll, Chicago bank roll, flash roll, Kansas City roll, nigger's bankroll (a roll of small bills wrapped in one large one); divvy (dividend); loose ends, mad money, money to burn (spare money); OPM (other people's money – invested in business); quick (instantly available money); rainy-day money (savings); slush fund (contingency fund); whip-round (instant collection of money); whack (a share)

7. *businessmen:* spec. breadhead (obsessed with money); damager (manager); jobber (freelance cabbie); Mr Ten Per Cent (an agent or middleman)

8. *locations:* Arthur (rhy.sl. = J. Arthur Rank), iron tank (rhy.sl.), jug, kaynab (backsl. = bank); Ma and Pa store, Mom and Pop store (corner shops); rip (off) joint (an exorbitantly expensive store); schlock shop (flashy dress shop)

9. *industrial relations:* compo (Aus.: industrial compensation); con and coal (rhy.sl. = dole); dole-bludger (Aus.: dole scrounger); greens (rhy.sl. = greengages = wages), rock of ages (rhy.sl.); time and a half (overtime); sweetheart contract, yellow-dog contract (contracts that favour the company)

10. *cost, bill:* Beecham's pill (rhy.sl.), damage, nut, tab; spec. swindle sheet (expense account)

11. spec. action (business deal); bottom line, real deal (end result, basis); cherry-picking (reviewing rival business ideas); dog (unsaleable item); Jewish piano, – typewriter (cash register); quick and dirty, quick fix (instant remedy); bob a nob (a shilling each)

v. 12. *to spend money:* push the

boat out, splurge; spec. blew in, do one's dough (waste money); bounce (pass a dud cheque or have the bank refuse payment on the cheque); catch a cold, hold the baby (lose money on investments)
13. *to invest:* bankroll; spec. pick up the tab (pay a bill)
14. *to earn money:* knock out (plus sum), make change (US black), pull down (plus sum)
15. *to become rich:* carve a slice, coin (it), make a bomb, – a killing, rake it in, scoop the pool, strike it rich
16. *to sell:* flog, hype, push; spec. whack for (to charge); go like hot cakes (for a commodity to sell fast)
17. *to cost:* set (one) back
18. spec. headhunt (to recruit executives)
adj. 19. *expensive:* pricey, through the nose
20. *free:* buckshee, on the house
adv. 21. spec. hanging-up (cab use: refusing to take unprofitable fares); on the clock (freelance taxi-driving); in the barrel (about to be dismissed); staked long and deep (US black: investing heavily)
phr. 22. *deriding a small sum of money:* don't spend it all at once

509. Names for Money
n. 1. *money:* ace, ackers, beans, bees and honey (rhy.sl.), billies, boodle, brass, bread, cabbage, cake, clams, cod's roe (rhy.sl. = dough), coin, dibs, dinero, do-re-mi, dough, duckies (US black), gelt, gold, gravy, green, greenbacks, greenies, guineas, hard money, hoot (Aus.), Jimmy O'Goblins, kale, kylege (WI), lean green, lettuce, lolly, long green, loot, mazuma, moolah, mulla, oscar (rhy.sl. = Oscar Asche = cash), potatoes, readies, ready, rhino, roll, sausage and mash (rhy.sl. = cash), scramble, scratch, shekels, simoleons, smash, spondulicks, sugar, tusheroon (US black), wampum, whistle and toot (rhy.sl. = loot), wonga, yennom (backsl.); spec. crackle, folding stuff, soft money (paper money); long-tailed 'un (large sterling note); paper (money orders, etc.)
2. *pound sterling:* bar, doonups (backsl.), funt (Yid.), oncer, nicker, note, quid, smacker, smackeroo, sov
3. *dollar bill:* clam, skin, slab (see also: green, greenbacks, long green, etc. in n. 1)
4. *small cash sums:* spec. Abergavenny (rhy.sl. = penny), yenep (backsl. = penny); Susy (rhy.sl. = Susy Anna = tanner), tanner (sixpence); tosheroon (half a crown); caser, dollar, Oxford scholar (rhy.sl.) (five shillings); calf (rhy.sl.), cows (rhy.sl. = cow's calf = half), half a bar, – a sheet (ten shillings, 50p); pony in white (£1.25 in silver); deuce ($2.00); nickel (5 cents; dime (10); quarter (25)
5. *five pounds, five dollars:* fin, finnif, pound note ($5.00); half a cock (rhy.sl. = half a cock and hen = half of ten), Jacks (rhy.sl. = Jack's alive = five)
6. *ten pounds, ten dollars:* sawbuck, sawski ($10.00); cock and hen, cockle and hen (rhy.sl. = ten)
7. *twenty dollars, twenty pounds:* double sawbuck, double sawski ($20); score (£20)
8. *twenty-five pounds:* macaroni (rhy.sl. = pony), pony
9. *fifty dollars:* half a yard
10. *one hundred pounds, one hundred dollars:* big one, C, C-note, century, hun, one bill, yard ($100); big one, century (£100)
11. *one hundred and fifty dollars:* buck and a half
12. *two hundred pounds:* twoer
13. *five hundred pounds:* monkey

14. *one thousand pounds, one thousand dollars:* G, grand, K

510. Loans; Debts, etc.
n. 1. *usurer:* loan shark, shark, shy, shylock; spec. Uncle (pawnbroker)
2. *credit:* drip, never-never, slate, sub, tick; spec. lay-by (Aus.: deposit paid in a shop); sharking (practising usury)
3. *interest:* juice, vig, vigorish
4. *location:* hockshop
v. 5. *to loan:* spot, sub (for); spec. nail (charge with a debt); hold paper on (stand as creditor)
6. *to pawn:* hock
7. *to purchase on credit:* drip it up, put on the slate, – on tick, etc. (see adv. 10)
8. *to pay one's debts:* ante up, brass up, pony up; spec. welch (to refuse to pay debts)
adj. 9. spec. financial (Aus.: in credit, solvent); in hock, to the bad, up the spout (in debt)
adv. 10. *owing:* into (one for)
11. *on credit:* on the cuff, – the slate, – tick; spec. on the drip, – the never-never (on hire purchase); on appro (on approval)

GAMBLING
511. Gambling and Wagering
n. 1. action; spec. Lombard Street to a China orange (the longest possible odds); cert, dead cert, million (certain winner); on the Murray cod (Aus. rhy.sl.), on the nod, payday stakes (betting on credit)
2. *gambler:* high roller, punter; spec. mug punter (foolish gambler)
3. *money:* bundle (large sum); short-end money (betting on a loss); smart money (bets made by experts)
4. *locale:* spieler (gambling club): plot (site of a three-card monte game); blower (tannoy system in a betting shop)

v. 5. *to bet:* play, punt, put one's shirt on, spiel (Yid.), splosh it on; spec. go for the doctor (Aus.), shoot for the sky, – for the moon (bet all one's money)
6. spec. make book (work as a bookmaker)
adj. 7. big (multiples of ten thousand; thus 'big nickel' = $5,000)
adv. 8. *at stake:* on the line; spec. on the short end (the unfavourable end of the odds)
phr. 9. spec. put up or shut up (bet, don't talk)

512. Winning and Losing
n. 1. *a win:* motsa (Aus.), skinner (Aus.); spec. dirty money (dishonourable gains)
2. *loss:* tap city
3. *loser:* provider, pooch
v. 4. *to lose:* dog it
5. *to beat:* clean out, take to the cleaners
6. *to pay debts:* come across; spec. welch (to refuse to pay debts)
adj. 7. *impoverished:* skinned, tapioca, tapped out
adv. 8. *winning:* hot, in the money, on a roll, – a rush
9. *losing:* in the hole

513. Persons
n. 1. *gambler:* punter; spec. hustler (professional gambler)
2. spec. hot dog (successful); hardnose (cautious); knocker (one who defaults on debts); kibitzer, railbird, sightseer (watchers, not players); shill, steerer (house player); sucker-bait (female used to lure gamblers); take-out guy (member of card-sharping team)

514. Horse-racing
n. 1. airs and graces (rhy.sl. = races)
2. *horses:* gee-gees; spec. pelter (fast horse); dead cert (a winning

horse); dead 'un (Aus.), quitter, stiff 'un, undertaker job (a losing horse); closer (horse on whom odds shorten); underlay (horse on whom odds increase)

3. *locations:* canal boat (rhy.sl. = the Tote); flapping track (small, unlicensed track); smoked haddock (rhy.sl. = the paddock)

4. *people:* chalk eater (one who bets on favourites only); horseplayer (better); hot walker (groom who walks horses after the race)

5. *the race:* boil over (Aus.: an upset); dead cert, romp (absolute certainty); the off (start)

6. *betting:* dope sheet, morning line, scratch sheet (racing form); Heinz (a combination bet); on the nose (a bet to win rather than place or show)

v. 7. spec. dope, dope out, – the ponies (to work out bets); go for the doctor (Aus.: for a horse to draw ahead); go through the card (bet on every horse); nobble (interfere with a horse); play the gee-gees (bet on races); pull (deliberately pull up a horse)

515. Cards
n. 1. bladder of lard (rhy.sl.), broads, flats, Wilkie Bard (rhy.sl.); spec. readers (marked cards); case card (last card of the four suits in each denomination to turn up); bullet (ace), deuce (two), trey (three), trips (three of a kind), whore (the queen)

2. *card games:* skin game (US black); spec. find the lady, monte, three-card monte ('the three-card trick')

3. spec. mechanic (cardsharp); tells (tics and mannerisms that betray poker bluffing)

v. 4. *to play cards:* spread the broads; spec. kibitz (watch a game)

5. *spec. poker uses:* bring it in (for the lowest card to start betting);

coffeehouse (to bluff); fold (cease betting on a hand); sandbag (bluff by checking the bet); tight-weak (weakness in play)

adj. 6. *marked deck:* spooked

excl. 7. *deal the cards:* hit me!

516. Dice; Bingo, etc.
n. 1. *dice:* African dominoes, bones, tatts; spec. flats, tops (doctored dice)

2. *dice player:* gunner, shooter

3. *playing dice:* fading game (players bet against each other and not against a bank); hard way (throwing pairs to make even points in craps); jacking off (shaking dice up and down)

4. spec. numbers, policy ('numbers' gambling); April fools (rhy.sl. = football pools)

5. *names of points in craps:* snake-eyes (pair of one 1s; 2); ace-deuce, trey (3); little Josie, little Joe (from Kokomo) (4); fever in the South, five in the South, (Little) Phoebe (5); Jimmy Hix, sixty days (6); craps (2, 7 or 12 as a loss), natural (7 as a win or 11); Ada from Decatur, eighter from Decatur (8); Nina from Carolina, Nina with her hair down (9); big Dick (from Boston) (10); box cars (12)

6. *names of numbers in bingo (many are rhy.sl.):* buttered scone, Kelly's eye (1); dirty old Jew, me and you (2); you and me (3); knock at the door (4); God's in heaven (7); garden gate, Harry Tate (8); doctor's orders (9); cock and hen, Downing Street (10); legs eleven (11); monkey's cousin (12); unlucky for some (13); rugby team (15); never been kissed (17); blind twenty (20; thus 'Blind thirty', 'Blind forty', etc.); all the twos (22; thus 'all the threes', 'all the fours', etc.); two ducks, dink-do (22); Pompey whore (24); bed and breakfast, half a crown (26); speed limit (30); all the

steps (39); half-way house (50); all the beans (57); stop work (65); clickety click (66); was she worth it? (76); two little crutches (77); two fat ladies (88); top of the house (99 or 100)

phr. 7. *toss the dice:* roll them bones!

Guide to Using the Index

1. This Index has been prepared on a computer database and as such conforms in its alphabetical order to the rules that are part of the standard ASCII (American Standard Code for Information Interchange) data transmission system. In practical terms, as experienced by the user of such an alphabetical system, ASCII listings work as follows.

Assuming that a list contains a number of examples of the same word, differentiated by capitals, punctuation marks and so on, the ASCII system will sort them thus: Fully capitalised words, initially capitalised words, lower case words, words incorporating a bracket, words incorporating a punctuation mark (!?*), words incorporating a hyphen. Thus:

AND 76.3	and 20.15	and! 94.5
And 234.1	and (and) 23.1	and-some 272.3

This order, when capitals, punctuation marks, etc. have to be considered, supercedes any non-computer-based alphabetical rules. Other than these differences, the basic alphabetical listing of individual words remains as would be expected in any dictionary.

2. For the purposes of this Thesaurus, the words listed in this Index have been designated typographically as follows.

LOVE 123–127: a comprehensive section of the book, comprising a number of subsections and identifying a wide-ranging topic which has been broken down into a number of more specific sections.
Love 123: a single sub-section of the book dealing with a single specific topic.
Love 125.1: a keyword as listed within a specific sub-section; usually one of the parts of speech defined within that sub-section.
love 125.17: the slang words included at large within the Thesaurus.

Index

blabs in labs 179.4
black 279.7, 496.1, 505.4
black Maria 475.3
black Pak 506.1
Black Power dance 479.1
black and white 75.4,
  475.2
black beauties 504.2
black bird 384.3
black bomber 504.2
black dog 279.2
black dust 384.3
black gang 456.1
black gold 67.6
black gungeon 506.2
black justice 320.1
black moat 506.2
black on black 76.7
black Russian 506.2
black sensibility 260.2
black taxi 75.2
black 360 degrees 384.2
black widow 504.2
black wings 360.4
blackjack 217.2
blackleg 241.9, 453.5
blacks (by blacks) 384.2
blacks (by whites) 384.1
blacktop 47.1
bladder 194.3
bladder of lard 515.1
blade 69.9
blag 310.4, 479.4
blagger 458.7
blah (on) 146.6
blah 19.2, 124.4, 146.3,
  185.1, 185.2, 299.2
blah! 292.8
blam 2.11, 135.1, 164.11
blame 18.10
blame 316
blame unfairly 316.3
blamed 28.2, 189.4
blamelessness 305.2
blanco 384.12
Blanco 179.8
blank 150.2, 200.1, 200.2,
  224.3, 493.3, 502.5
blanket man 458.9
blanket party 494.7
blankety 18.8, 18.10,
  28.2, 189.4
blap 164.11
blarney 183.2, 183.19,
  184.1, 287.1, 287.2
blart 183.9

blast 113.4, 276.3, 337.7,
  363.1, 506.6
blasted 101.3, 189.4
blat 183.9
blather 146.3, 184.1
blatherskite 146.2, 299.1,
  401.1
blaze on 338.4
blazes 326.2
blazing (down) 66.1
blazing 18.8
bleary 101.3
bleat 188.1, 188.2, 289.2,
  493.5
bleed (white) 368.3
bleed 384.2
bleed the liver 119.8
bleeder 377.1
bleeding 18.10, 189.4
bleeding dirt 496.1
bless me! 189.5
bless my heart! 189.5
bless my soul! 189.5
bless you! 285.5
bless your little cotton
  socks 328.10
blessed 18.8, 189.4
blessed event 110.1
blew in 508.12
blighter 377.1
blighty 45.1
blimey! 189.5
blimp 427.2
blind 18.10, 98.1, 101.3,
  116.37, 311.2, 317.2
blind Freddy 414.1
blind pig 104.2
blind staggers 101.1
blind twenty 516.6
blinder 344.1
blinding 27.3
blindside 173.3
blinker 195.9, 486.2
blinking 18.8, 18.10, 22.6,
  189.4
blip 164.11
blister 397.1
blithering 189.4
blitzed 101.3
blob 16.2, 95.11
block 116.4, 494.2
blockbuster 18.1, 386.4
blocked 507.8
blocker 458.15
blockhead 431.1
blockheaded 145.3

bloke 377.1, 379.1
Blondie 179.11
blood 116.28
blood 384.2, 438.1
blood claat 396.1
blood oath! 199.3
blood wagon 75.11
bloody 18.8, 18.10, 96.1,
  189.4
bloody-minded 206.2
blooey 258.4
blooey! 146.11
blooie 7.4
bloomer 165.1
blooming 18.8, 22.6,
  189.4
blooper 183.1
blop 41.5, 135.1, 164.11
blort 505.3
blossom 180.1
blot 116.29
blot one's copybook 165.3
blotch 69.18
bloviate 183.9
blow (it) 233.4
blow (it)! 54.6, 189.5
blow (n.) 337.2
blow (off) 184.2
blow (oneself out) 89.7
blow (out) 25.4
blow (up) 7.4
blow 7.8, 54.1, 54.3,
  183.7, 211.3, 235.4,
  360.12, 502.4, 505.3,
  505.11
blow Black 299.2
blow a fuse 147.4, 280.3
blow a gasket 280.3
blow a raspberry 292.3
blow ass 49.4
blow away 113.4, 173.3,
  337.7
blow by 361.4
blow down one's ear
  183.8
blow fire 239.4
blow great guns 66.8,
  289.2
blow hard 183.9, 299.2
blow heavy 299.2
blow in 52.1, 52.2, 53.1
blow in one's ear 202.4
blow it 127.1, 216.5,
  280.3
blow it out (your arse)!
  292.7

bogtrotter 383.12
bogue 12.4, 503.6
boho 147.5
bohunk 390.3, 427.1
boil 88.4
boil over 280.3, 514.5
boiled 101.3
boiler 77.1, 382.3
boilerplate 4.8
boiling 18.8
boing-boing 447.2
boko 116.4, 116.9
bold 347.4
bold as brass 347.4
boldacious 231.5
bollick 291.2
bollix up 254.2
bollixed 7.13
bollock 364.2
bollock naked 117.6
bollocking 291.1
bollocko 117.6
bollocks 116.36, 146.2
bollocks up 254.2
bollocksed (up) 7.13
bollox 146.2
bologna 146.2
boloney 19.2, 146.2
bolshy 342.4
boltop 191.5
bomb 28.1, 258.2, 504.2
bomb off 258.2
bomb out 258.2
bombed 101.3, 507.8
Bomber 179.8
bomber 504.2, 506.2, 506.3
bombshell 173.1
bonaroo 27.3
bonce 116.4
bonds 498.5
bone 116.35
bone idle 245.1
bone to pick 334.2
bone up (on) 190.9
bone yard 48.6, 112.3
bone-shaker 75.3
boned 337.10
bonehead 431.1
boneheaded 145.3
boner 118.4
bones 506.3, 516.1
bong 73.1, 135.1
bonified 253.7
bonkers 145.3
bonzer 27.3

boo 165.1, 506.2
boo-boo 165.1
boob 165.1, 165.3, 390.3, 391.1, 431.1, 494.1
boob-tube 82.21, 195.1
booboisie 390.1
booby hatch 147.2
boodle 509.1
boofer box 69.25
boofhead 431.1
booful 180.1
boog 384.1
boogaloo 276.5, 364.3
boogie 276.5, 364.3, 384.1
boogie-woogie 54.3
boogieman 325.4
boogying 364.1
boohoo 281.3
boojie 451.1
book (the joint) 132.6
book 190.7
book 54.3, 194.3, 489.2
book it 190.9
book up 190.9
boola-boola 188.1
boolhipper 82.12
boom 73.1
boom-boom 119.3
boomer 18.1
boondocks 46.1
boondoggle 235.3
boong 384.1
boonie 390.2
boonie hat 82.17
boonie rat 456.1
boonies 46.1
booshwah 146.2
boost 285.2, 286.1, 286.2, 341.1, 341.2, 341.3, 479.4
booster 458.15, 479.3
boosting 479.1
boot (around) 337.4
boot (out) 24.5, 63.2
boot 32.3, 63.1, 94.8, 118.13, 224.2, 242.4, 384.2, 454.1
boot-out 63.1
booted 63.4
bootlick 287.3
bootlicker 418.1
booty 116.40, 380.1
booze 94.1, 97.3
booze artist 92.3
booze hound 92.3
booze it up 97.3

booze joint 104.1
booze-up 98.1
boozed 101.3
boozed up 101.3
boozer 78.6, 92.3, 104.1
boozing 97.1
bop 41.5, 56.1, 59.2, 73.1, 135.1, 338.3, 338.5
bopper 381.5
boppers 82.15
bopping 364.1
bopping club 378.3
bopping gang 378.3
boracic 376.5
borax 146.2
borders 504.3
bore 272.3
bore stiff 272.3
bore the pants off 272.3
bore to tears 272.3
bored 272.6
bored stiff 272.6
bored to tears 272.6
boring 272.5
born days (all one's) 1.2
born tired 245.1
born under a bad sign 215.9
born with a silver spoon in one's mouth 215.5
borrow 489.2
borrower 417
borrowing 368
Borscht Belt 43.3
bosh 28.1, 146.2, 184.1, 299.1
boss 27.3, 457.1
Boss Charlie 387.1
boss player 430.2, 498.4
boss-eye 428.4
bossman 457.1
bot 368.2
botch up 33.3
bother 252.1, 252.4
botheration 168.1
botheration! 189.5
bottle (up) 218.2
bottle 295.1
bottle and glass 116.30
bottle baby 92.3
bottle blonde 117.9
bottle out, 33.2, 296.3
bottle-a-day man 92.3
bottled 101.3
bottler 394.4, 403.1
bottom drawer 354.1

bust a gut 205.2, 238.5, 280.3

bust caps 73.3

bust in 53.1, 53.2

bust loose 309.3

bust loose on 318.4

bust one's arse 205.2, 238.5, 241.6

bust one's hump 238.5, 241.6

bust one's nuts 238.5, 241.6

bust some booty 359.6

bust-out 18.10, 89.5

bust-up 7.4, 10.2, 331.1, 356.1

busted 376.5

buster 178.3, 382.1

busting 263.4, 264.3

bustle-punching 496.1

busy 241.10

busy 495.2

busy as a one-armed paper-hanger (with the itch) 241.10

but good 27.1

Butch 179.10

butch 404.1

butcher 456.2

butcher's 124.4, 132.1

butcher's window 116.40

butt 106.2, 106.3

butt in 183.15

butt out 249.4

butt out! 201.6, 292.7

butt-fuck 360.15

butt-plunger 436.4

butter 116.30, 380.1

butter baby 425.1

butter one's corn 360.19

butter up 287.2

butter-and-egg man 413.1

butterball 427.3

butterbox 383.5, 404.5

butterboy 454.1

buttercup 180.1, 404.1

buttered 84.3

buttered bun 437.3

buttered scone 516.6

butterfingers 254.1, 393.1

butterflies (in one's stomach) 283.1

butterfly 401.5

butterhead 384.2, 395.1

buttfucker 404.1

buttinski 398.1

buttocks 116.30

button 116.23, 116.42, 495.1, 505.4

button man 458.3

button mob 495.4

button one's lip 201.1

button up 201.1

button up! 201.5

button your lip! 201.5

button-down 227.3

buttoner 480.3

buttonhole 360.20

butty 86.4, 438.1

buy 160.2, 502.2

buy a (wolf) ticket 344.5

buy drugs 502.9

buy the (whole) farm 112.5, 160.2

buy the ring 360.15

buyer 458.10

buzz 60.4, 94.8, 192.2, 195.11, 196.1, 273.1

buzz around (like a blue-arsed fly) 236.4

buzz around like a one-armed paper-hanger 236.4

buzz off 54.3

buzz off! 54.6

buzz the nab 211.3

buzzard 426.2

buzzed 101.3

buzzer 181.1, 495.6

BVDs 82.10

by a nose 38.6

by George! 189.5

by golly! 189.5

by gorry! 189.5

by gosh! 189.5

by guess and by gosh 163.6

by gum! 189.5

by jimminy! 189.5

by jingo! 189.5

by jove! 189.5

by the book 4.8

by the great horn spoon! 189.5

BYO 98.1

c 16.4

C 509.10

c. 505.3

c-note 509.10

cabbage 509.1

caboodle 16.1

caboose 116.30

cabs 75.13

cache 203.3

cachunk 135.1

cack-hand 254.2

cackle 183.7, 184.1

cad 75.4

Caddy 75.4

cafe 78.7

caff 48.6, 78.7

caginess 149.1

cahoots 339.1

Cain and Abel 81.4

Cairo crud 119.5

cake 509.1

cake 86.12

cakehole 116.7

cakes 116.31

calaboose 494.1

calf 509.4

California bankroll 508.6

California roll 462.1

call (one) out 294.6, 344.5

call (v.) 188.2

call (n.) 188.1

call all bets off 10.7, 209.3, 302.2

call boy 497.9

call for Hughie 118.13

call for Ralph 118.13

call house 500.1

call it (right) 174.2

call it a day 10.6, 63.2, 112.5, 209.2, 239.6, 241.8, 302.2, 331.2, 356.2

call it quits 10.6, 112.5, 239.6, 241.8, 302.2, 331.2, 356.2

call of nature 119.1

call one's (best) shot 174.2

call the punches 216.3

call the shots 216.3

call the turn on 316.2

call-girl 497.2

calling down 291.1

calls to eat 89.9

calm (adj.) 265.6

calm down 265.4

calm down! 265.7

calm one down 265.5

calmness 265

camp 358.4

camp 80

catch a buzz 118.14,
360.19
catch a cold 125.16
catch a cold 252.5, 508.12
catch a listen 134.3
catch asleep at the wheel
173.2
catch bending 162.5,
173.2, 259.3
catch cold 162.5
catch flat-footed 173.2
catch forty winks 247.5
catch hell 291.3
catch it (hot) 291.3
catch it 318.6
catch off-base 173.2
catch on the hop 162.5
catch one's (big fat) tit in
a wringer 252.5
catch one's death 125.16
catch out 162.5
catch some rays 65.3,
346.4
catch up with 162.3
catch venereal disease
125.15
catch with one's pants
down 162.5, 173.2
catch with one's trousers
down 162.5, 173.2
catch you later 54.7, 346.4
catered food 89.2
cathouse 500.1
catnip 502.5
cats and kitties 116.31
catting 352.1
cattle car 475.3
catty-cat 116.40
caught by the short and
curlies 252.12
caught in a snowstorm
505.14
caught red-handed 489.5
caught short 119.6
cauliflowers 116.11
cause bad luck 215.7
cause trouble 250.1, 252.6
cause trouble for 334.3
caution 406.1
caution sign 451.2
cavalier 116.37
cave in 33.2, 258.2
cave-in 302.1
CCW 466.5
cease 10.6
cecil 505.3

celeb 139.7, 387.1
celebrate 276.5
celebration 276.3
celebrity fucker 439.2
celibate 436.11
cell 494.3
cell task 494.7
cement kimono 485.1
cement overcoat 485.1
cement-head 431.1
cemetery 112.3
censor 202.3
censure 290
central cut 116.40
centreman 494.4
century 16.4, 509.10
cereb 453.3
cert 159.1, 511.1
certain 159.3
certainly 159.4
certainly! 199.3
certainly not! 200.3
certainty 159
certificate 181.2
cessation 10.2
Cestrians 179.1
cha-cha 359.6
chair 492.1
chair 81.5
chalice 503.3
chalk 384.12
chalk eater 514.4
Chalk Farm 116.45
Chalkie 179.8
chalkie 456.10
Chalky 179.8
challenge 344.5
challenges 344.8
champagne 95.4
champagne trick 499.1
champers 95.4
champing at the bit 264.3
CHANCE 214–215
chance 38.1
chance one's arm 214.5
chance one's luck 214.5
chancer 402.1
chancy 151.6
CHANGE 11–13
change direction 51.3
change one's tune 209.4
chap 379.1
chapper 495.1
chappie 379.1
character 137
character 14.1

charas 506.1
charge (n.) 490.4
charge 273.1, 506.2, 507.2
charge him! 490.10
charged up 507.8
charity girl 437.3
charity moll 497.3
charlatan 323.3
Charlie 179.8
charlie 283.6, 384.12,
404.2, 497.2, 505.3
Charlie Cooke 132.1
charlie horse 125.4
Charlie Ronce 498.2
charlie's dead 85.7
charlies 116.31
Charlotte the Harlot
179.9
charmer 425.1
charming 137.5
charming wife 69.9
charver 359.6
chase away 224.4
chase the dragon 505.11
chase up 88.1
chasm 116.40
chassis 116.1
chastisement 318.2
chat 176.1, 183.2, 352.4
chat up 350.3
chateaued 101.3
Chats 179.8
chatter (v.) 184.2
chatter 184.1
chatter box 69.25
Chatty 179.8
chazerali 28.1
cheap 19.7
cheap 374.4
cheap and cheerful 151.2
cheap Charlie 399.1
cheap spirits 95.6
cheap wine 95.3
cheapie 28.1, 399.1
cheapskate 399.1
cheat (sexually) 353.3
cheat the starter 109.3
cheated 310.11
cheaters 83.6, 132.3
cheating 310.10
check 166.5, 340.5
check! 199.3
check and double check
164.12, 166.5, 340.5
check and double check!
199.3

Cons 179.2
cons 494.6
consarn(ed) 189.4
consent 222
consent 222.2
conservative person 407
consideration 329
consistent 4.8
consult Dr Jerkoff 360.19
contemptible person 396
contented 275.6
contention 344
contentment 275
continue 8.4
contraceptive devices 69.27
contraceptives 83.12
contract 113.1
contribute 370.3
CONTROL 216–218
convention 227
conventional 227.3
conversation 186
convictitis 494.5
convulse 274.5
cooch 116.40
cook (the books) 311.3
cook 456.25
cook 505.10
cook cucumbers 360.20
cook one's goose 250.1, 371.4
cook the mark 480.6
cook up 203.7, 232.4, 240.1
cooked (up) 311.5
cooked 258.4
cooked up 203.9
cooker 505.9
cookie 380.1, 425.1
cookie-pusher 446.1
cookies 357.1
cooking 270.4
cooking/eating utensils 91
cool (off) 265.5
cool 27.3, 143.6, 265.1, 265.4, 345.1
cool cat 389.1
cool down 265.3, 265.4
cool head 394.1
cool it 265.3, 265.4, 265.7, 266.1
cool off 265.4, 272.4
cool the rock 265.4
cooler 48.6, 494.2
coolie 458.2

coon 384.1
coon's age 1.2
coon-lover 438.2
coop 494.1
COOPERATION 339–341
cooping 495.11
coot 116.40, 380.1, 431.1
cootie 381.6
cooties 115.4
cooze 116.40, 437.3
cop 162.3, 166.2, 365.2, 482.4, 495.1, 498.6
cop a cherry 359.11
cop a decko 132.6
cop a dose 125.15
cop a drop 482.4
cop a feel 351.3
cop a gander 132.6
cop a heel 487.5, 494.8
cop a listen 134.3
cop a moke 487.5
cop a packet 257.2
cop a plea 491.4
cop a sight (of) 132.6
cop a snooze 247.5
cop a squat 346.3
cop an attitude 183.17
cop and blow 498.7
cop and heel 487.5
cop (for) 502.9
cop for 498.6
cop it 318.6
cop one's bird 360.12
cop one's joint 360.12
cop out (on) 472.3
cop out 211.3, 296.3, 491.4
cop shop 460.1
cop (some) Zs 247.4
cop the laughs (laffs) 277.2
cop the lot 20.4, 257.2
copacetic 27.3
copasetic 255.5
copout 403.1
copper 472.3, 495.1
copper jitters 496.1
copper-hearted 472.4
coppernob 428.1
copping 495.11
copping clothes 498.5
copulate enthusiastically 359.7
copy 15.5
copycat 15.3

cor! 189.5
corked 101.3
corker 27.1, 35.2
corksacking 189.4
corn 272.2
cornball 142.3
corned 101.3
corner 481.1
corner cowboy 412.12
cornfed 37.3
cornflakes 404.5
cornhole 116.29, 360.15
cornpone 385.1
corny 142.3
Corp 179.18
corporation cocktail 95.11
corpse 112.2, 429.5
corpse 250.1
correct 164.10
correspondence 191
corrode 288.3
corroded 36.2
corrupt 482.5
corruption 482.1
cosmetics 83.13, 120.7
cossie 82.13
cost (v.) 508.17
cost (n.) 508.10
cost ya! 292.7
cot-case 429.3
cottage 47.4, 362.2
cotton 116.39, 505.9
cotton-picking 28.2
cough (up) 319.1, 319.2, 370.2
cough 125.7
cough 193.3, 472.3, 490.6
cough and a spit 19.3
cough-drop 409.1
could be worse 123.4
couldn't find his arse with both hands 145.2
couldn't find one's way to first base 145.2
couldn't organise a fuck in a brothel 254.7
couldn't run a piss-up in a brewery 254.7
council houses 82.11
count 16.6, 139.2
count me in 340.5
count me out! 288.5
count out 25.4
counter to threats of violence 336.4
counterfeit money 483.1

338.4, 359.6, 363.1, 507.4
do a Melba 185.2
do a bit 239.8, 494.8
do a brodie 7.5
do a bunk 54.3, 54.4
do a crib 479.4
do a dry waltz with oneself 360.19
do a fade (on) 209.5
do a fade 211.3
do a fair lick 49.4
do a favour 341.7
do a job 478.2
do a job on 7.10, 310.6, 337.4
do a kindness 359.6
do a mischief (to) 485.3
do a number (on) 219.4
do a number 54.3, 263.3, 506.6
do a powder 54.3
do a runner 54.3, 211.3, 487.5
do a solid 341.7
do a thing 505.10
do a ton 60.4
do a twos 107.4
do a vanishing act 132.9
do any which way 151.3
do as one damn well pleases 213.2
do as you like 75.10
do brown 7.10, 310.4, 310.6
do down 310.4
do easily 251.4
do everywhichway 151.3
do for 318.4
do in 7.10, 113.4, 243.3, 505.10
do in the eye 310.4
do it for oneself 496.2
do it like Mommy 239.2
do it up (right) 239.4
do like a dinner 259.3
do one dirt 308.2
do one's best 238.6
do one's bit 339.4
do one's block 280.3
do one's darnedest 238.6
do one's dough 508.12
do one's head 507.5
do one's level best 238.6
do one's nut 280.3

do one's own thing 213.2, 230.2
do one's share 339.4
do one's stuff 239.4
do one's thing 212.3
do oneself in 112.7
do oneself off 360.19
do over 7.10, 33.3, 243.3, 252.10, 310.6, 337.4, 338.5
do rag 83.11
do roughly 239.3
do say! 173.9
do skippers 247.4
do something stupid 146.5
do successfully 257.3
do tell! 173.9
do the Dutch 112.7
do the business on 33.3, 113.4
do the crazy act 146.5
do the dirty (on) 308.2, 314.2
do the disappearing act 211.3
do the do 359.6
do the full sesh 204.2
do the handsome thing 305.4
do the honours 363.4
do the job (on) 113.4
do the lolly 280.3
do the nasty 359.6
do the natural thing 359.6
do the party 480.6
do the pussy 359.6
do the vanishing act 211.3
do the whole bit 239.4
do the works 239.4
do to a turn 259.3, 338.5
do up (brown) 7.8, 33.3, 338.5
do up (like a kipper) 7.10, 162.5
do up 4.4, 6.3, 33.3, 338.4, 505.10, 507.4
do up right 162.5
do well 239.4, 253.4
do with 268.2
do you get me? 166.6
do you get my meaning? 166.6
do you need a boy? 502.15
do you read me? 166.6
do you understand? 166.6

do you want drugs? 502.15
do-dad 69.2
do-hickey 69.2
do-jigger 116.34
do-re-mi 509.1
do-right man 407.1
DOA 459.2
dob in 193.4, 252.8, 370.2, 490.6
dobbin 115.10
dock 41.4, 218.2
dock asthma 490.3
docker 456.15
doctor (up) 203.7, 234.3
doctor's orders 516.6
doctored (up) 203.9, 311.5
doctors 456.2
doddle 251.1
dodge 210.1, 307.1, 310.2, 481.1
dodge the column 210.5
Dodger 179.8
dodgy 28.2, 482.5
dodo 407.1, 431.1
does a bear shit in the woods? 199.3
does a lot of shitting but his pants aren't down 435.4
does the bear shit in the woods! 299.4
does the Pope shit in the woods? 199.3, 299.4
does your mother know you're out?! 292.7
doesn't cut the mustard 33.1
doesn't have a clue 145.2
doesn't have a pot to pee in 376.5
doesn't know a mule's ass from a lemon 145.2
doesn't know enough to come in out of the rain 145.2
doesn't know enough to pound sand in a rathole 145.2
doesn't know from Adam 145.2
doesn't know from the man in the moon 145.2
doesn't know his ass from

face-ache 433.1
face-fucking 360.2
faced 101.3
facer 168.2, 252.1
facial 499.2
facial characteristics 117.8
FACILITY 251–254
factory 460.1, 495.8
facts 164.
fad 270.2
fade 7.5, 211.3, 259.3, 384.6, 487.1
fade away 54.3
faded boogie 384.6, 473.2
fadeout 112.1, 258.1
fading 20.1
fading game 516.3
fag (out) 243.3
fag 106.2, 241.1, 272.2
fag boy 497.9
fag tag 82.18
fag your face! 292.7
fag-end 106.3
fagged (out) 243.4
faggotter 498.4
faggy 33.6
fag hots 501.2
fail 258.2
fail to agree 343.1
failed 258.4
failing 258.3
failure 258
faint 125.17
fair crack of the whip! 305.9
fair dinkum 159.4, 305.9
fair dos! 285.5
fair enough! 285.5
fair go 214.2
fair go 305.1
fair one 338.1
fair pop 214.2
fair shake 305.1
fair shake of the dice! 305.9
fair to middling 123.4
fair-haired boy 387.1
fairy snuff! 285.5
fairy story 198.2
fake (up) 203.7, 233.1
fake 311
fake evidence 486.7
fake illness 124.3
fake it 311.4
fake jewellery 463.2
fake on (one) 150.1

fake up 232.4
faked 311.6
fall (all) over oneself 49.5
fall (for) 160.2, 258.1, 489.3
fall 56.1, 56.2
fall about 274.4
fall apart 127.1, 283.2
fall by 361.4
fall down on 282.2, 307.2
fall down on the job 258.2
fall flat 258.2
fall for (like a ton of bricks) 349.2
fall for 267.2, 310.8
fall guy 391.1
fall money 462.2, 494.7
fall off the wagon 97.3
fall out 247.3, 274.4
fall to pieces 127.1
fallen off the wagon 101.3
false 311.5
false alarm 282.1
false appearance 481.2
false information 192.4
falsehood 312
falsies 82.10
falsification 311
falsify 311.3
family jewels 116.33, 202.1
famous 139.7
famous last words! 292.7
fan 298.2, 318.5, 479.4, 488.3
fan one's ass 352.5
fan one's butt 49.6
fan one's pussy 352.5
fanatically 270.6
fancy! 173.8
fancy crib 48.2
fancy pants 161.3
fang 368.2
fanning (one's arse) 318.3
fanny 116.30, 116.40, 312.1
Fanny 179.8
fantabulous 27.3, 273.6
fantasising 175.3
fantasy 175
far 38.5
far gone 101.3
far out 22.5
far out! 27.4
faraways 38.5
fare 499.1

farm 48.6, 97.3
farmer 390.2
Farmington 44.2
fart 118.2, 118.8
fart about 146.4, 244.1
fart around 146.4, 207.2, 244.1
fart off 244.1
fartarse around 244.1
fascinate 349.3
fashion 229
fashionable 229.4
fast 309.4, 359.14
fast 49.9
fast black 75.13
fast lane 47.3
fast mover 71.3
fast one 253.2, 277.1, 310.2
fast shuffle 310.3
fast track 500.2
fast-fuck 359.2
fast-talking Charlie 384.8
fat 109.4
fat 37.3
fat chance 158.2
fat chance! 200.3
fat city 117.1, 257.1
fat knot 508.1
fat lip 183.1
fat lot 18.2
fat-assed 37.3
fatheaded 145.3
father and mother of 18.8
father and mother stuff 485.1
fatigue 243
fatmouth 152.3
Fats 179.13
Fatso 179.13
fave 212.1
fave rave 27.1, 212.1
fay 384.12
faze 169.3
fazed 169.4
fear 296.2
feast 89.5
feather 122.1
featherbedding 251.1
feature 139.4
feature 18.6
feature with fill one up 359.6
FEB 86.5
fed up 284.5
fed up with 272.6

gink 431.1
ginnal 458.8
ginned (up) 101.3
ginney 383.13
ginormous 18.7
ginzo 383.13
girl 505.3
girl's blouse 403.1
girlfriend 441.3
gism 67.7
gissa job! 242.9
gissum 116.28
git 431.1
git-down time 497.13
git-em-up guy 479.3
git-go 9.1
gitty-gap 69.2
give (it) a miss 150.1
give (it) a name 193.3
give (it) a tumble 144.3
give (it) all one's got 238.6
give (it) the (old) heave-ho 209.2
give (it) the ear 134.3
give (it) the go-by 150.1
give (it) the gun 60.4
give (it) the herbs 60.4
give (merry) hell 318.4
give (one) a bell 195.11
give (one) a buzz 195.11
give (one) a fast shuffle 310.4
give (one) a piece of one's mind 291.2
give (one) lead poisoning 337.7
give (one) the business 310.4
give (one) the office 494.8
give (one) the old boracic 186.7
give 193.3, 197.1
give 370.2
give a bad moment 296.5
give a bang 273.4
give a basting 318.5
give a black eye 20.3
give a body 473.3
give a break 341.5
give a bronx cheer 293.6
give a buzz 273.4
give a chance to 341.5
give a charge 273.4
give a clouting 318.5
give a coating 495.10

give a cut 367.3
give a dose 318.4
give a dressing-down 318.4
give a fair crack of the whip 305.4
give a fair shake 305.4
give a fourpenny one 337.4
give a fucking 310.6
give a going-over 132.6, 154.3
give a leg-up 341.2
give a little leg 312.2
give a nod (to) 222.2
give a piece 367.3
give a raspberry 293.6
give a roasting 154.3
give a rumble 162.3
give a screwing 310.6
give a share 367.3
give a shit 270.3, 283.2
give a sob story 261.4
give a song and dance 317.4
give a square shake 305.4
give a squeeze 341.5
give a tumble 162.3, 267.2
give a turn 296.5
give a whirl 238.3
give a wide berth 210.4
give a workover 154.3
give an orgasm 359.9
give an out 317.3
give cone 360.12
give enough rope 213.3
give false information 192.6
give freedom 284.2
give half a chance 341.5
give head 360.12
give her a length 359.6
give her one 359.6
give in 302.2
give it a burl 238.3
give it a fling 238.3
give it a fly 238.3
give it a go 214.5, 238.3
give it a miss 302.2
give it a tumble 238.3
give it all that 299.2
give it hot and heavy 291.2
give it the E 209.2
give it the chuck 209.2

give it the elbow 209.2
give it the toss 209.2
give it to (one) good 338.5
give it to 318.4, 337.7, 485.3
give jiggs 149.5, 255.4
give lumps 338.5
give one Larry Dooley 318.4
give one a (good) talking to 291.2
give one a (nasty) jolt 173.2
give one a (nasty) turn 173.2
give one a headache 278.4
give one a miss 362.4
give one a pain (in the neck, arse) 284.2
give one a pain 278.4
give one a pain in the arse 278.4
give one a song and dance 186.7
give one a tumble 359.6
give one in the neck 278.4
give one rocks 357.4
give one some curry 291.2
give one some funny business 313.2
give one some stick 291.2
give one the belt 348.2
give one the brush (off) 348.2
give one the brush 331.2
give one the brush-off 331.2
give one the business 291.2, 293.5
give one the cold shoulder 348.2
give one the creeps 283.4
give one the freeze (out) 348.2
give one the frost 348.2
give one the go-around 348.2
give one the leather 337.4
give one the leg 293.5
give one the pink slip 370.2
give one the runaround 348.2
give one the shaft 313.2
give one the works 291.2

good-time Charlie 447.1
goodbye! 346.4
goodbye 54.7
goodies 116.40, 365.1
goodness 27
goods (on) 162.1
goods 137.2, 164.4, 192.1, 253.1, 464.1, 486.1
gooey about 349.4
gooey over 349.4
goof 165.3, 409.1, 431.1
goof bender 276.2
goof off 210.5, 244.1
goof on 274.4
goofball 409.1, 504.3
goofed 507.8
goofer 497.9
goofy 101.3, 145.3, 169.5
Goofy 179.16
goofy about 349.4
gook 384.11, 431.1
goolies 116.36
goombah 395.2
goon 395.2, 433.3, 453.5
goon squad 433.3, 453.5
goop 67.7, 390.3, 431.1
goopy 145.3
goose 129.2, 284.8, 310.5, 351.3, 451.1
goose's neck 508.3
gooseberry 350.7
gopher 453.2
gor 325.1
gor blimey! 189.5
Gordon and Gotch 83.9
Gordon Bennett! 189.5
gorge out 112.7
gorilla 18.1, 29.1, 257.1, 338.6, 433.3, 499.2
gorilla in the washing machine 360.13
gorilla pimp 498.4
gork 429.3
gorm 143.1
gorra 325.1
gorry 325.1
gosh 9.2, 325.1
gosh! 189.5
gosh-almighty 189.5
gosh-damned 189.4
gosh-danged 189.4
gosh-darn! 189.5
gosh-dern 189.4
gospel 164.2
gossip (person) 420.2
gossip (v.) 196.3

gossip 196
gossiping 196.4
got it 166.5
got up 84.3
got you 166.5
gotcha 166.5
gourd 116.3
goy 384.10
goyim 384.10
grab 267.3, 489.2, 494.7
grab a bite 89.6
grab a chair 56.3
grab a flop 56.3
grab a listen 134.3
grab a little shuteye 247.5
grab one's fifteen minutes 139.4
grab-arse 146.4
grab-bag 16.1
grabby 268.5
grade A 20.2, 87.4
graduate 143.4
graft 241.1, 241.4, 307.1, 482.1
grafter 453.4
gramps 382.2, 444.8
grand 16.4, 299.2, 509.14
grand bag 116.36
grand duchess 404.1, 404.5
grandiloquence 185
grandparents 444.8
grandstand 298.2
Granny 179.8
granny 481.3
granny-jazzer 395.1
grape 456.1
grapefruits 116.31
grapes 116.31
grapevine 196.2
grass (up) 193.4
grass 116.39, 472.2, 472.3, 473.3, 506.2
grass-eater 482.3
grassed (up) 193.8
grassed up 473.5
grassfighter 405.2
Grauniad 179.5
graveyard shift 1.10, 241.3
gravy 20.2, 27.1, 509.1
gravy 86.23
gravy train 251.1
gray 384.12
greapha 506.2
grease 86.1, 113.4, 120.8,

287.2, 370.4, 372.3, 482.2
grease job 287.1, 372.1
grease one's palm 372.3
grease one's pipe 360.19
grease the gash 360.20
grease the wheel 251.2
grease-gun 71.1
greaseball 383.15
greased lightning 49.3
greaser 383.15, 451.1
greasers 378.3
greasy spoon 48.6
great! 285.5
great Caesar's ghost! 189.5
great Scott! 189.5
Great Unwashed 390.1
great in degree 18.8
'*great love*' 441.6
great outdoors 64.1
great shakes 27.3
great snakes! 189.5
greatness 18
Grecians 179.1
greedy 268.5
greedy person 399
greefo 506.2
greek 167.1
Greek 383.9
Greek culture 360.5, 499.4
green (as grass) 254.5
green 509.1
green as owlshit 145.3
green ashes 505.4
green hornet 495.3
green house 502.2
green light 222.1
green nigger 383.12
green thumb 415.1
greenbacks 509.1
greener 431.1, 454.1
greenhorn 431.1, 454.1
greenie 95.1
greenies 509.1
greens 508.9
greet with mutual palm-slapping 346.2
greeting 346
Gregory Peck 116.21
grey 227.3, 384.4, 407.1
grey ghost 495.3
grey matter 143.1
grief 281
griefo 506.2

H² 351.4
ha'penny 116.41
habe 217.1
habit 503.5
habituated 226.2
hack (it) 190.9
hack (it out) 190.8
hack 118.13, 238.2, 253.3, 453.3, 456.3, 456.13, 494.5
hack around 235.5, 277.3
hack it 239.5, 257.2, 257.3
hack one's mack 360.19
hack out 151.3
hack up 290.2
hacked 280.6
hacker 456.13
hackie 456.13
hacking (it out) 190.1
had 359.15
had it (with) 278.6, 284.5
hades 326.2
haemorrhoids 125.11
hair 116.2
hair 295.1
hair of the dog 102.3, 97.2
hair pie 116.40
hairbag 426.2
haircut 491.3
hairstyle 120.1
hairy 262.6, 380.1
hairy-assed 262.6
Hairy Mary 179.9
half 3.10
half a bar 16.3, 509.4
half a cock 16.3, 509.5
half a crown 516.6
half a dollar 16.3
half a mo! 248.5
half a sheet 16.3, 509.4
half a stretch 491.3
half a yard 16.3, 509.9
half and half 207.3
half gone 101.3
half past two 384.8
half saw 16.3
half seas over 101.3
half shot 101.3
half slewed 101.3
half step 244.1
half the bay over 101.3
half your luck! 292.7
half-and-half! 357.9
half-arsed 151.7, 235.9, 254.3
half-assed 28.3

half-baked 28.2, 145.3, 254.5
half-brass 497.3
half-cock(ed) 237.6
half-cocked 19.6, 28.3, 151.7
half-cracked 138.4, 147.5
half-crazy 138.4
half-cut 101.3
half-gone 147.5
half-inch 479.4
half-iron 439.3
half-lo 502.4
half-ounce 310.6
Half-Pint 179.14
half-pint 19.6, 388.1, 427.4
half-portion 19.6, 427.4
half-saved 409.1
half-there 147.5
half-way house 516.6
half-wide 143.6
halfpenny dip 75.8
hallucinogens 506.4
halvers 26.2
ham and egger 451.1
ham hocks 116.18
hambone 85.4
hamma 425.1
hammer 20.3, 60.4, 76.3, 116.34, 290.2, 318.5, 425.1
hammer 69.6
hammer ass 241.6
hammer away (at) 205.2
hammer away 241.7
hammer away at 153.4
hammer man 387.1
hammer out 240.1
hammered 101.3
hammered down 37.2
hammerhead 431.1
hammers 116.18
Hammers 179.1
hampsteads 116.8
Hampton Wick 116.34
hampton rock 116.34
hand (out) a line 146.6, 183.19
hand 8.2
hand a (cock-and-bull) story 198.7
hand a laugh 274.5
hand a lemon 310.4

hand a line (of bull) 198.7, 287.2, 310.7
hand gig 497.12
hand in one's chips 10.6
hand in one's dinner pail 112.5
hand in one's dinner plate 54.3
hand job 360.9
hand out 370.2
hand out a bit of stick 337.3
hand out a line of bull 146.6
hand out a line of crap 146.6
hand out punishment 337.3
hand shandy 360.9
hand-gallop 360.19
hand-made cigarette 106.4
hand-me-downs 82.6
hand-reared 117.5
-handed 458.20
handful 168.2, 491.3
handkerchief 83.2
handkerchief head 384.6
handle 178.1, 190.3
handlebars 76.6
handout 370.1
hands 116.15
hands down 251.6
hands off your cocks and on your socks! 247.78
handsome 27.3, 370.7
handwriting 190.4
hang (it) up 209.2, 241.8
hang 492.3
hang 51.3, 241.1
hang a Lilly 51.3
hang a Louie 51.3
hang a Ralph 51.3
hang a U-ie 51.3
hang about 244.2, 248.5
hang around 244.2
hang around with 328.6
hang in (there) 4.5, 8.4, 13.1, 205.2, 266.2
hang in there! 295.6
hang it up 10.6
hang loose 222.2, 265.3
hang on! 266.4
hang one on 101.2, 337.4
hang one out to dry 338.5
hang one to the wall 318.4
hang out 41.6

hung for bread 376.5
hung up (on) 226.2
hung up 270.4
hung up on 270.5
hunger 90.2
hungry 236.8, 495.1
hungry 90.4
hungry croaker 50.23
hunk 390.3, 425.2, 427.1
hunkie 384.12
hunko 427.1
hunky 117.12, 390.3
hunky-dory 4.2, 27.3, 275.4
hunkydory 123.3
hunt 157.1
hunt 224.4
hurl 118.13
hurricane lamp 417.3
hurry 49.5
hurry up! 49.12
hurry-up 475.2
hurry-up wagon 475.3
hurt (v.t.) 485.3
hurt 337.8
hurt 337.8
hurt for 268.2
hurt one's feelings 301.3
hurt to 264.2
hurtin' for certain 36.2
hurting (for) 268.4, 503.7
hurting 264.3, 279.7, 376.5
hurting dance 281.1
husband 404.5
husband 444.4
hush money 372.2
hush my mouth! 173.7
hush one's mouth 136.3
hush up 136.3, 202.2
hush up! 136.4
hush your mouth! 201.5
hush-hush 202.5
husky 453.3
hustle 49.1, 232.1, 232.3, 236.1, 236.2, 236.3, 502.8
hustler 513.1
hydraulic 434.1
hygiene 120
hype 20.3, 187.2, 286.2, 503.2, 508.16
hyper 263.4
hypo 505.9
hysterical historical 198.5

I agree 340.5
I ain't just whistling (Dixie)! 199.3
I ain't just whistling Dixie 204.7
I am jealous 333.2
I am/was embàrrassed 301.4
I approve 285.5
I ask you 161.6
I can't get that together 167.5
I can't handle this 283.8
I could care 151.9
I could do that a favour 286.3
I disapprove 288.5
I don't believe it! 161.6
I don't believe this 161.6
I don't buy that 161.6
I don't care 271.7
I don't give a fuck 151.9
I don't know 271.7
I don't mean maybe! 199.3
I don't mind if I do 221.3
I don't think! 200.3
I don't understand 167.5
I dunno 271.7
I feel happy 273.7
I give in 302.5
I give up 145.5
I haven't the foggiest 145.5
I hear you! 199.3
I mean 9.2
I mean! 199.3
I mean it 204.7
I pass 145.5
I refuse! 223.1
I should be so lucky 158.7, 285.5
I should care 271.7
I should cocoa 146.11
I should live so long 158.7
I should say so! 199.3
I should worry 271.7
I suppose 116.9
I understand 166.5
I've won! 20.7
I want work 242.9
I want! 365.5
I wouldn't fuck her with a borrowed prick 359.20
I wouldn't fuck her with your prick 359.20

I wouldn't know 271.7
I wouldn't touch it with a (ten-foot) barge-pole 288.6, 359.20
I wouldn't touch it with yours 288.6, 359.20
I wouldn't trust him/her as far as I could throw him/her 307.5
I'll be a Dutchman! 189.6
I'll be a (lowdown) son of a bitch! 189.6
I'll be a Chinaman! 189.6
I'll be a dirty word! 189.6
I'll be a monkey's uncle! 173.7, 189.6
I'll be blowed 189.6
I'll be consarned! 189.6
I'll be damned (if I will) 223.1
I'll be damned if! 200.3
I'll be danged (if I will) 223.1
I'll be darned! 189.6
I'll be dashed (if I will) 223.1
I'll be fucked 173.7
I'll be fucked if! 200.3
I'll be hanged (if I will) 223.1
I'll be hanged 189.6
I'll be jiggered! 189.6
I'll be shot (if I will) 223.1
I'll be shot 189.6
I'll be . . .! 189.6
I'll eat my hat! 161.6, 199.3
I'll eat my head! 199.3
I'll freeze 345.5
I'll go for that 340.5
I'll say 340.5
I'll say! 199.3
I'll say she does 164.12
I'll say.you do 164.12
I'll see you in hell first! 223.1
I'm bored 272.7
I'm on 340.5
I'm with you 340.5
ibble out 89.7
IBM 116.34
IC 379.1
ice 83.10, 113.4
ice 67.4
ice cream 86.29
ice cream machine 116.34

judgement 163
judy 380.1
judy with the big booty 427.3
jug 95.1, 494.1, 508.8
jug-up 494.7
jugged 494.11
jughead 92.3
jugheaded 145.3
juice 32.1, 67.5, 94.1, 216.1, 219.1, 276.1, 372.3, 510.3
juice house 104.1
juice man 485.2
juice-freak 92.3
juice-head 92.3
juiced 101.3
juicy 306.5
juke 363.3, 364.3
juking 364.1
jumble 383.6
Jumbo 179.13
jump 9.1, 54.2, 236.1, 338.7, 359.6
jump all over 291.2, 338.5
jump at 310.8
jump bad 231.4
jump bail 487.5
jump down one's throat 280.3
jump off one's perch 300.3
jump on (with both feet) 291.2, 300.3, 318.4
jump salty 280.3, 284.3
jump steady 94.1
jump street 9.1
jump tables 88.2
jump the gun 9.3, 54.4
jump the last hurdle 112.5
jump the rails 216.5, 280.3
jump to (it) 241.5
jump to it 49.7, 148.2
jump up and down 359.6
jump up and down on 291.2
jump-up man 458.7
jump-up merchant 458.7
jumped up 142.2
Jumper 179.8
jumper 465.1
jumping 270.4
jumping Jehosaphat! 189.5
jumping cat 389.1, 413.1

jumps 263.1
jumpy 283.6
jungle 80.1
jungle bunny 384.1
jungle juice 94.7
jungle mouth 125.5
jungly 142.3
junior jumper 458.6
junk 69.2, 209.2, 235.2, 505.2
junk food 86.1
junk hawk 503.2
junker 75.3
junkie 503.2
junky 235.9
just like mother makes it 27.3
just one's speed 253.8
just quietly 328.8
just the job 27.3
just the ticket 27.3
just what the doctor ordered 27.3, 94.5, 164.10
justifying possession of stolen goods 481.6
juvie 494.1

K 16.4, 509.14
ka-ka 119.3
kack up 219.6
kak 118.13, 119.3
kaker 28.1, 506.1
kale 509.1
kanaka 383.10
kanga 69.12
kangaroo 384.8
Kangaroo Valley 44.1
Kansas City roll 508.6
karsy 79.1
Kate and Sidney 86.5
kate karney 179.3
kaycuff foe! 54.6
kaylack 183.1
kaynab 508.8
kayo 27.1, 337.5
kayrop 86.5
KB 63.1, 200.1, 200.2, 494.7
kecks 82.10
keel over 112.5, 243.1
keen 123.3, 229.4, 253.7, 273.6, 285.5
keen (-o) 27.3
keen-looking 35.7
keeno 253.7, 285.5

keep (one) cool 275.2
keep (one) guessing 168.3
keep (one) on a string 310.7
keep (one) sweet 275.2
keep a low profile 300.2
keep a secret 202.2
keep a stiff lip 202.2
keep a stiff upper lip 266.2, 295.4
keep a tight asshole 265.3
keep ahead of the game 216.3
keep banker's hours 244.1
keep cave 149.5, 255.4
keep chickie 149.5
keep decko 255.4
keep in the clear 305.5
keep it dark 202.2
keep it down 202.2
keep it on one's chest 201.3
keep it under one's hat 201.3
keep jiggers 255.4
keep KV 149.5, 255.4
keep mum 201.1, 202.2
keep mum! 201.5
keep nit 149.5
keep on ice 374.3
keep on tap 234.2
keep on the q.t. 203.6
keep on the straight and narrow 230.2
keep on the strict q.t. 202.2
keep one's chin up 295.4
keep one's cool 265.3
keep one's ear to the ground 149.5
keep one's end up 230.2, 339.4
keep one's eye on the ball 148.1
keep one's eyes peeled 149.3, 149.4
keep one's hair on 265.3
keep one's head down 149.3
keep one's nose clean 139.2, 230.2, 305.5
keep one's pants zipped 230.2
keep one's pecker up 266.2, 295.4
keep one's shirt on 50.2

look fit to kill 35.5
look out 256.6
look out for number one 149.2, 213.2
look sharp 49.5, 84.2, 148.1, 149.4
look slippy 148.1, 149.4
look some 35.5
look what the cat's brought in 346.3
look what the wind's blown in 346.3
look-out 458.13
look-see 132.1, 156.1
lookalike 15.1
looker 35.2, 425.1, 436.12
looking green about the gills 34.2
looking like a dog's dinner 34.2
lookism 132.1
looks 34
looks like a wet weekend 118.15
looks like he/she lost a pound and found sixpence 282.5
looksee 132.1
loon 431.1
loon about 276.6
loon pants 82.11
looney doctor 456.2
looniness 147.1
loony 124.7, 147.5, 431.1
loony bin 48.6, 147.2
loony farm 48.6
loop-the-loop 86.25
looped 101.3
loopy 124.7, 138.4, 147.5
loose ends 508.6
loose up top 147.5
loosen up 193.3, 309.3
loot 509.1
lor 325.1
Lord Lovel 69.11
lord love a duck! 189.5
Lord Mayor 189.3
Lord Muck 401.4
Lord Right 441.2
lordy 325.1
lose 369.2
lose a bet 512.4
lose control 216.5
lose importance 19.5
lose money 376.4

lose one's bottle 33.2, 210, 296.3
lose one's cool 280.3
lose one's doughnuts 118.13
lose one's erection 359.13
lose one's gender 358.2
lose one's groceries 118.13
lose one's hair 280.3
lose one's lunch 118.13
lose one's marbles 147.4, 280.3
lose one's rag 280.3
lose one's rudder 101.2
lose one's shirt 369.2
lose one's temper 280.3
lose out 258.2, 282.3
lose reputation 140.3
lose the ball 258.2
lose the combination 171.1
loser 512.3
losing at gambling 512.9
losing streak 369.1
loss 369, 512.2
loss of reputation 140.2
lost in thought 153.9
lot 14.1
Lottie 179.8
loud 131.5
loud and clear 134.6
loudmouth 183.9, 299.2, 420.1, 456.4
loudtalk 299.2
lounge lizard 446.1
louse (one) up 334.3
louse up 7.8, 165.3
lousy with 22.4, 366.5
lout 390.3
love 178.3, 180.1, 328.10
LOVE 349–356
love it to death 273.7, 276.4
love letter 191.6
lovely 425.1
lovely grub! 199.3
lovers 441
lovers' codes on envelopes 191.5
lovey 178.3, 180.1, 328.10
lovey-dovey 180.1, 349.4, 351.1
low down 28.2
low in the saddle 101.3
low rent 7.14, 28.2, 140.6

low-down 140.5, 306.3, 308.3
low-life 140.5, 278.5
low-rent 278.5, 306.3, 308.3
lowdown (on) 162.1
lowdown 192.1, 192.2, 194.2
lower (it) 89.6
lower one's flag 300.4
lower than a snake's belly 279.7
lower than the spots on a snake's ass 396.1
lower than whale shit 396.1
lower the boom on 291.2
lowest of the low 140.5
lowlife 392.1, 433.1, 433.3
lox jock 384.8
LSD 506.4
LTR 355.2
lube 67.6
lubricated 101.3
luck 215
luck into 215.5
luck out 215.5
lucky 215.8
Lucozade 384.1
Lucy Law 495.1
Lucy Locket 82.19
ludes 504.4
luggage 366.2
lugger 479.3, 494.4
lulu 27.1
lumber 250.1, 312.2
lumme! 173.7
lummocks 395.1
lump 337.4, 390.3, 427.1, 454.3
lumpy chicken 134.6
lunch 360.1, 360.2
lunchbox 431.1
lunchtime intercourse 359.3
lunchy 145.3, 229.5, 274.9
lunk 431.1
lunkhead 390.3, 431.1
lunkheaded 145.3
lurk 307.1
lurkola 508.5
lurky 307.4
lush 92.3, 97.3
lush it around 97.3

niggly 280.5
night 3.9
night clothes 82.1
night-cap 97.2
night-club 363.2
nighthawk 479.2
nightstick 447.1
nignog 384.1
-nik 10.4
Nina from Carolina 516.5
Nina with her hair down 516.5
nine day blues 125.10
nine-to-five 226.1, 241.1
nineteenth hole 78.6
ning-nong 431.1
nip 162.3, 337.8, 365.2, 383.14, 383.14
nipper 381.3
nisht 16.2
nit 431.1
nit-nit 201.5
nitro 67.5
nitty gritty 18.3, 144.1, 162.1, 164.1, 164.3
nitwit 431.1
nitwitted 145.3
nix 200.1, 200.2, 224.1, 225.1, 288.1, 288.3
nix! 200.3, 225.3
nix on that (stuff) 225.3
no! 200.3, 225.3
no account 235.8
no better than he/she should be 437.6
no big deal 28.1, 388.1
no biggie 271.7
no bon 28.2
no can do 254.3
no can see 167.2
no chance 214.4
no chance! 214.11
no chicken 111.4
no deal 343.2
no deal! 223.1, 343.2
no dice 158.7, 258.1, 282.1
no dice! 200.3, 223.1
no fear 158.7
no flies on (him, her, etc) 143.6, 253.7
no freak 499.2
no go 28.2, 258.1, 343.2
no go! 223.1
no great catch 19.4, 140.6

no great shakes 19.1, 19.4, 140.6, 388.1
no holds barred 213.5
no ifs and buts 159.3
no ifs or buts 164.8
no joy 282.1
no kick 275.4
no kid(ding)! 199.3
no kidding 161.6, 204.7
no laughs (laffs) 252.11
no longer addicted 503.12
no muss no fuss 265.7
no oil painting 36.1
no picnic 252.11
no prize 36.1
no punches pulled 213.5
no rest for the wicked 241.11
no risk 199.3
no sale 258.1, 343.2
no sale! 200.3
no savvy 167.2
no shit 159.4, 161.6, 164.12, 204.7
no shit! 173.9, 199.3
no siree (bob)! 200.3
no skin off my arse 271.7
no skin off my nose 271.7
no slouch 35.7, 430.2
no soap 158.7, 258.1, 282.1, 343.2
no soap! 200.3, 223.1
no squawk 275.4
no strings (attached) 213.5
no stuff 305.1
no sweat 251.6, 275.4, 345.4
no sweat! 285.5
no thank-you 345.5
no two ways (about it) 159.3
no two ways about it 212.2
no way 158.7, 343.2
no way! 146.11, 200.3, 225.3, 288.5
no-brand cigarette 506.3
no-hope 278.5
no-hoper 140.5, 414.1
no-name cigarette 506.3
no-no 158.2, 200.1, 200.2, 306.1, 431.1
noah's ark 472.2
nob 448.1
nobbing 359.1

nobble 7.4, 514.7
nobby 141.1
Nobby 179.8
nobody to write home over 388.1
nobody's fool 430.2
Nocky 179.8
nod 182.1, 507.5
nod and a wink 285.1
nod out 507.5
noddy 475.2
noffka 497.2
noise (light, splashing) 135.2
noise (loud) 135.3
noise (of a blow) 135
noise (of a crash) 135
noise 131.5, 183.1
nola 404.1
Nola the Bowler 179.9
nommus! 256.6
non 393.2
non compos 147.5
non-Jews (by Jews) 384.10
non-alcoholic drinks 87
nonce 436.5
nonchalant 271.6
nondescript 475.2
nong 431.1
nonsense 146
nonsense 146.2
noodle 431.1
nookie 359.1
nooner 359.3
nope! 200.3
NORWICH 191.5
nose 472.2, 505.3
nose around 249.2
nose candy 505.3
nose in 53.2
nose-dive 56.1, 140.2, 258.1
noseful 22.1
nosh 86.1
nosh-up 89.5
nosing around 249.1
nosper 377.1
nosy 155.2
not a bean 376.2
not a bite 258.1
not a brass razoo 376.2
not a cat's chance in hell 214.4
not a Chinaman's chance 214.4
not a hope 214.4, 258.1

not a hope in hell 158.7, 214.4
not a lick 23.3
not a nibble 258.1
not a sausage 16.2
not a smell 23.3
not a sniff 23.3
not a snowball's chance in hell 214.4
not all that it seems 311.5
not all there 101.3, 145.3, 147.5, 150.2, 169.5, 254.3
not amount to a hill of beans 19.4
not amounting to a piss in the ocean 140.6
not an earthly (chance) 214.4
not an earthly 158.7
not backward in coming forward 142.2, 236.8
not be all there 147.3
not bleeding likely! 200.3
not cricket 308.1
not cut it 258.2
not cut out for 237.6
not feel like anything 124.1
not feel too hot 124.1
not feel up to scratch 124.1
not feel up to snuff 124.1
not fucking likely! 200.3
not get past first base 258.2
not give a damn (for) 151.3
not give a damn 150.1, 271.2
not give a darn 271.2
not give a (flying) fuck 271.2
not give a fuck (for) 151.3
not give a fuck 150.1
not give a good goddam 271.2
not give a hoot 271.2
not give a monkey's 271.2
not give a rap (for) 271.2
not give a shit 150.1, 271.2
not give a stuff 271.2
not give a tinker's cuss 271.2
not give a tumble (for) 150.1

not give a tuppeny fuck 271.2
not give up the ship 205.2
not go for (it) 161.1
not go for 288.3
not go nap on 332.2
not hack it 258.2
not half! 285.5
not have a Chinaman's chance 158.4
not have a dog's chance 158.4
not have a hope (in hell) 158.4
not have a pot to piss in 376.3
not have a prayer 376.3
not have a red cent 376.3
not have all one's marbles 147.3
not have the first idea 167.2
not have the foggiest 167.2
not having both oars in the water 147.5
not hit a lick 258.2
not hold together 165.2
not hold water 165.2
not hurry 50.2
not in the game 21.3
not in the picture 21.3
not in the same league 21.3
not know the score 192.8
not know whether you're on your head or heels 169.2
not let it get one down 266.2
not let it get to one 266.2
not let the cat out of the bag 202.2
not miss a trick 148.1, 214.9
not much chop 28.2
not much you wouldn't! 146.11
not on the job 150.2
not on your life! 223.1
not on your Nellie! 158.7, 200.3
not on your tintype! 200.3, 223.1
not peep 202.2

not playing with a full deck 147.5, 254.3
not quite there 147.5
not ready for people 145.3
not see (it) 161.1
not so bad 123.4
not so dumb 143.5
not so dusty 124.4, 143.5, 27.5
not so hot 124.4
not spill the beans 202.2
not stand a cat's chance in hell 158.4
not stand a snowball's chance in hell 158.4
not stick one's head out 149.3
not stick one's neck out 149.3
not swallow (it) 161.1
not take any wooden nickels 148.1, 149.3
not tell t'other from which 15.4
not the full quid 147.5
not to be sneezed at 285.5
not to be sniffed at 285.5
not to have the breaks 215.6
not to matter 19.4
not tolerate 266.3
not tonight Josephine 351.5
not turn a hair 265.3
not up to scratch 237.6
not up to snuff 254.3
not with it 169.5
not worth a bumper 19.1, 19.4
not worth a fart in a noisemaker 19.4, 235.10
not worth a fart in a thunderstorm 19.4
not worth a hill of beans 19.1, 19.4
not worth a light 19.4, 235.10
not worth a pisshole in the snow 19.4, 235.10
not worth a plugged nickel 19.1
notch 394.1
notch above 17.1
note 509.2

phone freak 499.2
phoney 499.1
phonus balonus 146.2, 311.1
phony 311.1, 311.5
phooey! 146.2, 292.8
photo finish 95.1
photographer 195.9
phut 135.1
physical breakdown 127
physical condition 122
physical exercise 121
physical injury 126
physical strength 32.2
physically affectionate 351.4
physics for poets 179.4
pi 303.3, 321.3
piano 86.5
piccolo and flute 82.2
pick 479.3
pick a bone with 344.3
pick 'em up 49.6
pick the plums 371.5
pick up 350.3
pick up 352.7
pick up brownie points 139.4
pick up fag ends 183.15
pick up the soap for 360.16
pick up the tab 304.1, 370.5, 508.13
pick up the vibrations 360.22
pick-me-up 97.2
pick-up 441.11
pickaninny 384.1
pickings 365.1
pickled 101.3
picklepuss 426.1
pickles 86.21
pickpocket 458.14
picnic 11.1, 251.1
piddle 119.4, 119.8
piddle about 244.1
piddle around 244.1
piddle away 235.4
piddling 19.6
pie 251.5, 425.1
pie in the sky 175.1, 371.1
pie-eater 458.3
pie-eyed 101.3
piece (of the action) 23.1
piece 14.1, 38.1, 38.3,

70.1, 71.1, 367.1, 380.1, 411.1, 437.3, 502.4
piece of ass 380.1, 437.3
piece of cake 251.1
piece of crap 278.1, 396.1
piece of fluff 411.1
piece of one's mind 291.1
piece of piss 251.1
piece of shit 278.1, 396.1
piece of tail 380.1, 437.3
piece off 372.3
pieces 82.1
piffle 146.2
pig 399.3, 427.2, 427.3, 437.3, 495.1
pig brother 472.2, 473.2
pig heaven 460.1, 89.5
pig it 142.1, 268.3
pig out 89.7
pig sty 460.1
pig style 142.6
pig-headed 206.2
pig-ignorant 145.3
pigeon 391.1, 480.4
pigger 427.3
pigging 18.10
pigging it 142.6
Piggy 179.8
piggy 180.1, 268.5
pighead 399.4
pigmouth 427.3
pigs 383.25
pigs! 189.5
pigshit 146.2
pigshit! 189.5
piker 399.1, 412.12
pikey 417.3
pile 18.2, 359.6, 375.2, 508.1
pile in 241.5
pile into 84.1
pile it on (heavy-thick) 286.2, 310.7, 312.2
pile it on 185.2
pile up 7.11
pile up some Zs 247.4
pile-up 7.3, 75.14
Pilgrims 179.1
pill 397.1, 452.2
pill out 60.4
pill-popper 503.1
pill-taker 503.1
pilled up 507.8
pillhead 503.1
pillow 81.3
pillow biter 404.1

pills 128.3, 504
Pills 179.8
pimp 27.3
pimp 498.2
pimp dust 498.5, 505.3
pimp fronts 498.5
pimp post 76.4
pimp ride 498.5
pimp shades 498.5
pimp socks 83.5
pimp sticks 70.4
pimp stride 59.1
pimp tints 498.5
pimp's arrest 498.5
pimp-crazy 497.11
pimped down 84.3
pimple and blotch 95.5
pimpmobile 75.2
pimps & pimping 498
pimpsy 251.5
pin (something) on 316.2
pin 132.11
pin money 508.2
pin on 193.4, 473.3
pin one's ears back 291.2, 292.3
pin-jabber 503.2
pinch 479.4, 489.1, 489.2, 502.4
Pincher 179.8
pinch-hit 12.2, 341.2
pine overcoat 112.4
pineapple 72.1
pinhead 431.1
pink 384.12, 501.4
pink elephants 102.1
pink lady 504.2
pinkie 384.4
pinko 383.19, 456.9
pinktea 422.1
pinktoes 384.13
pinky 404.2, 404.4
pinned 503.11
pint-size 388.1, 427.4
pip 27.1, 35.2
pip emma 3.8
pip-pip 346.4
pipe 132.1, 132.6
pipe down! 136.4
pipe one's eye 281.3
pipes 183.6
pipped 21.3
pipper 457.2
pippin 27.1, 35.2
pips 181.1
pipsqueak 388.1, 427.4

pirates 495.3
piss (in) one's pants 296.4
piss 94.1, 119.4, 119.8
piss about 146.4, 207.2
piss and vinegar 236.2, 347.1
piss around 146.4, 207.2, 235.5
piss artist 92.3
piss away 235.4
piss blood 283.2
piss broken glass 125.15
piss down 66.7
piss elegant 84.3, 298.5
piss it 251.4, 253.4
piss off 280.4, 284.2, 54.3
piss off! 54.6, 278.7
piss on one's parade 282.2, 7.12
piss oneself 274.4
piss, or get off the pot 241.11
piss-ant 388.1
piss-cutter 395.1
piss-take 293.5
pissed (off) 284.5
pissed 101.3
pissed as a fart 101.3
pissed as a newt 101.3
pissed as a rat 101.3
pissed off (with) 278.6
pissed off 280.6
pissed to the ears 101.3
pissed up 101.3
pisser 277.1, 410.1
pisshole 48.8, 79.1
pisshouse 79.1
pissing 189.4
pissing down 66.3
pissing oneself 296.7
pisspoor 28.2
pisspot 92.3
pissy-ass 19.6
pit 5.1, 116.40
pit city 278.1, 279.8, 281.1
pit-a-pat 57.1
pita 497.1
pitch 312.1, 426.2, 480.1, 500.3
pitch a bitch 298.2
pitch and toss 387.1, 457.1
pitch camp 41.6
pitch in 89.7, 241.5
pitch in! 89.9
pitcher 404.5

pitchman 420.4
pits 278.1, 279.2
Pitt Street farmer 456.16
pitty 36.2
pixie 404.1
pixillated 101.3
pizza 86.20
pizzazz 229.1, 236.2, 269.1
pjs 82.14
PLACE 41–48
place 41.4
place of entertainment 78.8
place of intercourse 359.4
placer 458.10
places in prison 494.2
placket 116.40
plaguey 189.4
plain 95.1
plain sailing 251.5
plan (v.) 232.3
PLAN 232–233
plank 41.5, 359.6
plant 41.4, 112.8, 203.5, 315.2, 486.6, 486.7
plant evidence 486.7
plant oneself 246.3
plants 114
plaster 113.4, 287.2, 337.4
plastered 101.3
plastic 15.6
plastic job 128.2
plate 360.12
plates 135.5
Plato to NATO 179.4
platters 135.5
plausible 160.5
play (along) 310.7
play (it) for all its worth 234.2
play (one) dirty 308.2, 313.2
play 165.1, 236.1, 511.5
play a flute solo on one's meat whistle 360.19
play a hunch 214.5
play around (with) 156.4
play around 352.5
play ball (with) 339.2
play cards 515.4
play checkers 352.5
play play chick 255.4
play chicken 255.4, 353.2
play dead 203.6
play dumb 311.4

play fathers and mothers 359.6
play footsie 351.3
play for a sucker 310.4
play funny buggers 276.6
play gooseberry 350.7
play hard to get 352.6
play hardball 204.2
play hide-and-seek (with) 210.2
play hookey 210.3
play hoop-snake with 360.12
play it cool 252.9, 271.3
play it square 305.3
play it straight (down the line) 305.4
play Judas 314.2
play mummies and daddies 359.6
play night baseball 359.6
play one too close 249.2
play one's cards right 257.2
play one's hand 214.9
play one's tune 275.2
play out of the pocket 310.8
play past 239.5
play pocket billiards 118.14, 360.19
play possum 203.6
play practical jokes 277.5
play records 135.8
play ring a rosie 244.1
play second fiddle 302.3
play silly buggers 276.6
play stuff 312.2
play the Tom 302.3
play the chill (for) 209.5
play the con 310.4
play the dozens 294.4
play the duck 210.2
play the dummy 202.2
play the field 352.5
play the fool 145, 276.6
play the game 305.4
play the gee-gees 514.7
play the giddy goat 309.2
play the heel 278.3
play the male organ 360.19
play the nut role 310.4
play the piano 135.7
play the white man 305.4
play too close 494.8

prisons 44.3
prissy 303.3
privileged information 194.2
privileged worker 453.6
privy queen 404.5
prizing tool 69.5
pro 456.24, 497.2
probability 158
problem 168.2, 252.1
process 120.3, 120.9
prod 359.6
production 240
profanity 189
professional woman 497.2
profit from crimes (v.) 462.3
prohibit 225.1
prohibition 225
proletariat 449
promiscuous 359.14
promiscuous female 437.3
promiscuous lesbian 437.5
promiscuous male 437.2
promiscuous male homosexual 437.4
promiscuous persons 437
promise the truth 164.7
promo 187.2
promote 232.3, 310.6
promote 242.4
promote for 365.4
promoted pimp 498.4
prompt one's porpoise 360.19
prompt 2.14
prong 359.12
pronto 2.10, 2.14
prop up 312.2, 350.4
property 366
prophesy 144.7
propose marriage 354.3
proposition 377.1
prospect 454.1
prossie 497.2
prosso 497.2
prostitute 497.2
prostitutes working for a pimp 497.11
prostitutes' clients 499
prostitutes' services 499
prostitutes' working targets 497.13
PROSTITUTION 497–500
protect 255.2

protect oneself 255.3
protection 255
provider 512.3
provoke trouble 334.4
prune the fifth limb 360.19
pseud 430.1
pseudy Tudy 78.2
psych (oneself) up 204.3
psych out 173.3, 296.5
psyched (to death) 262.7
psyched up 204.6
psychedelic to the bone 507.8
psycho 409.1
PTA 426.2
pu the elop 109.4
public 78.6
public address 187
public house 78.6
public speaking 187
public transport 75.12
publicity 187.2
puck 451.1
pud 431.1
pudding 180.1
pudding club 109.1
puddinghead 431.1
puddle 67.2
pudge 427.2
puff 286.1, 286.2, 404.1
puff of a cigarette 107.1
pug 395.1
puggy 395.1
puke 118.13, 278.1
pukka 164.8
pull 219.1, 220.2, 239.2, 259.1, 488.3, 489.1, 489.2, 514.7
pull 61.2
pull a brodie 258.2
pull a caper 478.2
pull a fadeout 7.5
pull a fast one 277.4, 310.4
pull a job 478.2
pull a nifty 277.4
pull a quick park 350.4
pull a runner 211.3
pull a stroke 239.5
pull a train 360.17
pull an act 124.3, 310.4, 311.4
pull down 365.2, 508.14
pull funny faces 277.6

pull in one's horns 209.4, 265.4
pull in your ears! 136.4
pull in your horns 265.7
pull in your neck 249.4
pull it off 239.5
pull no punches 183.12
pull off a raw deal 308.2
pull off some funny business 308.2
pull one's coat 183.15, 202.4, 291.2
pull one's finger out 239.5
pull one's joint 118.14, 289.2, 360.19
pull one's leg 293.5, 310.5
pull one's pisser 293.5
pull one's pud 118.14, 360.19
pull one's pudding 118.14, 360.19
pull one's punches 218.4, 329.3
pull one's socks up 238.5
pull one's taffy 360.19
pull one's weight 339.4
pull one's wire 118.14, 360.19
pull oneself to pieces 6.2
pull oneself together 6.2, 274.6
pull out of it 6.2
pull something funny 308.2
pull strings 219.2
pull the juice 133.1
pull the other one (it's got bells on it)! 146.11, 278.7
pull the plug (on) 10.6
pull the pope 360.19
pull the rug from under 193.7
pull the wool over one's eyes 219.5, 310.5
pull through 6.2
pull time 491.5
pull to a set 98.2
pull to pieces 290.2
pull together 274.7
pull up stakes 54.3
pull wires 219.2
pull your head in! 292.7
pump 71.1, 154.3
pump jockey 456.19
pumping iron 121.2
pumpkin head 427.7

punch 94.8, 236.2, 359.6, 437.3
punch house 500.1
punch in the mouth 360.3
punch out 241.8
punch the clock 1.7, 241.4
punch up 236.5
punch-out artist 433.3
punch-up 338.1
punchy 145.3
punctual 2.14
puncture one's balloon 193.7, 282.2, 300.3
punish 318.4
punishment 318
punishment 360.2
punk 7.14, 124.4, 360.15
punk out 296.3
punks 378.2
punt (around) 214.5
punt 244.1, 511.5
punt it (up) 214.5
punt off 210.2
punter 377.1, 480.4, 511.2, 513.1
pup 381.4
puppethead 391.1
puppy 105.1, 381.4, 381.7, 442.1
puppy dog 381.6
purchase on credit 510.7
purler 56.1
purple heart 504.2
pursue 344.2
push 209.1, 236.3, 286.1, 286.2, 353.1, 378.1, 458.2, 508.16
push along 54.3
push off 54.3
puss off! 54.6
push one's face through the back of one's neck 338.5
push the boat out 508.12
push the thumb 60.7
push up the daisies 112.5
push-in job 485.1
pushed (for) 376.5
pushed out of shape 280.6
pusher 502.1
pushing iron 121.2
pushing up daisies 112.10
pushover 251.1, 391.1, 411.1, 437.3
pushy 236.8, 347.4
puss 404.4

puss gentleman 403.1
pussums 180.1
pussy 82.12, 380.1, 403.1
pussy game 497.1
pussy in a can 494.7
pussy posse 495.4
pussy-whipped 355.8
pussycat 400.1
pussyfoot 8.3, 207.2
pussyfooter 408.1
put (it) across 239.5, 257.3
put (it) away 10.7, 239
put (it) in cold storage 239.6
put (it) on ice 239.6
put (it) over 239.5, 257.3
put (one's business) on front street 196.3
put (one) away 337.5, 338.5
put (one) down 300.3
put (up) against the wall 251.10
put 41.4
put a body up 473.3
put a crimp into 218.2
put a few back 97.3
put a few down 97.3
put a flea in one's ear 291.2
put a hurting on 337.4
put a name up 193.4, 473.3
put a notice on 113.6
put a sock in it 136.3, 201.1
put a sock in it! 201.5
put a spell on 327.2
put a word in one's ear 192.4
put all at sea 169.3
put at a disadvantage 259.3
put at sixes and sevens 169.3
put away (the groceries) 89.6
put away 20.3, 87.6, 113.4, 274.5, 473.3
put down 290.2, 294.6
put down a routine 310.4
put down the soft pedal 136.2
put down with force 41.5

put in a (good) word for 285.4
put in a flat spin 169.3
put in cold storage 374.3
put in lights 18.6
put in one's papers 495.10
put in one's two cents 183.17
put in one's two cents worth 249.3
put in one's two pennorth 249.3
put in shtuck 252.10
put in stitches 274.5
put in the acid 473.3
put in the bag 233.1
put in the club 109.3
put in the family way 109.3
put in the frame 256.4, 315.2
put in the hot seat 154.3, 301.1
put in the know 192.4
put in the middle 256.4
put in the poison 196.3
put into disrepute 140.4
put it about 352.5, 357.5
put it across (on) 310.4
put it all together 257.2
put it around 472.3
put it in the wind 54.3
put it on the street 196.3
put it over (on) 20.3
put it there 340.5
put it there! 340.4
put it where the monkeys shove their nuts! 292.7
put lead in one's pencil 357.4
put money on 159.2
put next to 192.4
put on (the) dog 298.2, 298.4
put on 293.5
put on a crosstown bus 169.3
put on airs 298.4
put on dog 297.2
put on frills 298.4
put on hold 248.3
put on ice 10.7, 209.2, 233.1, 248.3
put on jam 298.2, 298.4
put on one's face 120.12

SHAPE 39–40
shape up 230.2, 495.10
share (v.) 367.2
share 23.1
share out (v.) 367.5
share out 464.3
sharing 367
sharing 367.6
shark 434.1, 510.1
sharking 510.2
sharp 123.3, 143.6, 148.7, 229.4, 253.7
sharp end 252.1
sharp-shooter 443.2
sharpen 170.3
sharpen up 237.2
sharpie 435.1
sharpies 378.3
shattered 263.5
shave 120.6, 120.11
shave 310.6
shaver 381.3
shazzam 236.4
she-man 404.1
shebang 69.1, 69.2, 78.1
shebeen 104.2
sheeny 384.8
sheep 403.1
sheepish 120.14
sheepskin 82.7
sheet 194.3, 494.6
sheet! 189.5
sheet music 135.4
sheila 380.1
shekels 509.1
shell out 370.2
shell-back 407.1
shell-road 352.10
shellac 318.5
shellacked 101.3
shellacking 318.2, 318.2
shemozzle 262.1
shenanigans 146.1, 231.1, 334.1
Sherlock Holmes 495.1
shicer 434.1
shicker 91.4, 97.3
shickered 101.3
shift arse 49.5
shift the weight 316.2
shikse 384.10, 455.1
shill 513.2
shilly-shallier 408.1
shilly-shally 207.2
shim-sham 263.1
shimmy up 55.2

shin 466.2
shin battle, 338.1
shindig 98.1, 276.3, 363.1
shindy 98.1, 231.2, 276.3, 363.1
shine 384.1
shone on 348.2
shine one's pole 360.19
shine up 170.3
Shiner 179.8
ship 75.8
shirt 82.18
shirt-lifter 404.1
shit 86.2, 119.3, 119.7, 168.2, 395.1, 505.2, 506.1
shit! 189.5, 278.7
shit a brick 296.4
shit a brick! 173.7
shit and derision! 189.5
shit and wish 279.3
shit bricks 296.4
shit city 252.2
shit detail 241.1
shit jacket 79.1
shit list 332.1
shit on a shingle 86.9
shit on a stick 395.1
shit on a string 168.2
shit on from a great height 252.6
shit oneself 296.4
shit or bust 204.2, 238.6
shit stompers 82.15
shit stopper 276.2
shit through one's teeth 312.2
shit, or get off the pot 241.11
shit-eating grin 274.3
shit-for-brains 395.1, 433.1
shit-hot 27.3
shit-scared 296.7
shit-stick 465.1
shit-stirrer 420.2
shit-stirring 294.2
shitbird 433.1
shitface 98.1
shitfaced 101.3
shithead 396.1, 433.1
shitheap 46.2
shitheel 396.1, 433.1
shithole 48.8
shithook 393.1

shithouse 79.1, 252.2
shitkicker 390.2, 431.1
Shitkicker, Ohio 43.2
shits 119.5
shitter 48.6, 79.1, 479.3
shitting 189.4
shitting bricks 296.7
shitting oneself 296.7
shitty 28.2, 252.11, 334.6
shitwork 241.1
shiv 69.9
shiver my timbers 173.7
shivers 129.1
shmeer 287.2
shmeggegge 414.1
shmooser 418.1
sho' 'nuff 159.4, 164.8
shock (v.t.) 262.5
shocker 198.4
shocks for jocks 179.4
shoe 450.1
shoes 82.15
Shoey 179.8
shonk 384.8
shonnicker 384.8
shoo-fly 495.2, 495.4
sho-in 159.1
shook on 270.5
shoot (off) 118.12
shoot (one's wad) 183.10
shoot 73.3, 113.5, 337.7
shoot 183.14
shoot! 189.5, 278.7
shoot a cat 118.13
shoot a line 183.7, 198.7, 287.2, 310.7, 352.7
'shoot a line' 186.7
shoot blanks 184.2
shoot down 292.3, 348.2
shoot for the moon 511.5
shoot for the sky 511.5
shoot from the hip 205.2
shoot gravy 505.10
shoot off (at one's mouth) 184.2
shoot off 49.4, 54.3
shoot off at the mouth 299.2
shoot on 293.5
shoot one's best mack 205.2
shoot one's bolt 204.2
shoot one's load 118.12
shoot one's marbles 147.4
shoot one's star 360.15
shoot one's wad 118.12

snow 310.4, 312.1,
383.25, 384.13, 403.1,
505.3
snow bird 503.2
snow bunny 437.3
snow job 186.2, 310.1,
312.1
snow-dropping 479.1
snowed over 349.4
snowed under 241.10
snowfall 310.1
snub (v.) 348.2
snub 348
snuff (out) 113.4
snuff it 112.5
snuff movie 195.3
snuggies 82.10
so 404.1
so busy I've had to put a
man on to help 359.10
so dumb he couldn't find
his ass with two hands
at high noon 145.3
so dumb he couldn't piss
out of a boat 145.3
so long 346.4
so low he can look up a
snake's asshole and
think it's the North Star
396.1
so what? 271.7
so's your old man! 292.7
so-and-so 69.2, 395.1
soak 92.3, 368.2
soaked 101.3
soap 183.2
soap dodger 384.1
soap opera 195.1
SOB 252.4, 395.1, 433.1
sob sister 456.3
sob story 198.3
sob stuff 183.2, 261.1,
281.1
sober 93.3
sociability 361
sociable 361.5
sociable person 446
social elite 448
social engagement 362
social entertainment 363
social error 231.3
social failure 452.2
SOCIAL LIFE 361–364
social remarks 345.2
socially inept 390.4
sock 32.3, 41.5, 94.8,

135.1, 164.11, 257.1,
292.2, 318.5, 337.4
sock it to me! 173.7
sock the clock 241.4
sockerino 257.1
sockeroo 32.3, 257.1
socking 18.10
socko 2.11, 27.3, 135.1,
236.2, 257.1
sockola 257.1
socks 83.5
sod 252.4, 395.1, 396.1
sod about 146.4, 244.1
sod all 23.3
sod off 54.3, 211.3
sod off! 54.6, 278.7
sod that (for a lark) 167.5
sod widow 444.9
sod you! 189.7
soda 87.5
sodded 101.3
sodding 18.10, 189.4
sodomise 360.15
sodomy 360.5
soft (in the head) 145.3
soft 275.5, 329.4
soft drug use 507.2
soft drug user 503.3
soft drugs 506
soft money 509.1
soft number 251.1
soft on 349.4
soft pedal 218.4
soft soap 183.19, 287.1,
287.2
soft touch 391.1, 400.1
soft-cop 391.1
softie 400.1
softy 403.1
soggies 86.17
SOHF 395.1
soil 5.4
soixante-neuf 360.1
sold 160.6
sold on 160.6, 268.4
soldier 210.5, 458.3
solid 27.3, 164.8, 275.4,
305.8, 339.6
solid! 285.5
solids hit the air
conditioning 252.2
solitary as a bastard on
Father's Day 279.7
solo 213.6
solo drinker 423.3
SOLUTION 162–163

solve 162.2
solved 162.7
some 18.8
some chance 158.2
some chance! 200.3
some hope 158.2
some hope! 200.3
some mothers do have
'em 145.4
some people! 290.3
some place 41.7
someone blew out his/her
pilot light 507.9
something awful 18.9
something bad 28.1
something beautiful 35.2
something difficult 252.4
something else (again)
26.1
something excellent 27.1
something fast 49.3
something fierce 18.9
something heavy 29.1
something in reserve 374.1
something large 18.1
something on one 259.1
something small 19.1
something tedious 272.2
something terrible 18.9
something the cat dragged
in 36.1
something to shout about
27.1
something to write home
about 18.3, 27.1
something ugly 36.1
something unpleasant
278.1
something worthless 19.2
something/body important
18.3
somewhere else 150.2
somewheres 41.7
son of a bitch 252.4, 433.1
song-and-dance 198.2,
317.2
sonofabitch 395.1
sonofagun 395.1
sook 403.1
soon 2.8
sooner 412.12
sop 403.1, 495.5
sop-can 442.1
sophisticated lady 505.3
sophisticated person 389
sopor 504.3

stoneface 271.5
stoneginger 159.3
stones & bones 179.4
stones 204.1, 295.1
stonewall 201.3
stonicky 465.1
stonkered 101.3
stony (broke) 376.5
stood up 282.4
stooge 241.4, 388.1
stooge for 287.3, 341.3
stool 193.4
stool-pigeon 472.2
stoolie 435.3, 472.2, 494.4
stoop 359.6
stop 10.2, 10.6
stop and search 488.3
stop arsing around 146.7
stop being stupid 146.7
stop buggering about 146.7
stop by 361.4
stop drinking 93.1
stop it! 248.6
stop moing me! 292.7
stop one's clock 113.4
stop talking! 201.5
stop using narcotics 503.8
stop work 516.6
stoppo driver 475.1
storage enclosure 460.3
storefront preacher 420.1
stork 109.3
story 198
stoush 338.1
stove lid 384.1
stow away 89.6
stow it 10.6, 136.3
stow it! 10.9, 136.4, 201.5
stow the gab 136.3
straight 39.2
straight 106.2, 139.5, 305.6, 404.5, 407.1, 503.12
straight and narrow 303.1
straight arrow 432.1
straight dope 164.2
straight down the line 305.7
straight from the shoulder 305.7
straight goods 164.2, 192.3, 305.1
straight poop 164.2, 192.3, 305.1

straight shit 164.2, 305.1, 312.1
straight shooter 394.1
straight shooting 305.1
straight shot 359.1
straight up 164.8
straight up! 305.9
straight-out 22.6
straight-up 22.6
straighten 338.3, 372.3
straighten black hair 120.9
straightened black hair 120.3
straightener 372.2
straightness 39
strain the potatoes 119.8
strain the spuds 119.8
stranger 440
strap 490.5
strap oil 318.3
strapped (for cash) 376.5
strat 69.24
strawberry fields 506.4
streak (off) 49.4
streak 262.1
streak of lightning 49.3
streaker 62.2
street 47.2
street fighter 402.2
street people 417.3
street smart 143.6
street smarts 253.1
street wise 143.6
streetified 143.6
strength 32
strength 121.1
strength 164.1
strengthen 6.4
strep throat 125.7
stretch (one's neck) 492.3
stretch 1.1, 8.2, 491.3
stretched 101.3
strewth! 189.5
strict 216.6
strictly! 305.9
strictly from 15.6
stride 253.4
strides 82.11
strike a light! 173.7
strike all of a heap 173.3
strike home 183.16
strike it rich 257.2, 508.15
strike me blind! 173.7
strike me pink! 173.7
strike oil 257.2
strike one blind 173.3

strike one dead 173.3
strike one dumb 173.3
strike one pink 173.3
strike out 112.5, 258.2, 359.12
strike paydirt 257.2
strike the pink match 360.19
strike-breaker 453.5
strikers 69.16
string along 8.3, 310.4, 310.7
string bean 427.6
stringer 456.3
strings 219.1
strip (off) 85.3
strip my gears! 173.7
stripe 337.6
stripes 181.1
stroke 359.6
stroke book 194.4, 501.2
stroke one's beef 118.14, 360.19
stroke one's poker 360.19
stroke the dog 360.19
stroked (out) 243.4
stroll 500.3
stroll on! 146.11
strong 32.6
strong 306.5, 357.10, 501.5
strong arm stuff 337.1
strong it 297.2
strong on 267.4
strongarm 32.4, 217.2, 485.3
stroppy 284.5
struck on 267.4
strung out 279.6
strunz 146.2
strut one's stuff 298.2, 364.3
stub one's toe 254.2, 258.2
stubby 105.3
stuck on 270.5
stuck on oneself 297.3
stuck-up 297.3
stud 437.2, 441.6
study (v.) 190.9
study 156.5
study 155.1
stuff (on) 486.1
stuff 68.1, 69.2, 162.1, 164.4, 186.2, 335.2, 359.6, 505.1, 505.2

sweat 154.3, 252.1, 262.1, 264.1, 280.2, 283.2
sweat hog 426.2
sweat it out 241.6, 248.4
sweats 503.6
swede 390.2
Swedish culture 360.7, 499.4
Sweeney 495.4
sweep 433.1
sweep the board 20.3, 365.3
sweet (as a nut) 251.5
sweet (bleeding) Jesus 189.5
sweet 27.3, 180.1, 404.1
sweet chance 158.2
sweet daddy 441.2
sweet FA 16.2, 23.3
sweet Fanny Adams 505.5
sweet Jesus 505.5
sweet fuck all 23.3
sweet kid 494.4
sweet on 349.4
sweet patootie 441.3
sweet potato pie 425.1
sweet savagery 198.5
sweet talk 219.4
sweet-talk 352.7
sweetheart contract 508.9
sweetie 35.2, 180.1, 425.1, 441.1
sweetie-pie 180.1, 441.1
sweetman 498.2
sweetness 180.1
sweetness and light 261.1
sweetpea 441.3
sweets 180.1
swell 27.3, 139.6
swell (n.) 448.1
swell! 285.5
swellhead 401.1, 503.2
swelterer 3.1, 66.1
swift 143.6
swift 'un 489.1
swig 97.3
swill 97.3
swilling 97.1
swim in 366.3
swimming costume 82.13
swimming in 366.5
swindle (n.) 310.3
swindle (v.) 480.5
swindle sheet 508.10
swindler 458.8
swindling 480

swing (for it) 113.3
swing (it) 239.5, 253.6, 360.12
swing both ways 357.7
swing daddy 450.1
swing shift 1.10, 241.3
swing the lamp 299.2
swing the lead 124.3, 210.5, 244.1
swing with 276.4, 340.2
swinger 437.1
swipe 292.2, 479.2
swipe me! 173.7
swish 33.6, 318.5, 358.4, 404.1
Swish Alps 44.4
swishing 318.3
swiss 265.6
switch hitter 436.8
switched on 143.6
switcheroo 12.1
Swone One 44.1
swoop 488.1
swordsman 437.2, 443.2
swot 453.3
symbol 181
syph 125.10
sypho 125.10
syphon the python 119.8
syrup 120.5

T & A 499.3
T-bone 179.20
T-man 495.2
T-zoned 175.3
ta 345.3
ta muchly 345.3
tab 178.1, 194.3, 508.10
ta-ta 346.4
tabbed 84.3
tabbed to the bone 84.4
table 81.4
tack 86.1, 235.9
tack city 278.1
tackhead 426.2
tacky 36.2, 278.5
taco bender 383.15
taco head 383.15
tad 383.12
Taffy 179.8
taffy 383.22
tag 8.3, 178.1
Taig 321.1
tail 8.3, 132.7, 404.5
tailgate 60.6
tailormade 468.1

tails 82.3
take (for a ride) 480.5
take 365.1, 372.2, 372.4
take a (runout) powder 211.3
take a back seat 21.2, 300.2, 302.3
take a bath 21.2, 258.2
take a brodie 56.2
take a Brodie 112.7
take a chance 214.5
take a collection 322.1
take a crack at 337.7
take a crap 119.7
take a decko (at) 156.3
take a dive 233.4, 258.2
take a drag 107.2
take a drop 97.3
take a drug 507.4
take a dump 119.7
take a fall 258.2, 300.4, 489.3
take a few 97.3
take a flash at 132.6
take a flier 56.2
take a flying fuck! 292.7
take a gander (at) 132.6
take a gander (for) 157.1
take a header 258.2
take a hike 54.3, 54.6
take a hinge (at) 132.6
take a hit 506.6
take a jab at 291.2
take a leak 119.8
take a load off (your feet) 56.3
take a measure (of) 132.6
take a nap 247.5
take a nose-dive 7.5, 258.2
take a pee 119.7
take a pew 246.3
take a piss 119.8
take a pop (at) 238.3, 337.4
take a powder 49.4, 54.3, 112.7, 209.5
take a puff 107.2
take a pull 107.2
take a rain check 248.2
take a running jump! 292.7
take a runout powder 49.4, 54.3
take a runout powder on 209.5

the rabbit died 109.4
the real McCoy 94.5
the real stuff 94.5
the Revo 228.1
the rubout 25.2
the runaround 25.2
the score 472.1
the Scrubs 44.3, 494.1
the shaft 308.1, 313.1
the show on the road 9.3
the sky's the limit 213.5
the slip 25.2
the Smoke 43.1
the Squad 495.4
the street 500.3
the tape 156.1
the tops 123.3, 273.6,
  430.2
the tubs 75.8
the Ville 44.3, 494.1
the Water 44.1
the weed 479.1
the Widow 95.4
the wise guys 458.2
the word 256.2
the World 45.1
the works 113.1
the worst way 18.9
the Yard 495.1
theft 479
there (just) ain't such an
  animal 161.6
there with the goods
  143.5
there'll be blue murder if
  . . . 256.6
there's one born every
  minute 391.2
thespian 404.2
they give them away with
  a pound of the tea
  481.6, 479.7
thick 145.3, 153.7
thick head 101.1
thick liquid 67.7
thick with 328.7
thickie 431.1
thicko 431.1
thief 458.7, 479.2
thieving prostitute 497.10
thin 37.1
thin on the ground 19.6
thin person 427.6
thin time 278.2
thing 212.1
things in general 68.1

thingummibob 69.2
thingummijig 69.2
thingy 69.2
think 153.4
think about it! 153.11
think again 153.5
think one is 'it' 297.2
thinking 153
thinking about 153.10
thinks he/she is so nice
  his/her shit don't stink
  401.3
thinks he/she shits
  lollipops 401.3
thinks his/her ass is
  icecream and everyone
  wants a bite 401.3
thinks it's just to pee
  through 145.2
Third World briefcase
  69.25
third degree 154.2, 217.1,
  319.3, 490.2
third-rate 235.9
thirst 90
thirty-eight 71.1
this is where we came in
  2.7
this'll pin your ears back!
  173.7
thoroughbred 497.7
thoroughbred black 425.1
thoroughfare 47
thought 153.2
thousand eyes 82.15
thousand yard stare 175.1
thrash 60.4, 363.1
threads 82.1
threats of violence 336.3
three balls 384.8
three sheets to the wind
  101.3
three squares 89.1
three tears and a bucket
  271.7
three-bagger 257.1
three-bullet Joey 495.1
three-card monte 515.2
three-dollar bill 431.1
three-ed up 494.11
three-hour tour 272.1
three-letter man 404.1
three-sheet 219.5, 299.2,
  312.2
three-sheeting 299.1
three-time loser 494.4

three-way deal 360.6
three-way girl 497.12
threesome 360.6
thrift 374
thrill (v.) 273.4
thrill 273.1
thrill and chill 359.1
thriller 198.4
throat 453.3
throne 79.1
through 124.5
through and through
  394.1
through the nose 508.19
throw (a few) down 97.3
throw (for a loop) 168.3
throw (it) down 89.7
throw (one) down 97.3
throw 23.2, 273.4, 359.6
throw 62.1,
  62.3
throw a bash 363.4
throw a beano 363.4
throw a buttonhole on
  360.15
throw a curve (to) 310.5
throw a fit 280.3
throw a moody 263.3,
  279.3
throw a party 363.4
throw a punch 337.4,
  341.4
throw a scare into 296.5
throw a seven 125.17
throw a spanner in the
  works 250.1
throw a winging 280.3
throw a wobbler 125.17,
  263.3
throw down on 316.2
throw dust in one's eyes
  310.5
throw hands 337.4
throw in 24.1
throw in one's cards
  112.5, 302.2
throw in one's hands
  112.5, 209.2, 302.2
throw in the sponge
  112.5, 209.2, 302.2
throw in the towel 209.2,
  302.2
throw one for a loop
  283.4
throw one's cookies
  118.13

throw one's hat in the ring 205.2, 342.3

throw one's money away 373.2

throw one's voice 118.13

throw one's weight about 231.4, 297.2, 298.2

throw out a line 220.2

throw over 331.2, 353.5

throw overboard 209.5

throw some dirt (on) 196.3

throw the baby out with the bathwater 25.4

throw the book at 291.2

throw the hook at 154.3

throw the hooks into 368.2

throw up 118.13

thrower 480.3

throwing 62

throwing iron 121.2

thrown for a loss 258.4

thug 395.2, 433.3

thumb 338.1

thumb it 60.7

thumb the nose at 342.3

thumb-trip 60.7

thumbs-down 224.1, 225.1, 288.1

thumbs-up 222.1, 285.1

thump one's pumper 360.19

thumper 71.3

thumping (great) 18.7

thumping 18.2, 29.2, 312.3

thunder chicken 426.2

thunder-box 79.1

thunderer 179.5

thundering 18.10, 312.3

tick (one) off 267.3

tick 1.1, 388.1, 396.1, 399.1, 427.2, 510.2

ticker 69.17

ticket 164.1, 164.4, 377.1, 488.2

ticket 190.2

ticketty-boo 4.2

tickle (pink) 273.4

tickle 472.1

tickle one's funny bone 277.2

tickle one's pickle 118.14, 360.19

tickle one's tail 318.5

tickle palms 219.2

tickle the funny bone 274.5

tickle the ivories 135.7

tickle to death 273.4

tickled 273.5

tickled pink 273.5

tickled to death 273.5

tickled to pieces 273.5

tickler 453.2

ticky-tacky 28.2

tiddley-wink 383.4

tiddly 101.3

tidy step 38.2

tidy sum 18.2

tie 83.4

tie in with 328.6

tie into 339.2

tie off (v.) 505.10

tie on the feed-bag 89.6

tie on the nosebag 89.6

tie one on 97.3

tie the knot 355.5

tie up with 328.6, 339.2

tie-in 339.1

tie-up 233.1, 339.1, 340.1, 505.9

tied in 339.6

tied up 233.6, 241.10, 339.6

tiger (for) 270.5

tight 374.4

tight as Kelsey's nuts 399.1

tight as O'Reilly's balls 399.1

tight sweater 82.21

tight with 328.7

tight-assed 279.6

tightbuck 360.7

tightwad 399.1

Tijuana bible 194.4, 501.2

till hell freezes over 1.10

till the cows come home 1.10

tilly 495.1

Timber 179.8

TIME 1–3

time 491.1, 494.6

time and a half 508.9

tin 495.6

tin can 71.3

tin soldier 499.2

tin-arsed 142.5

tin-tack 242.2

tincture 97.2, 506.1

tinhorn 28.1, 28.2, 388.1

Tinker 179.8

Tinkle 179.8

tinkle 119.8, 195.11

tinnie 105.3

Tinseltown 43.1

Tiny 179.13, 179.14

tiny 427.5

tip (off) 256.3

tip (v.) 370.4

tip 97.3, 353.5, 472.1

tip in 193.4, 473.3

tip one's hand 193.6

tip one's hole-card 193.6

tip out 353.4

tip the nod 182.3

tip the wink (to) 222.2

tip the wink 182.3

tip-off 256.2

tipoff 182.1, 314.1

tippin' 216.6

tipster 400.5, 430.4

tipsy 101.3

tiptop 20.6

tiptop form 123.1

tire out (v.t.) 243.3

tired 101.3, 272.5

tired and emotional 101.3

tired people 403.1

tired woman 452.2

tiredness 243

tit 251.1

tit mag 194.4

tit man 441.10

Titch 179.14

titchy 37.2

titfer 82.17

title 178.2

tits and ass 499.3

tits up 459.2

tizzy 262.1, 280.2

Tizzie Lizzy 179.9

TJ 43.1

TL 396.1

TLC 329.1

TNT 18.10

to a degree 17.2

to a great extent 18.9

to be footloose and fancy-free 213.2

to be on a hiding to nothing 214.8

to beat all creation 18.9

to deal with 253.6

to die 27.3

tuna 380.1
tune in 166.2
tune off 265.5
turd 119.3, 396.1
turd-burglar 404.1
turd-packer 404.1
turf 46.1
turf out 63.2
turk 404.1
Turk McGurk / a cheat
435.1
turkey 258.1, 395.1
turkey on a string
391.1
turking 359.1
Turkish pollen 506.1
turn (one) around 219.4
turn (one) out 498.7
turn 173.1, 363.1
turn 8.2
turn a trick 239.5
turn against 314.3
turn in 247.3, 314.2
turn inside out 154.3,
318.4
turn into fish food 112.6
turn it on 49.4
turn it up 241.5
turn it up! 146.11
turn off 136.2, 356.3
turn off lights 133.1
turn off one's lights 112.7
turn on 273.3, 357.4
turn on the heat 73.3,
238.5
turn on the waterworks
261.4, 281.3
turn one around 472.3
turn one's face to the wall
112.5
turn one's nose up at
224.3
turn one's stomach 278.4
turn one's tum 278.4
turn out 360.17
turn over 488.3
turn the corner 358.5
turn the set 231.4
turn the tables 358.3
turn tricks 497.15
turn up one's nose at
288.5
turn up one's toes 112.5
turn up trumps 215.5,
257.2
turn upside down 157.1

turn-on 262.2, 273.1,
507.2
turn-up 173.1
turned on 143.6
turnip greens 506.2
turnout 34.1
turns one's crank 273.3
turnup (for the book)
215.2
turps 97.2
turtle 83.1
turtle-dove 180.1
tusheroon 509.1
tuskie 506.3
tux 82.3
TV 436.7
twaddle 146.2
twang 359.6
twang one's wire 118.14,
360.19
twak 499.2
twat 395.1
tweak one's twinkie
360.19
tweedler 75.4
tweedling 480.2
tweeked 101.3
twenties 480.2
twenty dollars 509.7
twenty pounds 509.7
twenty-five pounds 509.8
twenty-nine and a
wake-up 1.5
twerp 388.1
twig 132.6, 162.3, 166.2
twink 404.5
twinkies 404.5
twirl 255.1, 494.5
twist 160.1, 380.1, 404.4,
506.2
twist one's arm 217.2,
219.4
twisted 101.3, 147.5,
169.5, 284.5, 507.8
twister 69.13
twit 431.1
two 491.3
two and eight 262.1
two bricks short of the
load 147.5
two cents worth 153.3
two down 86.27
two ducks 516.6
two fat ladies 516.6
two fingers of scorn
293.3

two hundred pounds
509.12
two jumps ahead 20.5
two little crutches 516.6
two looking at you 86.27
two on a slice of squeal
86.27
two other guys 26.1
two pence short of a bob
147.5
two shakes of a lamb's tail
1.3
two with their eyes closed
86.27
two-bit 19.7, 28.2
two-bob 28.2
two-bottle man 92.3
two-dinners 37.3
two-dollar word 177.2
two-ed up 494.11
two-faced 313.4
two-holer 79.2
two-time 310.4, 313.3,
353.3
two-timer 435.1
two-timing 313.4
two-way man 497.9
twoer 509.12
twot 395.1
tying one on 97.1
tyke 115.1
typer 190.5
typewriter 190.5
tyres 76.5
tzuris 215.3

U-ie 51.1
UBs 82.10
ucky 278.5
Ugandan discussions
359.1
ugliness 36
ugly 36.2
ugly customer 433.3
UK football teams 179.1
UK newspaper nicknames
179.5
umbrella brigade 495.4
umpteen 16.5
ums 180.1
unarmed 466.6
unattached girl 445.2
unattractive male 426.3
unattractive people 426
unattractive woman 426.2
unbutton (one's lip) 193.3

READ MORE IN PENGUIN

In every corner of the world, on every subject under the sun, Penguin represents quality and variety – the very best in publishing today.

For complete information about books available from Penguin – including Puffins, Penguin Classics and Arkana – and how to order them, write to us at the appropriate address below. Please note that for copyright reasons the selection of books varies from country to country.

In the United Kingdom: Please write to *Dept. JC, Penguin Books Ltd, FREEPOST, West Drayton, Middlesex UB7 0BR*

If you have any difficulty in obtaining a title, please send your order with the correct money, plus ten per cent for postage and packaging, to *PO Box No. 11, West Drayton, Middlesex UB7 0BR*

In the United States: Please write to *Penguin USA Inc., 375 Hudson Street, New York, NY 10014*

In Canada: Please write to *Penguin Books Canada Ltd, 10 Alcorn Avenue, Suite 300, Toronto, Ontario M4V 3B2*

In Australia: Please write to *Penguin Books Australia Ltd, 487 Maroondah Highway, Ringwood, Victoria 3134*

In New Zealand: Please write to *Penguin Books (NZ) Ltd, 182–190 Wairau Road, Private Bag, Takapuna, Auckland 9*

In India: Please write to *Penguin Books India Pvt Ltd, 706 Eros Apartments, 56 Nehru Place, New Delhi 110 019*

In the Netherlands: Please write to *Penguin Books Netherlands B.V., Keizersgracht 231 NL–1016 DV Amsterdam*

In Germany: Please write to *Penguin Books Deutschland GmbH, Friedrichstrasse 10–12, W–6000 Frankfurt/Main 1*

In Spain: Please write to *Penguin Books S. A., C. San Bernardo 117–6° E–28015 Madrid*

In Italy: Please write to *Penguin Italia s.r.l., Via Felice Casati 20, I–20124 Milano*

In France: Please write to *Penguin France S. A., 17 rue Lejeune, F–31000 Toulouse*

In Japan: Please write to *Penguin Books Japan, Ishikiribashi Building, 2–5–4, Suido, Tokyo 112*

In Greece: Please write to *Penguin Hellas Ltd, Dimocritou 3, GR–106 71 Athens*

In South Africa: Please write to *Longman Penguin Southern Africa (Pty) Ltd, Private Bag X08, Bertsham 2013*

READ MORE IN PENGUIN

LITERARY CRITICISM

A Lover's Discourse   Roland Barthes

'*A Lover's Discourse* ... may be the most detailed, painstaking anatomy of desire we are ever likely to see or need again ... The book is an ecstatic celebration of love and language and ... readers interested in either or both ... will enjoy savouring its rich and dark delights' – *Washington Post Book World*

The New Pelican Guide to English Literature   Boris Ford (ed.)

The indispensable critical guide to English and American literature in nine volumes, erudite yet accessible. From the ages of Chaucer and Shakespeare, via Georgian satirists and Victorian social critics, to the leading writers of the 1980s, all literary life is here.

The Theatre of the Absurd   Martin Esslin

This classic study of the dramatists of the Absurd examines the origins, nature and future of a movement whose significance has transcended the bounds of the stage and influenced the whole intellectual climate of our time.

Introducing Shakespeare   G. B. Harrison

An excellent popular introduction to Shakespeare – the legend, the (tantalizingly ill-recorded) life and the work – in the context of his times: theatrical rivalry, literary piracy, the famous performance of Richard II in support of Essex, and the fire which finally destroyed the Globe.

Aspects of the Novel   E. M. Forster

'I say that I have never met this kind of perspicacity in literary criticism before. I could quote scores of examples of startling excellence' – Arnold Bennett. Originating in a course of lectures given at Cambridge, *Aspects of the Novel* is full of E. M. Forster's habitual wit, wisdom and freshness of approach.

READ MORE IN PENGUIN

LANGUAGE/LINGUISTICS

Sociolinguistics Peter Trudgill

Women speak 'better' English than men. The Eskimo language has several words for snow. 1001 factors influence the way we speak. Professor Trudgill draws on languages from Afrikaans to Yiddish to illuminate this fascinating topic and provide a painless introduction to sociolinguistics.

The English Language David Crystal

A guided tour of the language by the presenter of BBC Radio 4's *English Now*: the common structures that unify the language; the major variations from Ireland to the Caribbean; the 'dialects' of chemists and clergy, lawyers and truckers.

Bad Language Lars-Gunnar Andersson and Peter Trudgill

As this witty and incisive book makes clear, the prophets of gloom who claim that our language is getting worse are guided by emotion far more than by hard facts. The real truth, as Andersson and Trudgill illuminate in fascinating detail, is that change has always been inherent in language.

Our Language Simeon Potter

'The author is brilliantly successful in his effort to instruct by delighting ... he contrives not only to give a history of English but also to talk at his ease on rhyming slang, names, spelling reform, American English and much else ... fascinating' – *Higher Education Journal*

Grammar Frank Palmer

In modern linguistics grammar means far more than cases, tenses and declensions – it means precise and scientific description of the structure of language. This concise guide takes the reader simply and clearly through the concepts of traditional grammar, morphology, sentence structure and transformational-generative grammar.

Language and Learning James Britton

'The theoretical complexities of language acquisition and use are patiently presented and most skilfully and entertainingly illustrated with examples from children's speech and writing' – *Educational Review*

READ MORE IN PENGUIN

REFERENCE

Medicines: A Guide for Everybody Peter Parish

Now in its seventh edition and completely revised and updated, this bestselling guide is written in ordinary language for the ordinary reader yet will prove indispensable to anyone involved in health care – nurses, pharmacists, opticians, social workers and doctors.

Media Law Geoffrey Robertson, QC, and Andrew Nichol

Crisp and authoritative surveys explain the up-to-date position on defamation, obscenity, official secrecy, copyright and confidentiality, contempt of court, the protection of privacy and much more.

The Slang Thesaurus

Do you make the public bar sound like a gentleman's club? The miraculous *Slang Thesaurus* will liven up your language in no time. You won't Adam and Eve it! A mine of funny, witty, acid and vulgar synonyms for the words you use every day.

The Penguin Dictionary of Troublesome Words Bill Bryson

Why should you avoid discussing the *weather conditions*? Can a married woman be celibate? Why is it eccentric to talk about the aroma of a cowshed? A straightforward guide to the pitfalls and hotly disputed issues in standard written Englısn.

The Penguin Dictionary of Musical Performers Arthur Jacobs

In this invaluable companion volume to *The Penguin Dictionary of Music* Arthur Jacobs has brought together the names of over 2,500 performers. Music is written by composers, yet it is the interpreters who bring it to life; in this comprehensive book they are at last given their due.

The Penguin Dictionary of Physical Geography John Whittow

'Dr Whittow and Penguin Reference Books have put serious students of the subject in their debt, by combining the terminology of the traditional geomorphology with that of the quantitative revolution and defining both in one large and comprehensive dictionary of physical geography ... clear and succinct' – *The Times Educational Supplement*

READ MORE IN PENGUIN

REFERENCE

The Penguin Dictionary of Literary Terms and Literary Theory
J. A. Cuddon

'Scholarly, succinct, comprehensive and entertaining, this is an important book, an indispensable work of reference. It draws on the literature of many languages and quotes aptly and freshly from our own' – *The Times Educational Supplement*

The Penguin Spelling Dictionary

What are the plurals of *octopus* and *rhinoceros*? What is the difference between *stationery* and *stationary*? And how about *annex* and *annexe*, *agape* and *Agape*? This comprehensive new book, the fullest spelling dictionary now available, provides the answers.

The Roget's Thesaurus of English Words and Phrases
Betty Kirkpatrick (ed.)

This new edition of Roget's classic work, now brought up to date for the nineties, will increase anyone's command of the English language. Fully cross-referenced, it includes synonyms of every kind (formal or colloquial, idiomatic and figurative) for almost 900 headings. It is a must for writers and utterly fascinating for any English speaker.

The Penguin Dictionary of English Idioms
Daphne M. Gulland and David G. Hinds-Howell

The English language is full of pitfalls for the foreign student – but the most common problem lies in understanding and using the vast array of idioms. *The Penguin Dictionary of English Idioms* is uniquely designed to stimulate understanding and familiarity by explaining the meanings and origins of idioms and giving examples of typical usage.

The Penguin Wordmaster Dictionary
Martin H. Manser and Nigel D. Turton

This dictionary puts the pleasure back into word-seeking. Every time you look at a page you get a bonus – a panel telling you everything about a particular word or expression. It is, therefore, a dictionary to be read as well as used for its concise and up-to-date definitions.

FOR THE BEST IN PAPERBACKS, LOOK FOR THE 🐧

PENGUIN DICTIONARIES

Abbreviations
Archaeology
Architecture
Art and Artists
Biology
Botany
Building
Business
Chemistry
Civil Engineering
Computers
Curious and Interesting
   Words
Curious and Interesting
   Numbers
Design and Designers
Economics
Electronics
English and European
   History
English Idioms
French
Geography
German

Historical Slang
Human Geography
Literary Terms
Mathematics
Modern History 1789–1945
Modern Quotations
Music
Physical Geography
Physics
Politics
Proverbs
Psychology
Quotations
Religions
Rhyming Dictionary
Saints
Science
Sociology
Spanish
Surnames
Telecommunications
Troublesome Words
Twentieth-Century History